Computational Intelligence Techniques for Trading and Investment

Computational intelligence, a sub-branch of artificial intelligence, is a field which draws on the natural world and adaptive mechanisms in order to study behaviour in changing complex environments. This book provides an interdisciplinary view of current technological advances and challenges concerning the application of computational intelligence techniques to financial time-series forecasting, trading and investment.

The book is divided into five parts. The first part introduces the most important computational intelligence and financial trading concepts, while also presenting the most important methodologies from these different domains. The second part is devoted to the application of traditional computational intelligence techniques to the fields of financial forecasting and trading, and the third part explores the applications of artificial neural networks in these domains. The fourth part delves into novel evolutionary-based hybrid methodologies for trading and portfolio management, while the fifth part presents the applications of advanced computational intelligence modelling techniques in financial forecasting and trading.

This volume will be useful for graduate and postgraduate students of finance, computational finance, financial engineering and computer science. Practitioners, traders and financial analysts will also benefit from this book.

Christian Dunis is Emeritus Professor of Banking and Finance at Liverpool John Moores University, UK and Joint General Manager of global risk and new products at Horus Partners Wealth Management Group SA, Switzerland.

Spiros Likothanassis is Professor and Director at the Pattern Recognition Laboratory in the Department of Computer Engineering and Informatics at the University of Patras, Greece.

Andreas Karathanasopoulos is Senior Lecturer in Finance and Risk Management at the University of East London, UK.

Georgios Sermpinis is Senior Lecturer in Economics at the University of Glasgow, UK.

Konstantinos Theofilatos is a Post-Doctoral Researcher in the Department of Computer Engineering and Informatics at the University of Patras, Greece.

Routledge advances in experimental and computable economics
Edited by K. Vela Velupillai and Stefano Zambelli
University of Trento, Italy

Computational Intelligence Techniques for Trading and Investment

**Edited by Christian Dunis,
Spiros Likothanassis,
Andreas Karathanasopoulos,
Georgios Sermpinis and
Konstantinos Theofilatos**

Routledge
Taylor & Francis Group

LONDON AND NEW YORK

First published 2014
by Routledge
2 Park Square, Milton Park, Abingdon, Oxon OX14 4RN

and by Routledge
711 Third Avenue, New York, NY 10017

Routledge is an imprint of the Taylor & Francis Group, an informa business

British Library Cataloguing in Publication Data
A catalogue record for this book is available from the British Library

Library of Congress Cataloging in Publication Data
Computational intelligence techniques for trading and investment/edited
by Christian Dunis, Spiros Likothanassis, Andreas Karathanasopoulos,
Georgios Sermpinis and Konstantinos Theofilatos.
    pages cm
    Includes bibliographical references and index.
    1. Investments–Mathematical models. 2. Investment analysis–
    Mathematical models. 3. Speculation–Mathematical models. 4.
    Computational intelligence. I. Dunis, Christian.
    HG4515.2.C66 2014
    332.60285'63–dc23

                                                       2013036599

ISBN: 978-0-415-63680-3 (hbk)
ISBN: 978-0-203-08498-4 (ebk)

Typeset in Times New Roman
by Wearset Ltd, Boldon, Tyne and Wear

'To my family' Christian Dunis
'Dedicated to my daughter Kalliopi–Klelia' Spiros Likothanassis
'To my family' Andreas Karathanasopoulos
'To my beloved Fountouki' Georgios Sermpinis
'To my family and my beloved Zoi-Triantafyllia' Konstantinos Theofilatos

Contents

Figures

Tables

Contributors

Thomas Amorgianiotis, MCs student at Department of Computer Engineering and Informatics, University of Patras, Greece.

Grigorios Beligiannis, Assistant Professor, Department of Business Administration of Food and Agricultural Enterprises, University of Patras, Greece.

David de la Fuente, Department of Business Management, University of Oviedo, Spain.

Christos Dimitrakopoulos, PhD candidate at the Department of Biosystems Science and Engineering at the ETHZ University in Basel, Switzerland.

Christian L. Dunis, Emeritus Professor of Banking and Finance at Liverpool John Moores University, UK and Joint General Manager, Horus Partners Wealth Management Group, Geneva.

Efstratios Georgopoulos, Associate Professor at the Technological Educational Institute (TEI) of Peloponnese Kalamata, Greece.

Javier Giner, Department of Finance and Accounting, University of La Laguna, Spain.

Andreas Karathanasopoulos, Senior Lecturer at the University of East London, Royal Docklands Business School, UK.

Jason Laws, Senior Lecturer of Finance at the University of Liverpool Management School, UK.

Spiros Likothanassis, Professor at the Department of Computer Engineering and Informatics, University of Patras, Greece.

Manolis Maragoudakis, Assistant Professor at the Department of Information and Communication Systems Engineering, University of the Aegean, Samos, Greece.

Seferina Mavroudi, Assistant Professor at the Department of Social Work, School of Sciences of Health and Care, Technological Educational Institute of Patras, Greece.

Hans-Jörg von Mettenheim, Junior Professor, Leibniz Universität, Hannover, Germany.

Peter W. Middleton, Associate Researcher with CIBEF and Reader of Finance at the University of Liverpool Management School, UK.

Sovan Mitra, Lecturer at the Department of Law, Economics, Accountancy and Risk, Glasgow Caledonian University, UK.

Konstantina Pendaraki, Lecturer at the Department of Business Administration of Food and Agricultural Enterprises, University of Patras, Greece.

Rafael Rosillo, Lecturer at the Department of Business Management, University of Oviedo, Spain.

Georgios Sermpinis, Lecturer at the University of Glasgow Business School, University of Glasgow, UK.

Dimitrios Serpanos, Director of the Industrial Systems Institute, Patras, Greece.

Nikolaos Spanoudakis, Teaching Assistant at the Applied Mathematics and Computers Laboratory, Department of Sciences, Technical University of Crete, Greece.

Charalampos Stasinakis, PhD Candidate at the University of Glasgow Business School, University of Glasgow, UK.

Konstantinos Theofilatos, Post-Doctoral Researcher at the Department of Computer Engineering and Informatics, University of Patras, Greece.

Preface

The aim of this book is twofold. First it presents some well-known algorithms, methods and paradigms from Computational Intelligence (CI) to readers unfamiliar to the field. Second, it depicts how these methods, individually or combined (hybrid methods) can be applied to real-world problems, and specifically to time series prediction, financial forecasting and trading. Usually, these methods are data-driven techniques, thus they use historical data from the problem domain and extract knowledge from them in order to build a reliable model. These CI methods have been shown to be able to solve complicated real-world problems. Since financial data are usually noisy, dynamically changing and sometimes chaotic, and their amount quite big in size, the CI methods usually fail to produce directly accurate prediction models. However, if some filtering or dimension reduction methods are used, the performance of CI methods can be dramatically improved. Furthermore, if CI methods are combined such that some alleviate the disadvantages of the other, they have been shown to work quite efficiently.

In the last decades, trading and investing have attracted the attention of researchers from many domains such as mathematics, finance and computer science. The economic crisis that erupted in the United States in 2007 and in Europe in 2009 has strengthened the belief that traditional forecasting and trading techniques are not able to act as robust tools for investment and portfolio management. Especially in crisis periods, financial time series become extremely volatile and unpredictable. In this recent period, a boost to new advanced computational intelligent techniques has emerged: these techniques claim to be superior to traditional strategies and can act as alternative solutions as they are able to perform well with noisy data that are produced by the non-linearities of the global economy.

The development of accurate forecasting techniques is critical to economists, investors and risk analysts. This task is getting more complex as financial markets are becoming increasingly interconnected and interdependent. Traditional statistical techniques, on which market forecasters relied in previous years, seem to fail to capture this moving interrelationship among market variables. This context has led to a continuous search for techniques capable of identifying and capturing the non-linearities, discontinuities and high-frequency multi-polynomial components characterizing financial time series today. Classes of such techniques that have provided promising results in recent years are based on CI.

Modelling and trading financial variables is a very challenging open problem because of the complexity of financial data.

Existing statistical and linear models are unable to model real data complexity. The desired goal is the design and implementation of data-driven techniques able to extract profitable short-term trading models. Observed financial time series are non-normal, they show a slight skewness and high kurtosis and they are also non-stationary. This latter problem is addressed by transforming the time series into a stationary series of rates of return. Given the price level P_1, $P_2, \ldots, P_t$, the rate of return at time t is formed by:

$$R_t = \left(\frac{P_t}{P_{t-1}} \right) - 1$$

Percentage returns are linearly additive but log returns are not linearly additive across portfolio components. Based on these data, one has to construct a time series model that describes these data. In other words, one has to find the mapping:

$$R_{t+1} = \Phi(R_t, R_{t-1}, \ldots, R_0)$$

If Φ is a linear function (AR, ARMA, etc.) then one has to find the order and the coefficients of Φ. If Φ is non-linear, then the problem is complex. If Φ is non-linear and time varying, then the problem is even more complex. Traditional techniques solve the first model, but they fail for the last two approximate models and results suffer as a consequence from low prediction accuracy. Thus, more advanced techniques are needed to solve the non-linear/dynamical problem and produce more precise models for a better prediction accuracy. Such techniques are coming from CI – a sub-branch of Artificial Intelligence (AI) – and are primarily inspired by the laws of nature and adaptive mechanisms in order to enable or facilitate intelligent behaviours in changing complex environments. These mechanisms include the AI paradigms that exhibit an ability to learn and adapt to new situations, to generalize, abstract and discover. The following paradigms are commonly associated with CI: *artificial neural networks*, *evolutionary computation*, *swarm intelligence*, *support vector machines* and *fuzzy systems*. Individual techniques from these CI paradigms, as well as combinations (hybrid methods) of these paradigms, have been applied successfully to solve a variety of real-world problems. In particular, these have been widely applied to time series prediction, financial forecasting and trading. However, their practical utilization is not a trivial task and in order to be successful many 'parameters' should be examined and checked. Despite this, compared to the symbolic AI systems (Expert Systems – ES), the approximation of a realistic model is feasible and not time consuming. A traditional ES needs a knowledge engineer, at least a domain expert, and it will take 1–3 years to embed the expert's knowledge, to build and implement the inference mechanism (knowledge and rule bases) at a system prototype level. A similar CI model needs from some weeks to some months, since they are implemented using available open-source tools. Furthermore, these tools can be easily used by the domain experts.

This book focuses on current technological advances and challenges concerning the applications of CI techniques in financial time series forecasting and trading. It aims to provide an interdisciplinary view on current developments in financial time series forecasting, trading and investment. Existing approaches emphasize AI techniques or financial forecasting. Progress in the field has been extremely rapid in the past years, but novel methodologies and applications have not been included in existing books. This book intends to cover this gap.

The book is divided into five parts, all of which are focused on financial time series forecasting, modelling and trading.

The first part consists of two chapters which aim to introduce readers to the interdisciplinary field of trading with CI techniques. Specifically, the first chapter, 'Computational intelligence: recent advances, perspectives and open problems', provides an introduction to computational intelligence techniques, addressing the latest advancements and discussing outstanding problems and future directions. The second chapter, 'Forecasting and trading strategies: a survey', provides a small introduction to existing trading strategies and comparative characteristics of these strategies are discussed.

The second part is devoted to the applications of traditional CI techniques in the field of financial forecasting and trading. This part consists of two chapters, with the first one, 'Hidden Markov models: financial modelling and applications', analysing the applications of hidden Markov models in financial engineering and the second, 'Adaptive filtering on forecasting financial derivatives indices', applying adaptive filtering and ARMA modelling techniques to three forecasting and trading tasks.

The third part details more sophisticated methodologies in the form of neural networks. Its first chapter, 'Modelling and trading the corn–ethanol crush spread with neural networks', applies several neural network topologies including feedforward neural networks and recurrent neural networks, to the problem of forecasting and trading with a spread index. In the second chapter of this part, 'Trading decision support with historically consistent neural networks', a modern sliding window approach based on recurrent neural networks is presented and applied to several forecasting and trading tasks.

The fourth part is devoted to hybrid methodologies for trading and forecasting. Its first chapter, 'Advanced short-term forecasting and trading deploying neural networks optimized with an adaptive evolutionary algorithm', presents a novel portfolio management technique based on a hybrid evolutionary algorithm. Its second chapter, 'Using argumentation and hybrid evolutionary multi-model partitioning algorithms for efficient portfolio construction', introduces two novel hybrid techniques which combine a novel adaptive genetic algorithm with two classical neural network topologies: multilayer perceptrons and wavelet neural networks. These techniques are applied to two derivatives forecasting and trading tasks.

The final part comprises two chapters on the application of advanced computational intelligence modelling techniques to forecasting and trading. The first chapter, 'Forecasting DAX 30 using support vector machines and VDAX', deploys support vector machines for modelling and trading the DAX30 index. The second chapter, 'Ensemble learning of high-dimensional stock market data', introduces a novel random forest-based technique for financial trading.

The field of computational economics is quickly evolving and new computational intelligence techniques applications are published at an increasing pace. Moreover, the interdisciplinary nature of the field prevents existing CI and financial trading strategies articles from providing a set of unified information to students, researchers and practitioners. This volume will be useful for graduate and postgraduate students in computer science, financial engineering, finance and computational finance, both as a text and reference book. Practitioners, traders and financial analysts will also benefit from this book. Furthermore, since the same techniques can be used to process big data repositories, it could be very useful to scientists of other fields, such as bioinformatics.

Throughout the book, many applications are given which show the superiority of the new methods for trading and forecasting financial markets, while they explain how to preprocess the data (using filtering or wrapping methods), how to design different trading models/scenarios and how to implement the relative algorithms. Furthermore, the accompanying website of the book (http://prlab.ceid.upatras.gr/ACIFF) provides help to interested readers, in both the algorithms' modifications as well as implementation support. In a future edition we hope that all the methods presented, as well as some case studies, will be uploaded and available to readers on this website.

After reading this book, we hope that readers will have enjoyed this trip in the world of CI paradigms for financial forecasting, and even if they have not become an expert in the field 'you will arrive wise and experienced'.

Acknowledgements

We would like to thank all the contributors for their valuable research that they present in this book and the chapters' reviewers for the valuable critique. Credit need also to go to the entire editing and production team of Routledge and especially to our editorial assistant Natalie Tomlinson. Their efforts and support made this book a reality.

Part I
Introduction

Part 1

Introduction

1 Computational intelligence

Recent advances, perspectives and open problems

Konstantinos Theofilatos, Efstratios Georgopoulos,
Spiros Likothanassis and Seferina Mavroudi

1 Introduction

Machine intelligence dates back to 1936, when Turing proposed the idea of a universal processing machine (Turing, 1936), which composed the theoretical milestone in the theory of computability for the next years.

Having Turing's machine as a starting point, artificial intelligence (AI), in the last decades, focused on the principles, theoretical issues and design of algorithmic methodologies inspired by observations of the natural environment. Some striking examples are the artificial neural networks (ANNs), which are inspired by the mammalian neural system, and evolutionary algorithms (EAs), inspired by natural selection and genetic evolution in biology. These techniques, along with numerous others, have found their way in solving real-world problems in biology, medicine, business, technology and finance.

Computational intelligence (CI) (Engelbrecht, 2007) constitutes the subbranch of AI that includes the design and development of theories and methods with a sound biological understanding alongside their application to solve real-world problems. According to Bezdek (1994):

> A system is computationally intelligent when it: deals with only numerical (low level) data, has pattern recognition components, does not use knowledge in the AI sense and additionally when it (begins to) exhibit i) computational adaptivity, ii) computational fault tolerance, iii) speed approaching human-like turn around and iv) error rates that approximate human performance.

The above definition provides a central role for the definition of CI systems to the principles of computational adaptation, noisy data handling, computational speed and fault tolerance. The basic distinction of general AI systems and CI ones lies in their effort not only to imitate or surpass human intelligence, but also to aid humans to solve real-world problems more effectively, reducing their workload.

The necessity for fulfilling human tasks more conveniently, costlessly and faster, and the need for processing high volumes of data has led to the growth of the CI field in the last two decades, with the development of a series of high-performance algorithms.

The CI algorithms consist of models that are trained from examples with the aid of a tutor (*supervised learning*) and models that are self-adapted (*unsupervised learning*). The most significant applications of CI techniques in the financial forecasting and trading domain are financial time series forecasting, automatic trading and investment strategies extraction, portfolio management, bank failure, crisis predictions and, finally, risk management. These tasks are mainly supervised prediction problems and as historical data are available for most of the aforementioned tasks, the present chapter emphasizes supervised learning algorithms.

The high non-linearity and the noisy and adaptive nature of the underlying decision spaces requires the application of CI techniques which are designed to cope with such complex characteristics, and established them today as alternatives to more traditional, problem-specific financial engineering techniques.

In the rest of this chapter, the most important and well used CI techniques are introduced, emphasizing the analysis of their strengths and weaknesses, and discussing current open issues and future directions in the field.

2 Artificial neural networks

ANNs exist in several forms in the literature. In the present chapter the most popular architectures are presented by briefly describing their advantages and disadvantages.

2.1 Multilayer perceptrons

The first ANN architecture that was introduced for solving real-world problems is the multilayer perceptron (MLP). An MLP consists of a set of information-processing units called nodes. In the MLPs' topology these nodes are grouped together to layers which are interconnected serially to allow the nodes of one layer to be connected with the nodes of the previous and the next layer. The first layer is called the input layer (the number of its nodes corresponds to the number of the inputs for every examined problem). The last layer is called the output layer (the number of its nodes corresponds to the number of each problem's outputs). All the intermediary layers of nodes are called hidden layers. The number of hidden layers and the number of nodes composing them define the amount of complexity the overall neural network model is capable of fitting to the training data. Every node of the hidden and the output layers is acting as a classification hyperplane. Normally, each node of one layer has connections to all the other nodes of the next layer (fully connected). Moreover, the output's and the hidden layers' nodes have a connection with an extra input with constant value equal to one. This input is called the bias and its purpose is to remove the restriction that every node's corresponding hyperplane passes through the axis origin. Every connection of the MLP has a weight factor. In some cases an ANN could be not fully connected, meaning that connections between some nodes do not exist. In this case, the respective weights are equal to zero, and they are manipulated the same as the fully connected ones.

MLPs are feedforward neural networks and thus the information is processed starting with the input layer (input neurons are not processing units, which are often called sensory units; they just pass the input to the network) and finishing in the output layer. Specifically, the MLP network is processing the information, starting by passing the values from the input layer to the first hidden layer. These values are multiplied with the corresponding weights of the connections between the input and the hidden layer. Each node of the hidden layer processes the information through a non-linear activation function and passes it to the next hidden layer using the same procedure. This procedure is repeated step by step until the output layer and the final outputs are produced.

The training of the network (which is the adjustment of its weights and thresholds in a way that the network maps the input value of the training data to the corresponding output value) starts with randomly initialized weights and biases and proceeds by applying a learning algorithm. The most commonly used learning algorithm is called the Error Back Propagation (EBP) algorithm (Rumelhart *et al.*, 1986) and it simply tries to find those weights which minimize an error function (normally the sum of all squared differences between target and actual values). In order to apply the EBP algorithm, one has first to construct a *training set* (a set of N input–output pairs of the form (x_i, d_i) that are representative of the problem domain), and second to specify the network's architecture. The second part is the more difficult, since the training set specifies only the number of inputs and outputs of the network. The hidden layers of the network are a black box and the solution of this problem has been affected by the use of ANNs. Initially, this problem was handled using trial-and-error techniques. In recent years, new intelligent algorithms have been introduced in the literature, which perform the optimization of the network's topology automatically (Georgopoulos *et al.*, 2000; Yao, 1999). Many alternatives have been proposed in the literature and the strongest alternative to the EBP algorithm is the Extended Kalman Filter algorithm (Ruck *et al.*, 1992).

The network architecture of a 'standard' MLP is presented in Figure 1.1.

MLPs have been successfully applied in a variety of financial forecasting and trading tasks (Huang *et al.*, 2007). However, their training phase includes the very difficult tasks of obtaining their optimal network topology, weights and parameters. Dealing with these tasks requires time-consuming and risky steps of a repetitive trial-and-error procedure, which may lead to overfitting, low performance and data snooping effects (White, 2000). Moreover, this complexity regarding their training phase prohibits non-expert users from deploying them correctly.

2.2 Recurrent neural networks

A simple recurrent neural network (RNN) is a generalization of the MLP neural networks and has an activation feedback which resembles short-term memory. The architecture of RNNs is depicted in Figure 1.2.

The RNN architecture can provide more accurate outputs in time series forecasting tasks because the inputs are taken from as many previous values as

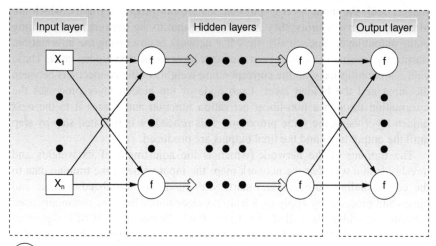

f : Neural network node with transfer function f

X₁ : Input node

——► : Weighted connection

Figure 1.1 The MLP neural network architecture.

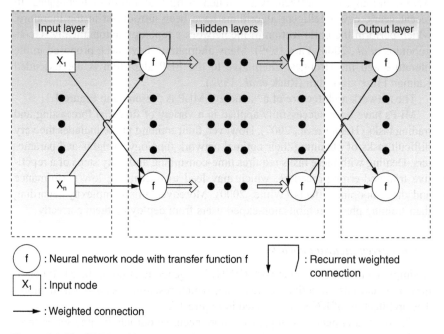

f : Neural network node with transfer function f

X₁ : Input node

——► : Weighted connection

: Recurrent weighted connection

Figure 1.2 The RNN architecture.

allowed by memory constraints. Despite the promising results of RNN applications in forecasting and trading tasks (Tenti, 1996; Dunis and Huang, 2002), they require substantially more connections and memory than standard MLPs and do not solve the overfitting, data snooping limitations; moreover, they cannot be easily used by non-experts.

For a more detailed presentation of recurrent networks, see Elman (1990).

2.3 Higher-order neural networks

HONNs are another generalization of the MLP neural networks which were initially designed to overcome the limitations of traditional NNs (Gils and Maxwell, 1987). They use simpler topologies as they do not have a hidden layer of nodes, but they can also operate as non-linear function approximators by using joint activation functions. This technique reduces the need for uncovering the relationships between inputs when training using complex architectures as these relationships are mapped to the extra inputs of the network. Moreover, this reduces the number of free parameters and reduces HONNs' training time complexity. Another advantage of HONNs is their reduced risks for overfitting and getting trapped in local optima due to the simplicity of their training. However, because the number of inputs can be very large for higher-order architectures, orders of four and over are rarely used. The topology of HONNs and an example of their correspondence with MLP neural networks are depicted in Figure 1.3. Furthermore, they are also prone to data snooping and their performance is constrained by their simplicity.

While HONNs have already experienced some success in the field of pattern recognition, their application in finance started only in the last decade (Zhang *et al.*, 2002). They have been successfully applied in a variety of forecasting and trading tasks, including trading exchange rates (Knowles *et al.*, 2011) and trading futures spread portfolios (Dunis *et al.*, 2008). These studies have proved their superiority over simple MLPs and RNNs in most of the examined indexes.

2.4 Radial basis function neural networks

A radial basis function (RBF) neural network in its generalized form is another feedforward neural network with one hidden layer where hidden units do not implement an activation function, but instead each one of them is an RBF. A generalized RBF neural network approximates a desired function by superposition of non-orthogonal, radial symmetric functions. They have been initially proposed by Broomhead and Lowe (1988).

Their architecture is depicted in Figure 1.4.

Compared to other simpler neural networks they are claimed to improve accuracy of artificial neural networks while decreasing training time complexity. This is attributed to their simpler and more straightforward training phase which includes the location of the optimal number of hidden nodes and the optimization of the parameters of the RBF. The optimization of the weights connecting

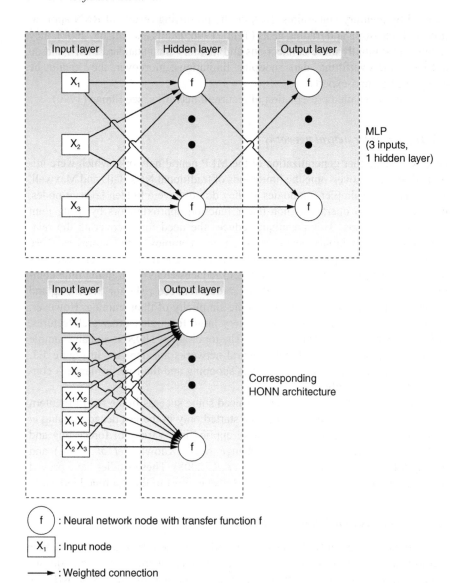

Figure 1.3 The HONN architecture.

the hidden with the output layer is straightforward as it could be deterministically achieved through solving a series of linear equations.

Regarding their financial applications, they have been widely used for predicting exchange rates (Yu *et al.*, 2008) and other financial indexes (Niu and Wang, 2013). Despite their learning phase being simpler than the MLP neural networks', it includes the hard task of finding the optimal parameter values for

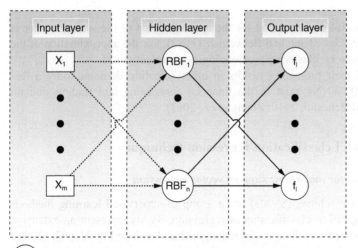

f_i : Neural network node with linear transfer function

RBF_i : Neural network node with radial basis transfer function

X_i : Input node

——► : Weighted connection

······► : Connection with fixed weight equal to 1

Figure 1.4 The RBF neural network architecture.

the RBF functions and their optimal number. To solve these issues, clustering methods such as Self Organizing Maps (Kohonen, 1982) and K-means (Lloyd, 1982), combined with a trial-and-error procedure, are usually applied. Lately, some metaheuristic algorithms (Sermpinis *et al.*, 2013) have been deployed to undertake this task, with very promising results.

2.5 *Wavelet neural networks*

Wavelet neural networks (WNNs) are a generalization of the RBF neural networks. Similar to RBFs they have the same three-layered structure as the one presented in Figure 1.4. In contrast to simple MLPs and RBFs, WNNs use radial wavelets as activation functions to the hidden layer, while using the linear activation function in the output layer. These wavelet functions are selected from three possible candidate ones: Mexican hat, Morlet and Gaussian wavelet function. Their training phase includes the determination of the optimal number of hidden neurons, the optimization of the parameters of the wavelet functions called scaling and translational vectors and the calculation of the weights that connect the hidden with the output layers, solving a set of linear equations.

The most well-known method for the approximation of the scaling vector is the one proposed by Zhang and Benveniste (1982). For the approximation of the translational vectors, clustering methodologies are mainly used.

In spite of their promising results in other scientific domains, only a few applications of WNNs exist in the financial forecasting and trading domain (Nekoukar and Beheshti, 2010; Zhang *et al.*, 2001).

3 Advanced CI classification/regression techniques

3.1 Support vector machines: support vector regression

Support vector machines (SVMs) are a group of supervised learning methods that can be applied to classification or regression. SVMs represent an extension to non-linear models of the generalized algorithm developed by Vapnik (2000). They have been developed into a very active research area and have already been applied to many scientific problems. SVMs are similar to an RBF neural network topology; however, their learning phase involves the application of Vapnik's generalized algorithm instead of other analytic, clustering or heuristic methods. Moreover, SVMs are not constrained to using RBFs – they can select between the large universe of kernel functions.

SVM models were originally defined for the classification of linearly separable classes of objects. For any particular linear separable set of two-class objects SVMs are able to find the optimal hyperplanes that separate them, providing the bigger (optimal) margin area between the two hyperplanes.

SVMs can also be used to separate classes that cannot be separated with a linear classifier. In such cases, the coordinates of the objects are mapped into a feature space using non-linear functions. The feature space in which every object is projected is a high-dimensional space in which the two classes can be separated with a linear classifier.

SVMs are classification techniques which, however, have been extended in order to enable their application in regression problems such as financial forecasting. This was accomplished through the introduction of the ε-sensitive loss function by Vapnik (2000) which established support vector regression (SVR) as a robust technique for constructing data-driven and non-linear empirical regression models.

SVMs and SVRs have already been applied in many prediction and classification problems in finance and economics (Cao and Tay, 2003; Huang *et al.*, 2005; Kim, 2003; Yeh *et al.*, 2011), although they are still far from mainstream in the financial forecasting domain.

Despite their strong theoretical background and their promising experimental results, they have not been not able so far to overcome the constraints of the curse of dimensionality, and parameter tuning and in some cases simple neural network topologies have been found to outperform them in practical problems.

3.2 Random forests

Another sophisticated machine learning method, alternative to SVMs, is the random forest (RF) method. RFs (Breiman, 2001) are ensemble classifiers that create in parallel many decision trees, with each tree's nodes being a random subset of the features considered. In particular, RFs are a combination of tree predictors such that each tree depends on the values of a random vector sampled independently and with the same distribution for all trees in the forest. The idea of growing an ensemble of trees and letting them vote for the most popular class has led to significant improvements in classification accuracy. The generalization error for the forest rises up to a limit as the number of trees in the forest becomes large. The generalization error for the forest of tree classifiers depends on the strength of the individual trees in the forest and the correlation between them. The applications of RFs in predicting the movement direction of financial time series remains nowadays quite limited, despite their high classification performance and ability to generalize on data that have not been used during their training phase (Ladyzynski *et al.*, 2013). Unfortunately, their supreme generalization and accuracy performance comes with limited interpretability. Moreover, their performance is highly dependent on the proper tuning of their parameters and the selection of a consistent and informative feature subset to be used as input.

4 Heuristic methods

Heuristic methods, which are mainly optimization techniques, are used to speed up the process of finding a good near-optimal solution, where an exhaustive search is infeasible. The term optimization refers to the efforts for bringing whatever is the examined object towards its ultimate state. In order to achieve this goal, heuristic methods are applied.

These methods require the definition of three quantities: a *representation* of a single solution for the examined problem, the *search space* and a *fitness function*. The *representation* is defined as a well-defined method to assign every solution of a problem to a well-structured, usually mathematical formation that could be easily used to extract the solution (known as coding). The most widely used representation forms are the ones of binary strings, real-valued strings and tree representation. Having selected a fixed representation schema for the solutions of a problem, the problem search space is defined as the set of valid solutions that could be represented with this schema. The fitness function is a mathematical equation which is used to measure the fitness-appropriateness of a solution given its representation. When the fitness function provides higher values for better solutions, the problem is formulated as a *maximization problem* and otherwise as a *minimization one*.

4.1 Classical deterministic methods

The most widely used deterministic heuristic methods are the *local search methods*, the *simplex* and *dynamic programming*.

All local search methods are based on the same principle: instead of searching exhaustively through the search space, these methods try to emphasize a small sub-space and search it. They start with a random solution in the search space and after evaluating this solution and its neighbouring solutions they select the current solution as the one with the best performance from the examined ones. This procedure is continued until the current solutions do not change for a series of the algorithm's repetitions. One of the most well-known representatives of the local search algorithms is the hill-climbing algorithm and its variations (Rosete *et al.*, 1999).

The simplex method (Nelder and Mead, 1965) can be applied to solve optimization problems when they can be defined as a system of linear equations. It consists of an iterative procedure that solves a system of linear equations in each of its steps, and stops when either the optimum is reached or the solution proves infeasible.

Dynamic programming (Bellman, 1954) is a method that applies the divide-and-conquer technique by breaking down complex search problems into simpler sub-problems. Its applicability is restricted by the nature of the problem at hand. Specifically, the problem should be easily divided to simpler ones which could be solved independently.

4.2 Meta-heuristic methods

Classical deterministic search methods have been proven to provide adequate results for simple problems with well-structured search spaces. However, real problems are not so easy to solve. Their search spaces are large, chaotic and include many local optimal solutions. Moreover, in most cases little is known a priori about the structure of the search space of the problem.

To deal with these hard optimization problems a variety of meta-heuristic methods have been proposed in the CI domain. These methods do not guarantee that the optimal solution of a problem will be found. Moreover, most of them do not have any strong mathematical background to justify their performance. They are inspired from nature observations to extract algorithmic solutions for *exploring* the search space as well as possible while *exploiting* its promising areas. The most important meta-heuristic methods are the evolutionary algorithms (Holland, 1992), the particle swarm optimization (Kennedy, 1997) and, more recently, some other promising methods that have been proposed, such as ant colony optimization (Dorigo *et al.*, 2006) and artificial bee colony algorithm (Karaboga and Basturk, 2007). The latter, despite their promising merit, are currently far from being considered as tested robust methods and in most practical applications they have been avoided so far.

All these methods are specifications of the flow chart depicted in Figure 1.5. They start with an initial construction of a set of solutions which they evaluate

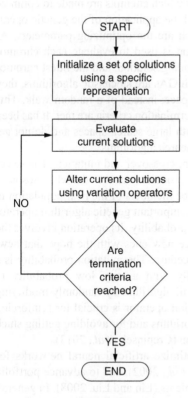

START

Initialize a set of solutions using a specific representation

Evaluate current solutions

Alter current solutions using variation operators

NO

Are termination criteria reached?

YES

END

Figure 1.5 Meta-heuristic algorithms flow chart.

using a fitness function, and alter them using a set of variation operators until some termination criteria are reached.

In the next subsections, the most important meta-heuristic methods, with many financial engineering applications, are briefly introduced.

4.2.1 Genetic algorithms

Genetic algorithms (GAs) (Holland, 1992) are the most widely used approaches to computational evolution for solving complex optimization problems with limited prior knowledge about the structure of their search space. Holland has presented GAs in a general theoretical framework for adaptation in nature. He attempted to understand and link diverse types of natural phenomena, but he has also proposed potential engineering applications of GAs. Since the publication of Holland's book, the field of GAs has grown into a significant sub-area of AI and machine learning.

GAs, as meta-heuristic algorithms, are useful and efficient if the search space is big and complicated or there does not exist any available mathematical analysis of the problem. Their operation starts with the random generation of a population of candidate solutions, called chromosomes, for which attempts are made to optimize through a number of evolutionary cycles and the application of the genetic operations. Chromosomes consist of genes, which are the optimizing parameters. At each iteration (*generation*), a fitness function is used to evaluate each chromosome, measuring the quality of the corresponding solution, and the fittest chromosomes are selected to survive. Thus, although GAs are stochastic algorithms, they perform a guided navigation in the search space, instead of a random walk. This evolutionary process is repeated until some termination criteria are met. It has been proved experimentally that GAs can deal with large search spaces and do not get trapped in local optimal solutions like other search algorithms.

Their main genetic operators are selection, crossover and mutation. The selection operator, imitating the natural selection process, reassures that chromosomes with higher performance are more likely to be members of the next population in an evolutionary cycle. Crossover is the most important genetic algorithm operator and is usually applied with a relatively high probability. Its operation involves the combination of existing solutions to produce new ones with the hope that new, better solutions will come up from this procedure. The mutation probability is a complementary one and is applied usually with a very low probability to strengthen the stochastic nature of the overall algorithm by randomly modifying small parts of the chromosomes. The mutation operator is crucial for reinforcing the exploration properties of the genetic algorithms and for avoiding getting stuck to local optima or the stagnation phenomenon (Crepinsek *et al.*, 2013).

GAs have been widely deployed to optimize artificial neural networks for forecasting and modelling tasks (Andreou *et al.*, 2002), and to advance portfolio management and investment allocation problems (Lin and Liu, 2008). In general, they are famous for their exploration properties, but they fail to perform robust local searching and thus have limited exploitation properties. Moreover, in spite of research attempts to design efficient operators for continuous variable optimization, they perform better in binary-represented problems.

4.2.2 Differential evolution

Differential evolution (DE) (Das and Suganthan, 2011) is considered as the prevalent stochastic real-parameter optimization algorithm in current use. DE operates through similar computational steps as employed by a standard GA. As an evolutionary algorithm, it iteratively applies selection, mutation and crossover operators until some termination criteria are reached. Its main variation operator, however, is the mutation operator which perturbs the current-generation population members with the scaled differences of randomly selected and distinct population members. Therefore, no separate probability distribution has to be used for generating the offspring. Since its introduction in 1995, DE has drawn the attention of many researchers, resulting in a lot of variants of the basic algorithm with improved performance.

Its superiority over traditional GAs has led to its extended use in various applications in finance (Krink and Paterlini, 2011; Donate *et al.*, 2013).

4.2.3 Genetic programming

Genetic programming (GP) (Koza, 1992) is a domain-independent problem-solving technique in which computer programs are evolved to approximately solve problems. It is an evolutionary algorithm and thus it follows the principles of the evolution theory of Darwin. In general, GP is a generalization of the GA, which considers computer programs as candidate solutions. This representation generalization enables it to provide solutions to a variety of problems, including classification, modelling and regression. In GP, the evolution operates on a population of computer programs of varying sizes and shapes and, as all meta-heuristic methods, starts with an initial population of thousands or millions of randomly generated computer programs composed of the available program-matic ingredients and then applies the principles of biological evolution to create a new (and often improved) population of programs. The generation of this new population is accomplished with specialized crossover and mutation operators for every representation schema. A computer program, which could be repres-ented also as a mathematical equation, that solves (or approximately solves) a given problem often emerges from this process. To represent computer programs as chromosomes of the GP method, the classical approach proposed by Koza (1992) is used, which deploys a tree-based representation schema. However, dif-ferent representations have been proposed in the literature and each one has led to a new GP method (Ferreira, 2001; Ciesielski, 2008).

The ability of GP to act as an alternative approach to ANNs, freeing the prac-titioners from their limitations, results in its application in various financial fore-casting and trading tasks (Vasilakis *et al.*, 2013; Sermpinis *et al.* 2012).

4.2.4 Particle swarm optimization

The particle swarm optimization (PSO) algorithm, proposed by Kennedy and Eberhart (1995), is a population-based heuristic search algorithm based on the simulation of the social behaviour of birds within a flock. In PSO, candidate solu-tions, which are referred to as particles, are placed initially randomly within the search space. Changes to the position of particles within the search space are based on the social-psychological tendency of individuals to emulate the success of other individuals. From its position, each particle is assigned a velocity value. This velocity indicates its movement in the search space, which will be conducted in the next iteration of the algorithm. Imitating the behaviour of birds flocking, the velocity of particles at every iteration is altered by attraction to the positions of good solutions of the present and past populations of solutions. Moreover, the velocity of its particle is attracted by its past good solutions. The consequence of modelling this social behaviour is that the search process is such that particles sto-chastically return towards previously successful regions in the search space. Many variations of the PSO algorithms have been proposed in the literature, with each of them proposing different equations for altering the velocity values and different methods to tune the parameters of the overall algorithm (Kameyama, 2009).

Compared to classical GAs, PSO presents better performance on optimizing continuous variables and, moreover, it is empowered with stronger local search properties. For these reasons it has been applied in many financial applications, with very promising results (Sermpinis *et al.*, 2013; Zhu *et al.*, 2011).

5 Discussion

Despite the very encouraging results of the aforementioned CI techniques in many engineering applications, there exist a lot of open problems and issues which cannot be handled by the current techniques. In this section the most important open problems are discussed, emphasizing the current research efforts for overcoming them.

5.1 Overfitting

One of the most important threats when applying a CI technique is overfitting. The term overfitting is used in supervised learning to define the state of a model that has been trained to become extremely specific in the training dataset of a problem, having very low performance on the testing dataset. Another facet of overfitting is the *bloat effect* which happens when a model becomes very complex, having very good performance in the training dataset and poor performance on the testing dataset. Both of these effects may lead to overestimating the power of a model and getting disappointing results when applying it in practice.

To overcome these issues the CI society has proposed many solutions.

A necessary step is to split the dataset to in-sample and out-of-sample datasets. In-sample datasets can be used to train a CI model and out-of-sample to evaluate it. A common error is to use the out-of-sample dataset to tune the parameters of a model. This technique treats the out-of-sample dataset as a part of the in-sample and thus contains the risks of overestimating the model's performance. However, even the proper utilization of the splitting technique is not sufficient to overcome the overfitting issues as it is only able to inform practitioners about its existence without providing solutions to avoid it.

The most commonly used approaches for avoiding overfitting are early stopping (Prechelt, 2012), cross validation (Prechelt, 1998), specialized fitness functions that favour simple models (Sermpinis *et al.*, 2013) and pruning techniques (Wang *et al.*, 2010). All of these techniques have been applied with satisfactory results, but they cannot solve the problem as single unit techniques. A combination of them is required to avoid overtraining, while also keeping the models as simple as possible.

5.2 Feature selection: curse of dimensionality

The problem of feature selection is twofold: first, the most informative features should be found and provided as inputs in the applied model; second, irrelevant features or features sharing the same information should be avoided. The higher the number of inputs a model has, the sparser the space when the training samples are projecting onto it. This is called the curse of dimensionality, which is responsible in most cases for the limited performance of models with many inputs.

To handle the curse of dimensionality, the scientific community has proposed the integration of a dimensionality reduction step in the classification or regression techniques. Dimensionality reduction techniques are divided into feature extraction and feature selection techniques. The distinction between the two categories is made by splitting them into those which do not preserve the data semantics in the process of reduction and those that do. The most important representative of the first category is the principal component analysis method (Jollife, 1986). Feature selection methods are further split into filtering, wrapper and embedded techniques. Filtering techniques, such as minimum redundancy maximum relevance (Peng *et al.*, 2005), act independently of the regression or classification model to select the most informative features. Wrapper and embedded techniques deploy a meta-heuristic method which is responsible for finding the optimal feature subset for a specific classification or regression model. Embedded techniques, in contrast to wrapper ones, do not deal with the utilized classification or regression model as a black box, but take feedback from it to fasten the feature selection procedure. Embedded techniques (Hsieh *et al.*, 2011) have been proved superior to all other techniques in performing feature selection tasks, but require higher execution time than the simple filtering techniques.

5.3 Interpretability: performance tradeoff

One of the most important drawbacks of CI techniques is the lack of interpretability. Most of the times, CI models are very complex and can only be handled by experts as black box approaches. This fact limits their further utilization by domain experts who could otherwise extract useful findings. On the other hand, when very simple models are considered, they usually present low performance. This tradeoff is called the interpretability–performance tradeoff and great efforts have been made to balance it in the last decade.

Lately, many approaches are trying to deal with this problem. One very crucial step, as already mentioned, is the feature selection step, which not only raises the extracted models' performance, but provides feedback about which inputs are significant for a given problem. Another technique for alleviating the interpretability need is the utility of the aforementioned techniques for avoiding overfitting. Keeping the models as simple as possible to avoid the bloat effect makes then more easily interpretable without harming their performance.

To further solve the interpretability–performance tradeoff, a variety of techniques have been proposed in the literature which instead of altering the classification or regression model, try to extract interpretable fuzzy rules from it. Techniques, following this idea, have been designed for both ANN (Kahramanli and Allahverdi, 2009) and SVM (Papadimitriou and Terzidis, 2005) models.

5.4 Parameter tuning

A vital point when training a CI classification or regression model is to tune its parameters properly. As already mentioned, this procedure should be accomplished only by using the in-sample datasets to avoid overfitting.

One simple technique is to apply a time-consuming step of trial-and-error experiments to properly tune the parameters of a model. However, this procedure is vulnerable to human error and to the data snooping effect. For this reason heuristic and meta-heuristic methods are designed and applied to undertake this task. Furthermore, this procedure is usually accomplished in parallel with the feature selection step by designing a simple meta-heuristic algorithm to deal with both optimization problems.

6 Conclusions

This chapter has briefly introduced the basic components of CI, focusing on techniques which are commonly applied to the financial engineering field. It is clear from the foregoing analysis that there does not exist a universal CI optimal solution for solving all problems of financial forecasting and trading. All CI techniques present some specific advantages and disadvantages which make them appropriate for usage in specific problems. Moreover, it is a prevalent trend that multiple CI techniques are combined to form hybrid techniques which tend to overcome the constraints of single techniques.

Other issues discussed in the present chapter are the open problems of CI techniques and the most significant future research directions. Specifically, the issues of overfitting, feature selection, interpretability–performance tradeoff and parameter tuning were discussed and analysed. To overcome these issues many new methods are being proposed by the scientific community. However, new methods require extended experimentation and testing and for this reason the CI community emphasizes the enhancement of existing techniques and their reinforcement with extra modules to surpass the current limitations.

References

Andreou, A., E. Georgopoulos and S. Likothanassis, 'Exchange-rates forecasting: a hybrid algorithm based on genetically optimized adaptive neural networks', *Computational Economics* 20(3), 2002, 191–210.

Bellman, R., 'The theory of dynamic programming', *Bulletin of the American Mathematical Society* 60, 1954, 503–516.

Bezdek, J., 'What is computational intelligence?' in L. Zurada, R. Marks and C. Robinson (eds.), *Computational Intelligence Imitating Life*, IEEE Press, New York, pp. 1–12, 1994.

Breiman, L., 'Random Forests', *Machine Learning* 45(1), 2001, 5–32.

Broomhead, S. and D. Lowe, 'Multivariate functional interpolation and adaptive networks', *Complex Systems*, 2, 1988, 321–355.

Cao, L. and F. Tay, 'Support vector machine with adaptive parameters in financial time series forecasting', *IEEE Transactions on Neural Networks* 14(6), 2003, 1506–1518.

Ciesielski, V., 'Linear genetic programming', *Genetic Programming and Evolvable Machines* 9(1), 2008, 105–106.

Crepinsek, M., S. Liu and M. Mernik, 'Exploration and exploitation in evolutionary algorithms: a survey', *ACM Computing Surveys Journal* 45(3), 2013, doi: 10.1145/2480741.2480752.

Das, S. and P. Suganthan, 'Differential evolution: a survey of the state-of-the-art', *IEEE Transactions on Evolutionary Computation* 15(1), 2011, 4–31.

Donate, J., X. Li, G. Sanchez and A. Miguel, 'Time series forecasting by evolving artificial neural networks with genetic algorithms, differential evolution and estimation of distribution algorithm', *Neural Computing and Applications Journal* 22(1), 2013, 11–20.

Dorigo, M., M. Birattari and T. Stutzle, 'Ant colony optimization', *IEEE Computational Intelligence Magazine* 1(4), 2006, 28–39.

Dunis, C. and X. Huang, 'Forecasting and trading currency volatility: an application of recurrent neural regression and model combination', *Journal of Forecasting* 21(5), 2002, 317–354.

Dunis, C., J. Laws and B. Evans, 'Trading futures spread portfolios: applications of higher order and recurrent networks', *European Journal of Finance* 14(5–6), 2008, 503–521.

Elman, J., 'Finding structure in time', *Cognitive Science* 14(2), 1990, 179–211.

Engelbrecht, A., *Computational Intelligence: An introduction*, John Wiley and Sons, Inc., New York, 2007.

Ferreira, C., 'Gene expression programming: a new adaptive algorithm for solving problems', *Complex Systems* 13(2), 2001, 87–129.

Georgopoulos, E., S. Likothanassis and A. Adamopoulos, 'Evolving artificial neural networks using genetic algorithms', *Journal of Neural Network World*, 4, 2000, 565–574.

Gils, L. and T. Maxwell, 'Learning, invariance, and generalization in high-order neural networks', *Applied Optics* 26(23), 1987, 4972–4978.

Holland, J., *Adaptation in Natural and Artificial Systems: An Introductory Analysis with Applications to Biology, Control and Artificial Intelligence*, Cambridge, MA: MIT Press, 1992.

Hsieh, T., H. Hsiao and W. Yeh, 'Forecasting stock markets using wavelet transforms and recurrent neural networks: an integrated system based on artificial bee colony algorithm', *Applied Soft Computing* 11(2), 2011, 2510–2525.

Huang, W., Y. Nakamori and S. Wang, 'Forecasting stock market movement direction with support vector machine', *Computers & Operations Research* 32, 2005, 2513–2522.

Huang, W., K. Lai, Y. Nakamori, S. Wang and L. Yu, 'Neural networks in finance and economical forecasting', *International Journal of Information Technology and Decision Making* 6(1), 2007, 113–140.

Jolliffe, I., *Principal Component Analysis*, Springer-Verlag, New York, 1986.

Kahramanli, H. and N. Allahverdi, 'Rule extraction from trained neural networks using artificial immune systems', *Expert Systems with Applications* 36(2), part 1, 2009, 1513–1522.

Kameyama, K., 'Particle swarm optimization: a survey', *IEICE Transactions on Information and Systems* E92-D(7), 2009, 1354–1361.

Karaboga, D. and B. Basturk, 'A powerful and efficient algorithm for numerical function optimization: artificial bee colony (ABC) algorithm', *Journal of Global Optimization* 39, 2007, 459–471.

Kennedy, J., 'The particle swarm: social adaptation of knowledge'. In *Proceedings of the IEEE International Conference on Evolutionary Computation*, Piscataway, NJ: Institute of Electrical and Electronics Engineers, 303–308, 1997.

Kennedy, J. and R. Eberhart, 'Particle swarm optimization', *Proceedings of the IEEE International Conference on Neural Networks* 4, 1995, 1942–1948.

Kim, K., 'Financial time series forecasting using support vector machines', *Neurocomputing* 55, 2003, 307–319.

Knowles, H., W. El Deredy, P. Lisboa and C. Dunis, 'Higher order neural networks with Bayesian confidence measure for the prediction of the EUR/USD exchange rate', in Zhang, M. (ed.), *Artificial Higher Order Neural Networks for Economics and Business*, IGI Global, New York, pp. 48–59, 2011.

Kohonen, T., 'Self-organized formation of topologically correct feature maps', *Biological Cybernetics* 43(1), 1982, 59–69.

Koza, J., *Genetic Programming: On the Programming of Computers by Means of Natural Selection*, MIT Press, Cambridge, MA, 1992.

Krink, T. and S. Paterlini, 'Multiobjective optimization using differential evolution for real-world portfolio optimization', *Computational Management Science* 8(1–2), 2011, 157–179.

Ladyzynski, P., K. Zbikowski and P. Grzegorzewski, 'Stock trading with random forests, trend detection tests and force index volume indicators', *Artificial Intelligence and Soft Computing, Lecture Notes in Computer Science* 7895, 2013, 441–452.

Lin, C. and Y. Liu, 'Genetic algorithms for portfolio selection problems with minimum transaction lots', *European Journal of Operational Research* 185, 2008, 393–404.

Lloyd, S., 'Least squares quantization in PCM', *IEEE Transactions on Information Theory* 28(2), 1982, 129–137.

Nekoukar, V. and M. Beheshti, 'A local linear radial basis function neural network for financial time-series forecasting', *Applied Intelligence* 33, 2010, 352–356.

Nelder, J. and R. Mead, 'A simplex method for function minimization', *The Computer Journal* 7(4), 1965, 308–313.

Niu, H. and J. Wang, 'Financial time series prediction by a random data-time effective RBF neural network', *Soft Computing*, 2013, 1–12.

Papadimitriou, S. and K. Terzidis, 'Efficient and interpretable fuzzy classifiers from data with support vector learning', *Intelligent Data Analysis* 9(6), 2005, 527–550.

Peng, H., F. Long and C. Ding, 'Feature selection based on mutual information: criteria of max-dependency, max-relevance, and min-redundancy', *IEEE Transactions on Pattern Analysis and Machine Intelligence* 27(8), 2005, 1226–1238.

Prechelt, L., 'Automatic early stopping using cross validation: quantifying the criteria', *Neural Networks* 11(4), 1998, 761–767.

Prechelt, L., 'Early stopping – but when? Neural networks: tricks of the trade', *Lecture Notes in Computer Science* 7700, 2012, 53–67.

Rosete, A., A. Ochoa and M. Sebag, 'Automatic graph drawing and stochastic hill climbing', *Proceedings of Genetic and Evolutionary Computation Conference, GECCO-99*, edited by Banzhaf, W., Daida, J., Eiben, A.E., Garzon, M.H., Honavar, V., Jakiela, M. and Smith, R.E., Morgan-Kaufmann, San Francisco, CA, Vol. 2, 1999, 1699–1706,.

Ruck, D., S. Rogers, M. Kabrisky, P. Maybeck and M. Oxley, 'Comparative analysis of backpropagation and the extended Kalman filter for training multilayer perceptrons', *IEEE Transactions on Pattern Analysis and Machine Intelligence* 14(6), 1992, 686–691.

Rumelhart, E., G. Hinton and R. Williams. 'Learning internal representations by error propagation', in Rumelhart, D.E., James L. McClelland and the PDP research group (eds), *Parallel Distributed Processing: Explorations in the Microstructure of Cognition, Volume 1: Foundations*, MIT Press, Cambridge, MA, 1986.

Sermpinis, G., J. Laws, A. Karathanasopoulos and C. Dunis, 'Forecasting and trading the EUR/USD exchange rate with gene expression and psi sigma neural networks', *Expert Systems with Applications* 39(10), 2012, 8865–8877.

Sermpinis, G., K. Theofilatos, A. Karathanasopoulos, E. Georgopoulos and C. Dunis, 'Modelling and trading the EUR/USD and EUR/GBP exchange rates with an adaptive RBF-PSO neural network', *European Journal of Operational Research* 225(3), 2013, 528–540.

Tenti, P., 'Forecasting foreign exchange rates using recurrent neural networks', *Applied Artificial Intelligence* 10(6), 1996, 567–581.

Turing, A., 'On computable numbers, with an application to the Entscheidungs problem', *Proceedings of the London Mathematical Society* 2(42), 1936, 230–265.

Vapnik, V., *The Nature of Statistical Learning Theory*, Springer, New York, 2000.

Vasilakis, G., E. Georgopoulos, K. Theofilatos, A. Karathanasopoulos and S. Likothanassis, 'A genetic programming approach for EUR/USD exchange rate forecasting', *Computational Economics*, 42, 2013, 415–431.

Wang, T., Z. Qin, Z. Jin and S. Zhang, 'Handling overfitting in test cost-sensitive decision tree learning by feature selection, smoothing and pruning', *Journal of Systems and Software* 83(7), 2010, 1137–1147.

White, H., 'A reality check for data snooping', *Econometrica Journal of the Econometric Society* 68(5), 2000, 1097–1126.

Yao, X., 'Evolving artificial neural networks', *Proceedings of the IEEE* 87(9), 1999, 1423–1447.

Yeh, C., C. Huang and S. Lee, 'A multiple-kernel support vector regression approach for stock market price forecasting', *Expert Systems with Applications* 38(3), 2011, 2177–2186.

Yu, L., K. Lai and S. Wang, 'Multistage neural network ensemble learning for exchange rates forecasting', *Neurocomputing* 71(16–18), 2008, 3295–3302.

Zhang, B., R. Coggins, M. Jabri, D. Dersch and B. Flower, 'Multiresolution forecasting for futures trading using wavelet decompositions', *IEEE Transactions on Neural Networks* 12(4), 2001, 765–775.

Zhang, M., X. Shuxiang and J. Fulcher, 'Neuron-adaptive higher order neural-network models for automated financial data modeling', *IEEE Transactions on Neural Networks* 13(1), 2002, 188–204.

Zhang, Q. and A. Benveniste, 'Wavelet networks', *IEEE Transactions on Neural Networks* 3, 1982, 889–898.

Zhu, H., Y. Wang, K. Wang and Y. Chen, 'Particle swarm optimization (PSO) for the constraint portfolio optimization problem', *Expert Systems with Applications* 38(8), 2011, 10161–10169.

2 Financial forecasting and trading strategies

A survey

Charalampos Stasinakis and Georgios Sermpinis

1 Technical analysis overview

Technical analysis is a financial market technique that focuses on studying and forecasting the 'market action', namely the price, volume and open interest future trends, using charts as primary tools. Charles Dow set the roots of technical analysis in the late eighteenth century. The main principle of his Dow Theory is the trending nature of prices, as a result of all available information in the market. These trends are confirmed by volume and persist despite the 'market noise', as long as there are not definitive signals to imply otherwise. Another interesting definition of technical analysis is given by Pring (2002, p. 2): 'The technical approach to investment is essentially a reflection of the idea that prices move in trends that are determined by the changing attitudes of investors toward a variety of economic, monetary, political, and psychological forces.' Furthermore, he adds that 'the art of technical analysis, for it is an art, is to identify a trend reversal at a relatively early stage and ride on that trend until the weight of the evidence shows or proves that the trend has reversed'.

In order to fully understand the concept of technical analysis, it is essential to clearly distinguish it from the fundamental one. It is also important to discuss the efficient market hypothesis and the random walk theory.

1.1 Technical analysis vs fundamental analysis

In order to fully understand the concept of technical analysis, it is essential to clearly distinguish it from the fundamental one. The premises of the technical approach are basically that market action discounts all available information, prices move in trends and history tends to repeat itself. On the other hand, fundamental analysis is based on information regarding supply and demand, the two major economic forces affecting prices' direction change. Both approaches aim to solve the same problem, but 'the fundamentalist studies the cause of market movement, while the technician studies the effect' (Murphy, 1999, p. 5).

In reality, the complete separation between the fundamentalist and the technician is not so easy, although there is always a basis of conflict. For example, institutions that need a long-term assessment of their stock turn to fundamental analysis, while short-term traders use technical ones. The company's financial health is evaluated with the technical approach, whereas its long-term potential is based on fundamental approximations. Such examples show that both techniques have advantages and disadvantages and one does not exclude the other. The greatest benefit derived from fundamental analysis is the ability to understand market dynamics and not panic in periods of extreme market volatility. On the other hand, technical analysis does not utilize any economic data or market event news, just simple tools that are easy to understand in comparison with fundamental indicators. The technicians are also able to adapt in any trading medium or time dimension and therefore they gain extra market flexibility compared to fundamentalists. In conclusion, technical analysis appears able to capture trends and extreme market events that the fundamental one discovers and explains after they have already been well established.

1.2 Efficient market hypothesis and random walk theory

Fama (1970) introduced the concept of capital market efficiency. This influential paper established the framework implied by the context of the term 'efficient market hypothesis'. According to Fama (1970), a market is efficient if the prices always reflect and rapidly adjust to the known and new information, respectively. The basis of this hypothesis is the existence of rational investors in an uncertain environment. A rational investor is following the news and reacts immediately to all important news that affects directly or indirectly his investment, capital, security price, etc. The efficient market hypothesis is also connected with the *random walk theory*, which suggests that the market price movements are random.

The assumptions of the efficient market hypothesis can be summarized as:

- prices reflect all relevant information available to investors;
- all investors are rational and informed;
- there are no transaction costs and no arbitrage opportunities (perfect operational and allocation efficiency).

Fama (1970) further classifies market efficiency into three forms, based on the information taken under consideration:

1 *The weak form* applies when all past information is fully reflected in market prices. The weakly efficient markets are linked with the random walk theory. If the current prices fully reflect all past information, then the next day's price changes would be the result of new information only. Since the new information arrives at random, the price changes must also be random.

2 *The semi-strong form* requires all publicly available information to be reflected in market prices. This form is based on the competition among analysts, who attempt to take advantage of the new information constantly generating from market actions. If this competition is perfect and fair, then there would be no analyst who would be able to make abnormal profits.

3 *The strong form* implication is that market prices should reflect all available information, including that available only to insiders. This form of market efficiency is the most demanding, because it concludes that profits cannot be achieved by inside information.

There is a general agreement that developed financial markets would meet the conditions of semi-strong efficiency, despite some anomalies. These anomalies are related to abnormal returns that can be evident simultaneously with the release time of the new information. On the other hand, the concept of strongly efficient markets is not easily accepted. This is because most of the countries already have anti-insider-trading laws, in order to prevent excessive returns from inside information.

Accepting or not the efficient market hypothesis is one of the core financial debates of our times. The relevant literature is voluminous (see, among others, Jensen (1978), LeRoy and Porter (1981), Malkiel (2003), Timmerman and Granger (2004), Yen and Lee (2008), Lim and Brooks (2011) and Guidi and Gupta (2013)). The empirical results of this extensive literature are ambiguous and controversial. Especially during the 1980s and 1990s, the efficient market hypothesis was under siege. Recent case studies present more results in favour of the market efficiency, but the debate is still ongoing. In fact, the main question remains: *'Does market efficiency exist?'* The practical market experience shows that trends are 'somewhat' existent and predictable, so strictly speaking the efficient market hypothesis can be stated as false (Abu-Mostafa and Atiya, 1996). There is also the opinion that science tries to find the best hypothesis. Therefore, criticism is of limited value, unless the hypothesis is replaced by a better one (Sewell, 2011).

1.3 Profitability of technical analysis and criticism

From all the above, it is clear that technical analysis is in contrast with the idea of market efficiency. The main reason for this conflict is that technical analysis opposes the accepted view of what is profitability in an efficient capital market. Technical analysis is based on the principal that investors can achieve greater returns than those obtained by holding a randomly chosen investment with comparable risk for a long time. Hence, the market can indeed be beaten.

However, claiming that there is a direct link between profitability and technical trading rules is justified. For example, Brock *et al.* (1992) in their pioneering paper present evidence of profitability of several trading rules using bootstrap methodology when applied to the task of forecasting the Dow Jones Industrial Average index. Bessembinder and Chan (1995) extend the use of those rules to predict Asian stock index returns with similar results. These studies created a research trend in technical analysis' efficiency and utility. Menkhoff and Schmidt (2005), Hsu and Kuan (2005) and Park and Irwin (2007) summarize relevant empirical evidence in surveys that focus on the profitability of the technical approach. Especially the latter provide an interesting separation of the corresponding literature into two periods: the early (1960–1987) and modern (1988–2004) studies periods. This classification is based on the available tools, factors, models, tests and drawbacks that the researcher of the period had to face (i.e. transaction costs, risk factor analysis, data mining and pattern recognition issues, parameter optimization, out-of-sample verification processes, bootstrap and white reality checks, neural networks and genetic programming architectures). Park and Irwin (2007) also note that most of the studies conducted in the 1960s were more or less published during and after the 1990s. The main reasons for that is, first, the fact that the computational resources 'flourished' during that period. Second, the benefits of technical analysis also emerged through several seminal papers, which till that period were not well known to the scientific public.

Taking all the above under consideration, it is very logical to wonder why technical analysis remains under constant criticism. Especially academics have an extreme and aggressive attitude towards the technical approach, which can be 'colourfully' described as follows:

> Technical analysis is anathema to the academic world. We love to pick on it. Our bullying tactics are prompted by two considerations: (1) the method is patently false; and (2) it's easy to pick on. And while it may seem a bit unfair to pick on such a sorry target, just remember: it is your money we are trying to save.
>
> (Malkiel, 2007, pp. 127–128).

The main reasoning for this critique can be summarized as:

- technical analysis does not accept the efficient market hypothesis;
- widely cited academic studies conclude that technical rules are not useful (Fama and Blume, 1966); Jensen and Benington, 1970);
- traders use the well-known charts and see the same signals. Their actions go in a way that the market complies with the overriding wisdom. Thus, technical analysis is a 'self-fulfilling prophecy';
- Chart patterns tell us where the market has been, but cannot tell us where it is going – in other words, the past cannot predict the future;
- the technical approach is 'trapped' between the psychology of the trader and the 'insensitivity' of an automatic computational system, where no human intervention is allowed in real time.

2 Technical trading rules

There is a wide variety of technical trading rules applied everyday by market practitioners, trading experts and technical analysts. This section attempts to present an overview of the 'universe' of these rules and to classify them in some basic categories.

2.1 The benchmark 'buy-and-hold' rule (BH)

The 'buy-and-hold' rule (BH) is a passive investment strategy which is thought to be the benchmark of all trading rules in the market. BH aligns with the efficient market hypothesis (see Section 1). Its principle is that investors buy stocks and hold them for a long period of time, without being concerned about short-term price movements, technical indicators and market volatility. Although BH is not a 'sophisticated' investment strategy, historical data show that it might be quite effective, especially with equities given a long timeline. Typical BH investors use passive elements, such as dollar-cost averaging and index funds, focusing on building a portfolio instead of security research. There is ground for criticism, especially from technical analysts, who after the Great Recession declared the death of BH rules. Corrado and Lee (1992), Jegadeesh and Titman (1993), Gençay (1998), Levis and Liodakis (1999), Fernández-Rodríguez et al. (2000), O'Neil (2001), Barber et al. (2006) and recently Szafarz (2012) perform competitions of trading strategies, with BH being the main benchmark. Although in most cases BH strategies are being outperformed, there are cases of returns of more than 10 per cent per annum.

2.2 Mechanical trading rules

Charting is subjective to the technician's interpretation of historical price patterns. Such subjectivity allows emotions to affect the technical decisions and trading strategies. The class of mechanical rules attempt to constrain these personal intuitions of the traders by introducing a certain decision discipline, which is based on identifying and following trends.

2.2.1 Filter rules (FRs)

Filter rules (FRs) generate long (short) signals when the market price rises (drops) multiplied by the per cent above (below) the previous trough (peak). This means that 'if the stock market has moved up "x" per cent, it is likely to move up more than "x" per cent further before it moves down by "x" per cent' (Alexander, 1961, p. 26). A trader using FRs, assumes that in each transaction he/she could always buy at a price exactly equal to the low plus x per cent and sell at the high minus x per cent, where x is the size of the filter (threshold). Such mechanical rules attempt to exploit the market's momentum. Setting up a filter rule requires two decisions. The first is the specification of the threshold. The second is the determination of the window length, meaning how far back the rule should go in finding a recent minimum. These decisions are obviously connected with the subjective view of the trader on the historical data at hand and the relevant past experience. Common threshold values fluctuate between 0.5 per cent and 3 per cent, while a typical window length is about five trading days.

FRs have a prominent place among the common tools in technical analysis, although the studies of the 1960s tend to understate their performance in comparison to the BH rule. Several examples in the literature show that filtering techniques are capable of exhibiting profits. Dooley and Shafer (1983) conduct one of the earliest studies that focus on applying FRs to trading in the foreign exchange market. Their results show substantial profitability for most thresholds implemented over the period 1973–1981 for the DEM, JPY and GBP currencies. Sweeney (1986) suggests that a filter of 0.5 per cent outperforms a BH of 4 per cent per annum strategy, using daily USD/DEM data during late 1970s. The bootstrap technique first used by Brock *et al.* (1992) and later by Levich and Thomas (1993) addresses the issue of the significance of such FRs' returns in the context of the stock market. Qi and Wu (2006) report evidence on the profitability and statistical significance of over 2,000 trading rules, including FRs with various threshold sizes. Dunis *et al.* (2008) forecast future spreads with neural networks and apply filter trading rules. In their approach, they experiment beyond the boundaries of the traditional threshold approaches by implementing correlation and transitive filters (see Guégan and Huck, 2004; Dunis *et al.*, 2005, respectively). These FRs, especially the transitive one combined with a recurrent neural network, present impressive results in terms of annualized returns. FRs can be used also as technical indicators that measure the strength of the trend. Dunis *et al.* (2011) also apply filter strategies to the task of forecasting the EUR/USD exchange rate. In their application, their confirmation filter does not allow trades that will result in returns lower than the transaction costs. Finally, Kozyra and Lento (2011) compare filter trading rules with the contrarian approach (see Section 2.4) and note that the filter technique is less profitable in periods of high market volatility in particular.

2.2.2 Moving average rules

Moving average rules (MAs) are also common mechanical indicators and their applications have been known for many decades in trading decisions and systems. In simple words, an MA is the mean of a time series, which is recalculated every trading day. Their main characteristic is the length window – namely the number of trading days that are going to be used to calculate the rolling mean of the high-frequency data. MAs are identifiers of short- or long-term trends, so the window length can be short (short MAs – 1 to 5 lags) or long (long MAs – 10 to 100 lags). The intuition behind them is that buy (sell) signals are triggered when closing prices cross above (below) the x day MA. Another variation is to buy (sell) when x day MA crosses above (below) the y day MA.

Assuming that the length window is n days, the current period's t closing price P_t, MAs can be further divided into three main categories:

Simple MA (SMA): $SMA_{t+1} = (1/n)(P_t + P_{t-1} + \dots P_{t-n+1})$ (2.1)

Exponential MA (EMA): $EMA_{t+1} = EMA_t + \alpha(P_t - EMA_t)$ (2.2)

Weighted MA (WMA): $WMA_{t+1} = [nP_t + (n-1)P_{t-1} \dots + 2P_{t-n+2} + P_{t-n+1})] / [n(n+1)/2]$ (2.3)

The SMA is an average of values recalculated every day. The EMA adapts to the market price changes by smoothing constant parameter α. The smoothing parameter expresses how quickly the EMA reacts to price changes. If α is low, then there is little reaction to price differences and vice versa. The WMA give weights to the prices used as lags. These weights are higher in recent periods, giving higher importance in recent closing prices. All these MAs are using the closing price as the calculation parameter, but open, high and low prices could also be used.

MAs are also well documented in the literature. Brock *et al.* (1992) and Hudson *et al.* (1996) analyse the Dow Jones Industrial Average and Financial Times Industrial Ordinary Index, respectively, with MAs and conclude that they have predictive ability if sufficiently long series of data are considered. Especially from the first study, it is suggested that the best rule is 50-day MA, which generates an annual mean return of 9.4 per cent. Applications of artificial intelligence technologies, such as artificial neural networks and fuzzy logic controllers, have also uncovered technical trading signals in the data. For example, Gençay (1998, 1999) investigates the non-linear predictability of foreign exchange and index returns by combining neural networks and MA rules. The forecast results indicate that the buy–sell signals of the MAs have market timing ability and provide statistically significant forecast improvements for the current returns over the random walk model of the foreign exchange returns. LeBaron (1999) finds that a 150-day MA generates Sharpe ratios of 0.60–0.98 after transaction costs in DEM and JPY markets over 1979–1992. LeBaron (2000) further examined their profitability and noted that it would be interesting to determine more complex combinations of MAs that are able to project even higher returns. Gunasekarage and Power (2001) apply the variable length MA and fixed length MA in forecasting the Asian stock markets. The first rule examines whether the short-run MA is above (below) the long-run MA, implying that the general trend in prices is upward (downward). The second rule focuses on the crossover of the long-run MA by the short-run MA. Their results show that equity returns in these markets are predictable and that the variable length MA is very successful.

On the other hand, Fong and Wong (2005) attempt to evaluate the fluctuations of the internet stocks with a recursive MA strategy applied to over 800 MAs. Their empirical results show no significant trading profits and align the internet stocks with the efficient market hypothesis. Chiarella *et al.* (2006) analyse the impact of long run MAs on market dynamics. When examining the case of the impact between fundamentalists and chartists being unbalanced, they present evidence that the lag length of the MA rule can destabilize the market price. Zhu and Zhou (2009) analyse the efficiency of MAs from an asset selection perspective and based on the principle that existing studies do not provide guidance on optimal investment, even if trends can be signalled by MAs. For that reason, they combine MAs with fixed rules in order to identify market timing strategies that shift money between cash and risky assets. Their approach outperforms the simple rules and explains why both risk aversion and degree of predictability affect the optimal use of the MA. Milionis and Papanagiotou (2011) test the significance of the predictive power of the MAs on the New York Stock Exchange, Athens Stock Exchange and Vienna Stock Exchange. Their contribution is that the proposed MA performance is a function of the window length and that it outperforms BH strategies. This happens especially when the changes in the performance of the MA occur around a mean level, which is interpreted as a rejection of the weak-form efficiency. Finally, Bajgrowicz and Scaillet (2012) revisit the historical success of technical analysis on Dow Jones Industrial Average index from 1897 to 2011 and use the false discovery rate for data snooping. In their review they present the profitability of MAs during these years, but call into serious question the economic value of technical trading rules that have been reported in the period under study.

2.2.3 Oscillators and momentum rules

The third class of mechanical trading rules consists of the oscillators (OTs) and momentum rules (MTs). OTs are techniques that do not follow the trend. Actually, they try to identify when the trend is apparent for too long or 'dying'. Therefore, they are also called *non-trending market indicators*. The main drawback of MAs is the inability to identify the quick and violent changes in price direction, which lead to capital loss by generating wrong trading signals. This performance gap is filled from OT indices. Their basic intuition is that a reversal trend is imminent when the prices move away from the average. Simple OT rules are based on the difference between two MAs and generate buy (sell) signals when prices are too low (have risen extremely). Nonetheless, being a difference of MA rules, OTs can also present buy and sell position, when the index crosses zero. The boundaries between OTs and MTs can be a bit vague depending on the case, because MTs can be applied to MAs and OTs. The main difference is that OTs are non-trend indicators, whereas MTs are capitalizing on the endurance of a trend in the market. A simple MT rule would be the difference between today's closing price and the closing price x days ago. The trading signal is generated based on this momentum. To put it simply, the buy (sell) signal is given when today's closing price is higher than the closing price x days ago. Setting properly the x day's price that is going to be used is also a matter of trader intuition, market knowledge and historical experience (five days and 20 days are common).

There are many types of OTs and MTs used in trading applications. Some typical examples are summarized, interpreted in short and followed by relevant research applications below:

- *Moving average convergence/divergence* (MACD): MACD is calculated as the difference between short- and long-term EMAs and identifies where crossovers and diverging trends generate buy and sell signals.
- *Accumulation/distribution* (A/D): A/D is a momentum indicator which measures whether investors are generally buying (accumulation) or selling (distribution) based on the volume of price movement.

- *Chaikin oscillator* (CHO): CHO is calculated as the MACD of A/D.
- *Relative strength index* (RSI): The RSI is calculated based on the average 'up' moves and average 'down' moves and is used to identify overbought (when its value is over 70 – sell signal) or oversold (when its value is under 30 – buy)
- *Price oscillator* (PO): PO identifies the momentum between two EMAs.
- *Detrended price oscillator* (DPO): DPO eliminates long-term trends in order to more easily identify cycles and measure the difference between closing price and SMA.
- *Bollinger bands* (BB): BB are based on the difference of closing prices and SMAs and determine whether securities are overbought or oversold.
- *Stochastic oscillator* (SO): SO is based on the assumptions that as prices rise, the closing price tends to reach the high prices in the previous period.
- *Triple EMA* (TRIX): TRIX is a momentum indicator between three EMAs and triggers buying and selling signals based on zero crossovers.

The exact specifications and formulas of the abovementioned indicators can be found in Gifford (1995), Chang *et al.* (1996) and Edwards and Magee (1997), or in any common textbook of technical analysis. Their utility, though, was eminent years before that. The pioneering paper of Brock *et al.* (1992) presents evidence of profitability of MACD, as for MAs and FRs mentioned above. Kim and Han (2000) propose a hybrid genetic algorithm–neural network model that uses OTs, such as PO, SO, A/D and RSI, along with simple momentum rules to predict the stock market. Leung and Chong (2003) compare the profitability of MA envelopes and BBs. Their results suggest BBs do not outperform the MA envelopes, despite being able to capture sudden price fluctuations. Shen and Loh (2004) propose a trading system with rough sets to forecast S&P 500 index, which outperforms BH rules. In order to set up this hybrid trading system, they search for the most efficient rules based on the historical data from a pool of technical indicators, such as MACD, RSI and SO. Lento *et al.* (2007) also present empirical evidence that prove BBs' inability to achieve higher profits compared to a BH strategy, when tested on the S&P/TSX 300 Index, the Dow Jones Industrial Average index, NASDAQ Composite Index and the Canada/ USD exchange rate. Chong and Ng (2008) examine the profitability of MACD and RSI using 60-year data of the London Stock Exchange and found that the RSI, as well as the MACD, rules can generate returns higher than the BH strategy in most cases.

Ye and Huang (2008) extend Frisch's (1993) damping OT with a non-classical OT. The non-classical OT introduces Quantum Mechanics in the market, which is treated as an apparatus that can measure the value and produces a price as a result. With the numerical simulations presented, the OT under study explains qualitatively the persistent fluctuations in stock markets. Aggarwal and Krishna (2011) explore support vector machines and decision tree classifiers in the task of direction accuracy prediction. In their application, the company's stock value history is evaluated based on the daily high, open, close, low prices and volumes traded over the last 5–10 years. The performance of their techniques provides impressive forecasting accuracy of over 50 per cent and is tested with several OTs and MTs (i.e. MACD, DPO, SO, A/D and RSI). Finally, Dunis *et al.* (2011) and more recently Sermpinis *et al.* (2012) forecast exchange rates with several neural networks. In those applications, MACD are used as benchmarks, but they do not present significant profitability.

2.3 Other trading rules

The rules presented above are the main market indicators of technical analysis, but their 'universe' is, in a way, limitless. Technical analysts and practitioners tend to create new trading rules, which in reality are small specification alternatives of the existing ones. Such offspring are commonly cited in the literature with different and more appealing names, despite their direct correlation with the basic mechanical rules presented in the previous section.

2.3.1 Contrarian rules

One such example is the contrarian approach in trading, or in other words the *contrarian rules* (CTs). Their logic and specification is very simplistic. For every simple trading rule that triggers a sell signal, there is the corresponding CT that triggers a buy signal and vice versa. Technical analysts that use the CR approach believe that the price changes can be temporary and the market tends to return to its steady state. Typical handbooks that refer to CTs are LeBaron and Vaitilingam (1999) and Siegel (2002). Forner and Marhuenda (2003) explore the profitability of the momentum and contrarian in the Spanish stock market. They find that a 12-month momentum strategy and the five-year contrarian strategy yield significant positive returns, even after risk adjustments have been made. Menkhoff and Schmidt (2005) compare BH, MT and CT traders and suggest that the latter are overconfident and willing to hold on against the market. In other words, contrarians are long-run arbitrageurs, but tend to perform worse than BH or MT traders. More recently, Park and Sabourian (2011) also compare the 'herding' and 'contrarian' psychology of trade agents. The 'herding' trader follows the trend, whereas a 'contrarian' goes against it. Their main conclusion is that herding and contrarianism lead to price volatility and lower liquidity. It is also noted that herding trades are self-enforcing, while contrarian trades are self-defeating.

2.3.2 Trading range break rules

Trading range break rules (TRBs) is also a class of technical rules in the literature. TRBs can be thought of as MT indicators, since their main premise is that a positive or negative momentum is built, when a stock breaks through or falls below its trading range after several days of trading. Trading range is the spread between the recent minimum and maximum of the current price. TRBs generate buy positions, when the current price exceeds the recent maximum by at least a band. Similarly, they emit sell signals when the current price falls below the recent minimum by at least the band. For example, Brock *et al.* (1992) and Bessembinder and Chan (1995) apply TRBs over the period 50, 150 and 200 days and use bands of 0 and 1 per cent. Coutts and Cheung (2000) investigate the applicability and validity of trading rules in the Hang Seng Index on the Hong Kong Stock Exchange for the period January 1985 to June 1997. Although TRBs are by far the most common, in terms of implementation they fail to provide positive abnormal returns, net of transaction costs and opportunity costs of investing. Park and Irwin (2007), in their technical analysis survey, also include TRBs in the pool of profitable trading rules. In a more recent application, Wang *et al.* (2012) present a weight reward strategy which combines MAs and TRBs to create a pool of 140 component trading rules. The proposed hybrid trading system employs a particle swarm optimization algorithm and the optimized combinations of MAs and TRBs are found to outperform the best individual MAs and TRBs.

2.3.3 Breakout rules

Another interesting category of trading rules is the *channel breakout* (CHB) and *volatility breakout* (VOLB) rules. The CHBs originate from Richard Donchian, a pioneer in futures trading (Kestner, 2003). The idea behind them is that a 'channel' of price changes is incorporated in the trading strategy. This '*x* days channel' is created by the plot of the high and lows of the price during *x* days and is also a measure of market volatility. Trading entries happen when prices remain in the channel. A buy (sell) position is taken when today's close is higher (lower) than the previous *x* day's close. The VOLBs entries are decided in a similar logic, but based on the three following parameters:

1 The reference value gives a measurement value to the price move.
2 The volatility measure is a computational calculation of the market volatility and is used to identify significant movements from random prices.
3 The volatility multiplier specifies how sensitive the price move is.

The combination of these parameters results in a high and low trigger point. This allows the trader to buy (sell) when the closing price is above the upper (below the lower) trigger. Levitt (1998) compared two trends following trading systems employing CHB and VOLB strategies using standard and daily market time data from 1987 to 1996. Both rules are profitable, but especially VOLB presents average annual returns of more than 10 per cent. Qi and Wu (2006) in their extensive search of profitable trading rules suggest that the best rule for trading the JPY and CHF exchange rate is the CHB rule. Marshall *et al.* (2008) examine the profitability of intraday technical analysis in the US equity market and compare FRs, MAs, TRBs and VOLBs. Their findings show that VOLBs are the most profitable family of trading indicators.

2.3.4 Pattern rules

Head-and-shoulders (HSs), *double-tops-and-double-bottoms* (DTBs), *triangles-and-rectangles* (TRs) and *flags-and-pennants* (FPs) are types of rules that attempt to identify and establish patterns on pricing charts. They can also be thought of as classes of MAs, OTs or MTs, and their short descriptions are given below:

- HS is a trading rule based on the tops of 'up-trends' and bottoms of 'down-trends'. In each period the higher price peak (head), the two higher picks before (left shoulder) and after the head (right shoulder) are identified. The two lowest prices (points) during this period create a line, called the HS 'neckline'. In an 'up-trend', a HS rule will act as a reversal point only when the price succeeds in breaking down the HS 'neckline'. Alternatively, it will go up and may retest the HS 'neckline' in the future. HSs are commonly used by daily currency traders.
- DTBs are also frequently used as reversal pattern indicators by the FOREX market participants. A 'double top' is formed by two price peaks at approximately the same level and the 'neckline' is similarly formed as in HSs. This pattern is completed when a price closes below the lowest price that has been reached between the two peaks.
- TRs are formed by two converging trendlines (triangles) or pairs of horizontal trendlines (rectangles), one connecting highest peaks and one connecting lower peaks. A triangle is completed when the closing price goes outside one of its trendlines (similar to the CHBs). The vertical line (called base) connecting the initial point of the converging trendline is called 'base' and the point of convergence is called 'apex of the triangle'. The 'base' and the 'apex' are used to identify price breakouts and moves, respectively. Similarly, a rectangle is completed when the prices closes out of the horizontal trendlines. In the rectangles there is no 'base' or 'apex', but the distance between the horizontal lines is always recalculated, if a rectangle is completed.
- FPs are indicators of pattern continuation. The 'flag' is a rectangle that slopes against the eminent trend, while 'pennants' form symmetrical triangles (see TRs). The FP patterns are completed when the closing price breaks through one of their trendlines.

The applications of the above pattern rules are quite extensive in the literature too. Clyde and Osler (1998) examine how graphical technical modelling methods may be viewed as equivalent to nonlinear prediction methods. Evidence in support of this hypothesis is presented by applying HS algorithm to high-dimension non-linear data and they suggest that HSs can be successful in pattern identification and prediction. Lo *et al.* (2000) develop a pattern-detection algorithm based on kernel regressions. Their methodology is able to identify price patterns, including HSs in the US stock market over the period 1962–1996. Lucke (2003) also explores whether HSs are profitable technical indicators in

FOREX markets. In the study many HS combinations are implemented, but the results present no significant or even negative returns. Hsu and Kuan (2005) reexamine the utility of technical analysis and in their survey pattern rules like HSs, DTBs, TRs and FPs have a prominent place in the 'universe' of the trading rules under study. Friesen *et al.* (2009) develop a theoretical framework that confirms the apparent success of both trend-following and pattern-based technical trading rules, as HSs and DBTs. Finally, extensive applications and specifications for the above pattern rules can also be found in Murphy (2012).

3 Automated trading strategies and systems

Many issues and variables have to be taken under consideration by managers and market practitioners in order to reach the final specification and implementation phase of a trading strategy. These can be summarized as follows:

- identifying trading opportunities
- trading schedule and timing
- trading costs
- price appreciation and market impact
- risk evaluation of alternative strategies
- ability of execution of each strategy.

All the above can be evaluated through fundamental or technical approaches. Nonetheless, the modern market practice has a tendency to turn to market technical indicators, whose variety and computational demands are increasing exponentially. This is the main reason that technical analysis and computing appear to be linked, now more than ever before. Charting software is applied everyday to actual or virtual financial markets. Optimization algorithms are automatically integrated in trading platforms, such as Bloomberg, and make the life of the intraday trader much easier. Consequently, modern trading projects aim to develop automated decision-support systems based on technical market technology and evolutionary computing. Fuzzy logic, artificial neural networks, genetic algorithms and programming are already established as the core of the automated trading approach (Deboeck, 1994).

Allen and Karjalainen (1999) present an automated decision tree that selects the optimal technical rules by genetic algorithms. Dempster and Jones (2001) also try to emulate successful trade agents by developing a rule system based on combinations of different indicators at different frequencies and lags, which are selected with a genetic programming optimization process. Shapiro (2002) notes that merging technologies, such as neural networks, evolutionary algorithms and fuzzy logic, can provide alternatives to a strictly knowledge-driven reasoning decision system or a purely data-driven one, and lead to more accurate and robust solutions. Thawornwong *et al.* (2003) evaluate the use of neural networks as decision makers to uncover the underlying non-linear pattern of these indicators. The overall results indicate that the proportion of correct predictions and the profitability of stock trading guided by these neural networks are higher than those guided by their benchmarks. Dempster and Leemans (2006) propose the use of adaptive reinforcement learning as the basis for a fully automated trading system application. The system is designed to trade foreign exchange (FX) markets relying on a layered structure consisting of a machine learning algorithm, a risk-management overlay and a dynamic utility optimization layer. Their approach allows for a risk–return tradeoff to be made by the user within the system, while the trading system is able to make consistent gains and avoid large drawdowns out-of-sample. Izumi *et al.* (2009) construct an artificial-market system based on support vector machines and genetic programming. Their system evaluates the risks and returns of the strategies in various market environments and tests the market impact of automated trading. Their results reveal that the market impact of the strategies may not only depend on their rule content, but also on the way they are combined with other strategies.

The above cited applications prove that automated trading is and will be dominant in financial markets and forecasting tasks, although its academic philosophy appears to be ambiguous. The utility of trading systems is usually criticized in the traditional financial literature because of their dependence on strict engineering and computational rules. The modern market reality, though, shows that returns are driven by trading systems' results, rather than human trading behaviour. On the other hand, automated trading applications and algorithms present practical drawbacks associated mainly with their parameter calibration. Therefore, financial researchers and computer engineers need to shed more light on this demanding and complex optimization problem.

References

Abu-Mostafa, Y.S. and Atiya, A.F. (1996) Introduction to financial forecasting, *Applied Intelligence*, 6, 205–213.

Aggarwal, S. and Krishna, V. (2011) CS698o: Project report stock price direction prediction, *Indian Institute of Technology Kanpur Working Paper*.

Alexander, S.S. (1961) Price movements in speculative markets: trends or random walks, *Industrial Management Review*, 2, 7–26.

Allen, F. and Karjalainen, R. (1999) Using genetic algorithms to find technical trading rules, *Journal of Financial Economics*, 51(2), 245–271.

Bajgrowicz, P. and Scaillet, O. (2012) Technical trading revisited: false discoveries, persistence tests, and transaction costs, *Journal of Financial Economics*, 106(3), 473–491.

Barber, B.M., Lehavy, R., McNichols, M. and Trueman, B. (2006) Buys, holds, and sells: the distribution of investment banks' stock ratings and the implications for the profitability of analysts' recommendations, *Journal of Accounting and Economics*, 41(1–2), 87–117.

Bessembinder, H. and Chan, K. (1995) The profitability of technical trading rules in the Asian stock markets, *Pacific-Basin Finance Journal*, 3(2–3), 257–284.

Brock, W., Lakonishok, J. and LeBaron, B. (1992) Simple technical trading rules and the stochastic properties of stock returns, *The Journal of Finance*, 47(5), 1731–1764.

Chang, J., Jung, Y., Yeon, K., Jun, J., Shin, D. and Kim, H. (1996) *Technical Indicators and Analysis Methods*, Jinritamgu Publishing, Seoul.

Chiarella, C., He, X.Z. and Hommes, C. (2006) A dynamic analysis of moving average rules, *Journal of Economic Dynamics and Control*, 30(9–10), 1729–1753.

Chong T.T.L and Ng, W.K. (2008) Technical analysis and the London stock exchange: testing the MACD and RSI rules using the FT30, *Applied Economics Letters*, 15(14), 1111–1114.

Clyde, W.C. and Osler, C.L. (1998) Charting: chaos theory in disguise?, *Journal of Futures Markets*, 17(5), 489–514.

Corrado, C.J. and Lee, S.H. (1992) Filter rule tests of the economic significance of serial dependencies in daily stock returns, *Journal of Financial Research*, 15(4), 369–387.

Coutts, J.A. and Cheung, K.C. (2000) Trading rules and stock returns: some preliminary short run evidence from the Hang Seng 1985–1997, *Applied Financial Economics*, 10(6), 579–586.

Deboeck, G. (1994) *Trading on the Edge: Neural, Genetic, and Fuzzy Systems for Chaotic Financial Markets*, Wiley, New York.

Dempster, M.A.H. and Jones, C.M. (2001) A real-time adaptive trading system using genetic programming, *Quantitative Finance*, 1(4), 397–413.

Dempster, M.A.H. and Leemans, V. (2006) An automated FX trading system using adaptive reinforcement learning, *Expert Systems with Applications*, 30(3), 543–552.

Dooley, M.P. and Shafer, J.R. (1983) Analysis of short-run exchange rate behaviour: March 1973 to November 1981, In Bigman, D. and Taya, T. (eds) *Exchange Rate and Trade Instability: Causes, Consequences, and Remedies*, Ballinger Pub. Co., Cambridge, MA.

Dunis, C.L., Laws, J. and Evans, B. (2005) Recurrent and higher order neural networks: a comparative analysis, *Neural Network World*, 6, 509–523.

Dunis, C.L., Laws, J. and Evans, B. (2008) Trading futures spreads: an application of correlation and threshold filters, *Applied Financial Economics*, 16(12), 903–914.

Dunis, C.L., Laws, J. and Sermpinis, G. (2011) Higher order and recurrent neural architectures for trading the EUR/USD exchange rate, *Quantitative Finance*, 11(4), 615–629.

Edwards, R.D. and Magee, J. (1997) *Technical Analysis of Stock Trends*, John Magee, Chicago, IL.

Fama, E.F. (1970) Efficient capital markets: a review of theory and empirical work, *The Journal of Finance*, 25(2), 383–417.

Fama, E.F. and Blume, M.E. (1966) FRs and stock-market trading, *The Journal of Business*, 39(1), 226–241.

Fernández-Rodríguez, F., Christian González-Martel, C. and Sosvilla-Rivero, S. (2000) On the profitability of technical trading rules based on artificial neural networks: evidence from the Madrid stock market, *Economics Letters*, 69(1), 89–94.

Fong, W.M. and Yong, H.M. (2005) Chasing trends: recursive moving average trading rules and internet stocks, *Journal of Empirical Finance*, 12(1), 43–76.

Forner, C. and Marhuenda, J. (2003) Contrarian and momentum strategies in the Spanish stock market, *European Financial Management*, 9(1), 67–88.

Friesen, G.C, Weller, P.A and Dunham, L.M. (2009) Price trends and patterns in technical analysis: a theoretical and empirical examination, *Journal of Banking and Finance*, 33(6), 1089–1100.

Frisch, R. (1933) Propagation problems and impulse problems in dynamic economics, In *Economic Essays in Honor of Gustav Cassel*, Allen & Unwin, London, 171–205.

Gençay, R. (1998) Optimization of technical trading strategies and the profitability in security markets, *Economics Letters*, 59(2), 249–254.

Gençay, R. (1999) Linear, nonlinear and essential foreign exchange prediction, *Journal of International Economics*, 47(1), 91–107.

Gifford, E. (1995) *Investor's Guide to Technical Analysis: Predicting Price Action in the Markets*, Financial Times, London.

Guégan, D. and Huck, N. (2004) Forecasting relative movements using transitivity? *Working paper, Institutions et Dynamiques Historiques de l'Economie.*

Guidi, F. and Gupta, R. (2013) Market efficiency in the ASEAN region: evidence from multivariate and co-integration tests, *Applied Financial Economics*, 23(4), 265–274.

Gunasekarage, A. and Power, D.M. (2001) The profitability of moving average trading rules in South Asian stock markets, *Emerging Markets Review* 2(1), 17–33.

Hsu, P.H. and Kuan, C.M. (2005) Re-examining the profitability of technical analysis with data snooping checks, *Journal of Financial Econometrics*, 3(4), 608–628.

Hudson, R., Dempsey, M. and Keasey, K. (1996) A note on the weak form efficiency of capital markets: the application of simple technical trading rules to UK stock prices – 1935 to 1994, *Journal of Banking and Finance*, 20, 1121–1132.

Izumi, K., Toriumi, F. and Matsui, H. (2009) Evaluation of automated-trading strategies using an artificial market, *Neurocomputing*, 72, (16–18), 3469–3476.

Jegadeesh, N. and Titman, S. (1993) Returns to buying winners and selling losers: implications for stock market efficiency, *The Journal of Finance*, 48(1), 65–91.

Jensen, M.C. (1978) Some anomalous evidence regarding market efficiency, *Journal of Financial Economics*, 6(2–3), 95–101.

Jensen, M. and Benington, G. (1970) Random walks and technical theories: some additional evidence, *The Journal of Finance*, 25(2), 469–482.

Kestner, L.N (2003) *Quantitative Trading Strategies: Harnessing the Power of Quantitative Techniques to Create a Winning Trading Program*, McGraw-Hill, Boston, MA.

Kim, Kyoung-jae and Han, Ingoo (2000) Genetic algorithms approach to feature discretization in artificial neural networks for the prediction of stock price index, *Expert Systems with Applications* 19(2): 125–132.

Kozyra, J. and Lento, C. (2011) FRs: follow the trend or take the contrarian approach?, *Applied Economics Letters*, 18(3), 235–237.

LeBaron, B. (1999) Technical trading rule profitability and foreign exchange intervention, *Journal of International Economics*, 49, 125–143.

LeBaron, B. (2000). The stability of moving average technical trading rules on the Dow Jones Index. *Derivatives Use, Trading and Regulation*, 5, 324–338.

LeBaron, B. and Vaitilingam, R. (1999) *The Ultimate Investor*, Capstone Publishing, Dover, NH.

Lento, C., Gradojevic, N. and Wright, C.S. (2007) Investment information content in Bollinger Bands?, *Applied Financial Economics Letters*, 3(4), 263–267.

LeRoy, S.F. and Porter, R.D. (1981) The present-value relation: tests based on implied variance bounds, *Econometrica*, 49(3), 555–574.

Leung, J.M.J. and Chong, T.T.L. (2003) An empirical comparison of moving average envelopes and Bollinger Bands, *Applied Economics Letters*, 10(6), 339–341.

Levich, R.M. and Thomas, L.R. (1993) The significance of technical trading rule profits in the foreign exchange market: a bootstrap approach, *Journal of International Finance and Money*, 12, 451–474.

Levis, M. and Liodakis, M. (1999) The profitability of style rotation strategies in the United Kingdom, *The Journal of Portfolio Management*, 26(1), 73–86.

Levitt, M.E. (1998) Market Time Data™: improving technical analysis and technical trading, *Working paper.*

Lim, K.P. and Brooks, R. (2011) The evolution of stock market efficiency over time: a survey of the empirical literature, *Journal of Economic Surveys*, 25(1), 69–108.

Lo, A., Mamaysky, H. and Wang, J. (2000) Foundations of technical analysis: computational algorithms, statistical inference and empirical implementation, *The Journal of Finance*, 55, 1705–1765.

Lucke, B. (2003) Are technical trading rules profitable? Evidence for head-and-shoulder rules, *Applied Economics*, 35(1), 33–40.

Malkiel, B.G. (2003) The efficient market hypothesis and its critics, *The Journal of Economic Perspectives*, 17(1), 59–82.

Malkiel, B.G. (2007) *A Random Walk Down Wall Street: The Time-Tested Strategy for Successful Investing*, Norton, New York.

Marshall, B.R., Cahan, R.H. and Cahan, J.M. (2008) Does intraday technical analysis in the U.S. equity market have value?, *Journal of Empirical Finance*, 15(2), 199–210.

Menkhoff, L. and Schmidt, U. (2005) The use of trading strategies by fund managers: some first survey evidence, *Applied Economics*, 37(15), 1719–1730.

Milionis, A.E and Papanagiotou, E. (2011) A test of significance of the predictive power of the moving average trading rule of technical analysis based on sensitivity analysis: application to the NYSE, the Athens Stock Exchange and the Vienna Stock Exchange. Implications for weak-form market efficiency testing, *Applied Financial Economics*, 21(6), 421–436.

Murphy, J.J (1999) *Technical Analysis of the Financial Markets: A Comprehensive Guide to Trading Methods and Applications*, New York Institute of Finance, New York.

Murphy, J.J. (2012) *Charting Made Easy*, Wiley, Ellicott City.

O'Neill, M., Brabazon, A., Ryan, C. and Collins, J.J. (2001) Evolving market index trading rules using grammatical evolution, *Applications of Evolutionary Computing, Lecture Notes in Computer Science*, 2037, 343–352.

Park, A. and Sabourian, H. (2011) Herding and contrarian behaviour in financial markets, *Econometrica*, 79(4), 973–1026.

Park, C.H. and Irwin, S.H. (2007) What do we know about profitability of technical analysis?, *Journal of Economic Surveys*, 21(4), 786–826.

Pring, M.J. (2002) *Technical Analysis Explained: The Successful Investor's Guide to Spotting Investment Trends and Turning Points*, McGraw-Hill, New York.

Qi, M. and Wu, Y. (2006) Technical trading-rule profitability, data snooping, and reality check: evidence from the foreign exchange market, *Journal of Money, Credit and Banking*, 38(8), 2135–2158.

Sermpinis, G., Theofilatos, K., Karathanasopoulos, A., Georgopoulos, E. and Dunis, C.L (2012) Forecasting foreign exchange rates with adaptive neural networks using radial-basis functions and particle swarm optimization, *European Journal of Operational Research*, 225(3), 528–540.

Sewell, M. (2011) History of efficient market hypothesis, research note, *UCL Department of Computer Science*.

Shapiro, F.A. (2002) The merging of neural networks, fuzzy logic, and genetic algorithms, *Insurance: Mathematics and Economics*, 31(1), 115–131.

Shen, L. and Loh, H.T. (2004) Applying rough sets to market timing decisions, *Decision Support Systems*, 37(4), 583–597.

Siegel, J.J. (2002) *Stocks for the Long Run*, 3rd edn, McGraw-Hill, New York.

Sweeney, R.J. (1986) Beating the foreign exchange market, *Journal of Finance*, 41, 163–182.

Szafarz, A. (2012) Financial crises in efficient markets: how fundamentalists fuel volatility?, *Journal of Banking and Finance*, 36(1), 105–111.

Thawornwong, S., David Enke, D. and Cihan Dagli, C. (2003) Neural networks as a decision maker for stock trading: a technical analysis approach, *International Journal of Smart Engineering System Design*, 5(4), 313–325.

Timmermann, A. and Granger, C.W.J. (2004) Efficient market hypothesis and forecasting, *International Journal of Forecasting*, 20(1), 15–27.

Wang, F., Yu, P.L.H. and Cheung, D.W. (2012) Complex stock trading strategy based on particle swarm optimization, *Computational Intelligence for Financial Engineering and Economics (CIFEr), IEEE Conference*, Piscataway, NJ: IEEE, pp. 1–6.

Ye, C. and Huang, J.P. (2008) Non-classical oscillator model for persistent fluctuations in stock markets, *Physica A: Statistical Mechanics and its Applications*, 387(5–6), 1255–1263.

Yen, G. and Lee, C.F. (2008) Efficient market hypothesis (EMH): past, present and future, *Review of Pacific Basin Financial Markets and Policies*, 11(2), 305–329.

Zhu, Y. and Zhou, G. (2009) Technical analysis: an asset allocation perspective on the use of moving averages, *Journal of Financial Economics*, 92(3), 519–544.

Part II

Trading and investments with traditional computational intelligence techniques

3 Hidden Markov models

Financial modelling and applications

Sovan Mitra

1 Introduction

Quantitative models have gained increasing interest within finance due to their wide-ranging applications (such as portfolio modelling, risk management and trading applications). Currently there are a multitude of models, each with different advantages and drawbacks. Although Markov models and hidden Markov models (from hereon MM and HMM, respectively) have been studied since the 1960s, their use in finance has not been as widespread as in other disciplines, such as engineering.

The basic theories of MM and HMM were published in a set of papers by Baum (see Baum and Petrie, 1966; Baum and Egon, 1967; Baum and Sell, 1968; Baum, 1972). The appeal of MM and HMM has arisen because they do not impose a stringent set of assumptions, yet they enable one to derive useful theoretical and computational results that one would not be able to achieve with other models. In the real world of finance, such modelling advantages are particularly valuable, enabling one to learn more about predicting price movements.

In this chapter we discuss MM and HMM in relation to trading and investment applications. First, we explain the theory of these models and their modelling advantages. We then explain the computational implementation: we introduce the calibration method that is most frequently applied in economic and financial research literature (Hamilton filter), but also a less well-known method: the Baum–Welch method. We discuss the superior qualities of the Baum–Welch filter (which is frequently used in science and engineering) compared to the Hamilton filter, and show how it offers a complete implementation of HMM (unlike the Hamilton filter). We then provide a practical study of the Hamilton filter and the Baum–Welch method applied to financial markets, discussing their results and comparing their performances. We then give a survey of current HMM applications in finance.

2 An introduction to Markov model and hidden Markov model theory

In this section we introduce the theory of Markov and hidden Markov models, explaining their advantages and properties.

2.1 Markov models

In Markov modelling we aim to model a system which consists of states and signals. A state is some arbitrarily chosen 'position' of a system, but is typically chosen to represent some useful information about the system. The signals represent the observable data that enable us to identify the state of the system – for instance a computer's power light bulb (the signal) has two colours that enable us to determine the two states of the computer: on or off. A red light signal may indicate the computer is in its on state, whereas white indicates it is in its off state.

Any MM or system consists of more than one state, so the system must either change state or remain in its current state, and this possibility occurs at discrete time intervals. The state changes are not governed by deterministic processes but by probabilities, known as *state transition probabilities*, and are sometimes provided in a state transition matrix (also called a transition kernel or a stochastic matrix). For instance, for an MM with two states called *A* and *B*, the state transition probabilities are the conditional probabilities: $p(A|A)$, $p(A|B)$, $p(B|A)$ and $p(B|B)$.

We can represent the MM state transitions by Figure 3.1. The outer arrows represent state transitions back to the same state again (governed by $p(A|A)$ and $p(B|B)$), whereas the inner arrows represent state changes from *A* to *B* or vice versa (which are governed by $p(A|B)$ and $p(B|A)$). Furthermore, as an MM must move from *A* to *A* or *B* with probability 1, then by the laws of probability $p(A|A)$ and $p(A|B)$ must sum to 1 (and so should $p(B|A)$ and $p(B|B)$).

In addition to modelling systems as states and signals, in MM we assume the *Markov property*: transition probabilities are independent of the history of previous states. If we denote the state of the system at time *t* by q_t, then by definition the state transition probabilities are denoted by $p(q_{t+1}|q_t)$ and the Markov property is expressed as:

$$p(q_{t+1}=i|q_t=j)=p(q_{t+1}=i|q_t=j,q_{t-1},q_{t-2}\ldots) \tag{3.1}$$

where *i, j* denote any possible state of the system. For example, for our two-state MM with states *A* and *B* we have:

$$p(q_{t+1}=B|q_t=A)=p(q_{t+1}=B|q_t=A,\ q_{t-1}=B,\ q_{t-2}=A)=p(q_{t+1}=B|q_t=A,$$
$$q_{t-1}=B,\ q_{t-2}=B)=p(q_{t+1}=B|q_t=A,\ q_{t-1}=A,\ q_{t-2}=B) \tag{3.2}$$

Figure 3.1 A diagram of a two-state Markov model with state transitions depicted by arrows.

Hence an MM is sometimes described as memoryless. Although such a property may be undesirable in some applications, in finance this is a highly attractive property due to its consistency with the efficient market hypothesis (EMH) and empirical price movements (this will be discussed in more detail in proceeding sections).

If we denote the state transition probability matrix by $\mathbf{A}$, with elements a_{ij} where

$$a_{ij} = p(q_{t+1} = j | q_t = i) \tag{3.3}$$

and i also refers to the matrix row number and j also refers to the column number of $\mathbf{A}$, then by the standard laws of probability we have:

$$0 \leq a_{ij} \leq 1, \text{ for all } i,j \tag{3.4}$$

and

$$\sum_{j=1...\infty} a_{ij} = 1 \text{ for all } i \tag{3.5}$$

We now give a definition of MM.

2.1.1 Definition (Markov model)

A Markov model is completely defined once the following parameters are known:

1 *State transition probability matrix A of size* R × R, *where* R *is the total number of states.*
2 *Initial state probabilities* p(q$_I$ = i), *for all* i.

In finance we may use MM to model the GDP growth rate by two states A and B (although theoretically we can choose any number of states we wish). We can choose to identify the GDP growth rate in state A (when the reported GDP growth rate is greater than 1 per cent per year) and in state B when the rate is less than 1 per cent per year. In modelling GDP growth rate as an MM we would hope to learn more about the GDP growth rate process, e.g. the probability of being in a recession.

2.2 Hidden Markov models

In MM the observed signals directly identify the state of the system; however, this assumption is too restrictive: in many realistic applications we may not be able to observe such a signal. For instance, observed signals in many cases are corrupted by noise and so we observe signals that have a probabilistic (rather than a deterministic) relation with the system's state. To return to the computer power light example, if we assume the light is faulty (so that it can be red when the computer is on or off) we can no longer determine the computer's state (on or off) with certainty from the light signal.

Instead of assuming a deterministic relation between observed signals and states, in HMM we assign a probabilistic relation between the system's state and the observed signals. Hence in the computer example we can relate the computer's state to its observed signals by a probability, e.g. $p(\text{light}=\text{red}|\text{computer}=\text{ON})=0.8$. A consequence of the probabilistic relationship between observed signals and states is that we cannot know with certainty the system's state and that we can only classify the system's state with a degree of probability. Since the states themselves are directly hidden from an observer we call such systems *hidden Markov models*.

We denote the probability of an observation signal O_t at time t, when the system is in state j, by $p(O_t|j)$ or alternatively in shorthand $b_j(O_t)$ (that is, $p(O_t|j)=b_j(O_t)$). The probabilities $b_j(O_t)$ are sometimes given in the observation matrix **B** or by a probability distribution for each state j. For instance, if we have an HMM with two states A and B and if the observation signals follow a normal distribution $N(\mu, \sigma)$ (with mean μ and standard deviation σ), then we may write:

$$b_{j=A}(O_t) \sim N(\mu_1, \sigma_1), \tag{3.6}$$

$$b_{j=B}(O_t) \sim N(\mu_2, \sigma_2). \tag{3.7}$$

In other words, in state A the observation signals follow a normal probability distribution given by $N(\mu_1, \sigma_1)$, whereas in state B the observation signals follow $N(\mu_2, \sigma_2)$.

Therefore to fully describe an HMM, in addition to the properties that describe an MM (state transition matrix and initial state probabilities) we require **B**. We now give this in a definition of HMM.

2.2.1 Definition 2 (hidden Markov model)

A hidden Markov model is fully defined once the following parameters are known:

1 *State transition probability matrix **A** of size R × R, where R is the total number of hidden states.*
2 *Initial state probabilities* $p(q_1 = i)$, *for all i.*
3 ***B**, the observation matrix.*

An application of HMM in finance would be classifying the stock market's phase in a bull or bear state. Since no signal exists to determine the stock market's bull or bear phase with certainty, these two states are therefore hidden for any observation signal we choose. We could use daily returns on the FTSE-100 stock index as our observation signal, as we would expect a probabilistic relation between these returns and the bull and bear states. Once we obtain the HMM of the FTSE-100 bull and bear phases we could obtain useful information about the market. For instance, the probability of a bull market occurring and the average duration of bull markets; such information is particularly useful to investors and traders.

2.3 Financial modelling using hidden Markov models: properties and advantages

HMMs have become a popular modelling method in finance because HMMs offer significant modelling advantages and properties, particularly in comparison to alternative methods (such as stochastic differential equations). We will now discuss these points in more detail.

2.3.1 Consistency with financial fundamentals

Using a Markov model to model asset prices ensures that our model is consistent with a number of fundamental empirical and theoretical properties in finance; this is particularly important for realistic modelling and trading strategies. First, to ensure theoretical consistency with fundamental theories in finance it is important asset price moves should follow a Markov process. This is because due to the EMH (Fama, 1965) it is important that asset prices follow a Markov process; a violation of this fundamental theory would cause theoretical inconsistencies in our model.

Second, the asset prices need to follow Markov processes for trading purposes. Many trading strategies are based on information releases (e.g. event-driven trading), hence it is important our model responds correctly with respect to information releases. According to the EMH, this is achieved if the asset prices follow a Markov process. Hence a Markov process is important to prevent traders making abnormal profits from information.

Third, asset prices should follow a Markov process for another important trading purpose. The EMH governs the relation between past and future prices (by the Markov property); since past prices are frequently used in trading (in particular technical analysis), it is therefore important to model this relation correctly. Moreover, it has been empirically validated by a large amount of literature that past prices follow a Markov process. Hence a Markov process is important to prevent traders making abnormal profits from past patterns generating from a trading model.

2.3.2 Model flexibility

HMM are extremely flexible models which provides the modeller with significant benefits and allow the modeller to apply them to a wide range of applications. First, the HMM method does not impose a large number of assumptions; consequently the modeller is able to apply HMM to a range of applications. This is particularly useful in finance as it is common that different applications have a different set of conditions imposed upon them. Moreover, we can adapt the HMM to take into account more realistic modelling features without violating HMM modelling theory.

The HMM modelling capabilities are in contrast to other modelling methods as they impose stringent or unrealistic assumptions, e.g. the standard price model for stock prices (geometric Brownian motion) places a number of unrealistic assumptions about the return distributions. The HMM can also be developed into more sophisticated stochastic models to incorporate a range of more realistic features. In fact, a range of HMMs variants exists: for instance, hidden semi-Markov models and layered HMMs. For other modelling methods it is difficult to develop models without incurring significant analytical or computational problems.

Second, the HMM provides a rich scope for designing a range of models with the ability to model dependencies on unobservable states. Such an ability is important in finance, where we require complex model structures that are typically governed by unobservable variables. We can apply arbitrary functions of observations to our models, provided they are functions of hidden states. The (hidden) states themselves can be chosen to be any aspect of the system the modeller chooses, provided the states follow the Markov property.

Third, the HMMs are capable of modelling systems with significant amounts of noise and without making any specific assumptions about the noise process; this is in contrast to other modelling methods that make specific assumptions about the noise process (e.g. Kalman filter). Such an application is particularly important in finance, where there exist numerous complicated sources of noise with non-normal distributions.

2.3.3 System behaviour and information

One of the main attractive features of HMMs is the ability to learn about a system and its properties. First, we can determine the behaviour of the underlying system from the state probabilities. From **A** we can determine the probability of a system to remain in its current state (a_{ii}) or change states (a_{ij}). Such information is particularly useful for investors to understand whether the market is likely to escape a bear market or possibly remain in it for some time (as in a depressed economy) when we model bull and bear markets as states.

Second, using the theory of Markov (and hidden Markov) processes it is possible to analytically forecast the probability of future state and observation sequences. For instance, we could forecast the probability of two quarters of negative GDP growth or two quarters of bear markets. Such information would be of particular interest to investors as it is not possible to directly determine whether a bear market occurs.

Third, HMM theory enables us to understand the long-term behaviour of such systems. We can analytically determine the probability that the system is in a particular state, regardless of the initial state, in the long term. We can also interpret the long-run probabilities of being in a particular state as also the mean percentage time spent in a particular state, in the long run. Hence the long run probabilities can tell us whether a particular stock market is, on average, in a bull or bear market. Furthermore, in the long run the HMM reaches an equilibrium state and exhibits a stationary distribution (also called the invariant or equilibrium distribution), enabling one to determine the long-term return distribution. Such long-term information is particular useful for trend analysis, but also evaluating long-term investment strategies, e.g. buy and hold.

Finally, HMM tend to be easier to understand and analyse compared to other modelling methods. The majority of mathematical finance models are based on stochastic differential equations (see, for instance, Scott, 1987; Heston, 1993; Bates, 1996). Such models require an understanding of stochastic calculus, hence the scope of model understanding, analysis and development is significantly limited. HMMs, on the other hand, do not require such theoretical knowledge and can be easily implemented on computer programs without significant mathematical knowledge.

3 Computational implementation of hidden Markov models: calibration

To model some empirically observed data using an HMM we require some calibration method to determine the HMM parameter values. The current method of calibrating HMM in finance/econometric literature has been popularly undertaken by the Hamilton filter. However, another method known as the Baum–Welch (BW) method, which has been widely used in engineering and the sciences for decades, is less commonly used in finance/econometrics. The BW method also offers more functionality that would be of benefit to traders and investors than the Hamilton filter (e.g. state sequence detection). The use of BW is therefore of importance to trading applications and so in this section we introduce both the Hamilton filter and the BW method. We then explain the advantages of the BW method.

3.1 Hamilton filter

In financial and economics literature the standard calibration method for HMM is the Hamilton filter (Hamilton, 1989), where HMMs are frequently referred to as regime switching models. This Hamilton filter works by maximum likelihood estimation (MLE): this is a general estimation method for a set of model parameters (denoted by θ) using some time series observations $O_1, O_2, \ldots, O_T$, assuming we know the function relating the observation's probabilities to model parameters.

The parameter estimation of θ is achieved by first determining the likelihood function $L(\theta)$ and maximizing $L(\theta)$ by varying θ; the values that maximize θ are our estimates of θ and is typically found using some search method. For Hamilton's HMM the general likelihood function $L(\theta)$ is given by:

$$L(\theta) = p(O_1|\theta)p(O_2|\theta,O_1)p(O_3|\theta,O_1,O_2) \ldots p(O_T|\theta,O_1,O_2,\ldots,O_{T-1}) \qquad (3.8)$$

where $p(O_{()}|\theta)$ is the probability of $O_{()}$, given model parameters θ. Now, by properties of logarithms, we have:

$$\log(L(\theta)) = \log(p(O_1|\theta)) + \log(p(O_2|\,\theta,O_1)) + \ldots + \\ \log(p(O_T|\theta;O_1,O_2,\ldots,O_{T-1})) \tag{3.9}$$

(As an example, assume we have a two-state HMM with observation signals as stock returns; each state models stock returns with a lognormal return distribution $N(\mu_i,\sigma_i)$ where μ_i and σ_i denote the mean and standard deviation of the distribution in state i. For the HMM we therefore would like to determine the parameters $\theta = \{\mu_1,\mu_2,\sigma_1,\sigma_2,a_{12},a_{21}\}$; note that by standard probability laws that $a_{22}=1-a_{12}$ and $a_{11}=1-a_{21}$, hence a_{22} and a_{11} do not require estimation.)

To obtain $p(O_t|\theta)$ for $t>1$, Hamilton showed it could be calculated by a recursive filter. We observe the relation:

$$p(O_t\,|\,\theta,O_1,O_2,\ldots,O_{t-1}) \sum_{q_t=1,2}\sum_{q_t=1,2} p(q_t q_{t-1},O_t\,|\,\theta,O_1,O_2,\ldots,O_{t-1}) \tag{3.10}$$

Now using the relation:

$$p(O,Q|\theta) = p(O|\theta,Q)p(Q|\theta) \tag{3.11}$$

where $Q=q_1q_2\ldots$ represents some arbitrary state sequence, we make the substitution of $p(q_t,q_{t-1},O_t|\theta,O_1,\ldots,O_{t-1})$ with

$$p(q_{t-1}|,O_1,\ldots,O_{t-1})p(q_t|q_{t-1},\theta)p(O_t|q_t,\theta) \tag{3.12}$$

Therefore with the substitution we have:

$$p(O_t\,|\,\theta,O_1,O_2,\ldots,O_{t-1}) \sum_{q_t=1,2}\sum_{q_t=1,2} p(q_{t-1}\,|\,\theta,O_1,\ldots,O_{t-1}) \tag{3.13}$$

$$p(q_t\,|\,q_{t-1},\theta)p(O_t\,|\,q_t,\theta)$$

where

- $p(q_t|q_{t-1},\theta) = p(q_t=\underline{j}|q_{t-1}=i,\theta)$ represents the transition probability a_{ij} we wish to estimate;
- $p(O_t|q_t=i,\theta) = p_i(O_t)$ where $p_i(.) \sim N(\mu_i,\sigma_i)$ and whose parameters μ_i,σ_i we wish to estimate.

Therefore to calculate $p(O_t|\theta,O_1,O_2,\ldots,O_{t-1})$ we require the probability $p(q_{t-1}|\theta,O_1,\ldots,O_{t-1})$ (summed over two different values of q_{t-1}). This can be achieved through recursion, that is the probability $p(q_{t-1}|\theta,O_1,\ldots,O_{t-1})$ can be obtained from $p(q_{t-2}|\theta,O_1,\ldots,O_{t-2})$. This can be understood as follows. First:

$$p(q_{t-1} \mid \theta, O_1,, \ldots, O_{t-1}) \sum_{i=1,2} \frac{p(q_{t-1}, q_{t-2} = i, O_{t-1} \mid \theta, O_1, O_2, \ldots, O_{t-2})}{p(O_{t-1} \mid \theta, O_1, O_2, \ldots, O_{t-2})} \qquad (3.14)$$

The denominator of this equation ($p(O_{t-1} \mid \theta, O_1, O_2, \ldots, O_{t-2})$) is obtained from the previous period of $p(O_t \mid \theta, O_1, O_2, \ldots, O_{t-1})$; so by inspecting the equation for $p(O_t \mid \theta, O_1, O_2, \ldots, O_{t-1})$ we can see it is a function of $p(q_{t-2} \mid \theta, O_1, \ldots, O_{t-2})$. The numerator of the equation for $p(q_{t-1} \mid \theta, O_1, \ldots, O_{t-1})$ is obtained from calculating equation $p(q_t, q_{t-1}, O_t \mid \theta, O_1, \ldots, O_{t-1})$ for the previous time period, which is also a function of $p(q_{t-2} \mid \theta, O_1, \ldots, O_{t-2})$.

To start the recursion of the equation for $p(q_{t-1} \mid \theta, O_1, \ldots, O_{t-1})$ at $p(q_1 = i \mid O_1, \theta)$ we require $p(O_1 \mid \theta)$. To obtain this Hamilton assumes the Markov chain has been running sufficiently long enough that we can assume the observations $O_1, O_2, \ldots, O_T$ are all drawn from the Markov chain's invariant distribution. Consequently, the following property of a two-state Markov chain can be applied:

$$\eta_j = p(q_t = j \mid q_1 = i) \text{ as } t \to \infty \text{ for any } i, \text{ and } \eta_1 = a_{21}/(a_{12} + a_{21}), \eta_2 = 1 - \eta_1 \quad (3.15)$$

The probability η_j tells us in the long run the (unconditional) probability of being in state j and this probability is independent of the initial state (at time $t=1$). Therefore:

$$p(O_1 \mid \theta) = p(q_1 = 1, O_1 \mid \theta) + p(q_1 = 2, O_1 \mid \theta) \qquad (3.16)$$

where $p(q_1 = i, O_1 \mid \theta) = \eta_j p_i(O_1)$ or $p(q_1 = i, O_1 \mid \theta) = \eta_j p(O_1 \mid q_t = i, \theta)$. We can therefore calculate $p(q_1 = i \mid O_1, \theta)$:

$$\begin{aligned} p(q_1 = i \mid O_1, \theta) = p(q_1 = i, O_1 \mid \theta) / p(O_1 \mid \theta) = \eta_j p(O_1 \mid q_t = i, \theta) / \\ (\eta_1 p_1(O_1) + \eta_2 p_2(O_1)) \end{aligned} \qquad (3.17)$$

Therefore $p(q_1 = i \mid O_1, \theta)$ can be obtained from estimating the parameter set θ, which is obtained when we estimate θ through MLE.

3.2 Baum–Welch method

The BW method estimates the HMM parameters, which we will denote by M, using the observation sequence $O = O_1 O_2 \ldots O_T$. Whereas the Hamilton filter estimates $\mathbf{A}, \mathbf{B}$ (in the case of a two-state HMM this is $\{\mu_1, \mu_2, \sigma_1, \sigma_2, a_{12}, a_{21}\}$), in the case of the BW method it estimates all the HMM properties, specifically $\mathbf{A}, \mathbf{B}$ and $p(q_1 = i)$. Therefore the BW, unlike the Hamilton filter, is able to determine the full HMM specification; moreover, it is also able to provide other modelling advantages for traders.

The BW algorithm determines the optimal estimates of M by iteratively calculating estimates of M, denoted by M'. Specifically, BW estimates M' such that it maximizes the likelihood of $p(O \mid M')$, where $p(O \mid M)$ is the probability of an observed time series sequence $O = O_1 O_2 \ldots O_T$ given all the HMM parameters are known. It has been theoretically proven BW is guaranteed to find the local optimum of M' for a given O (Rabiner, 1989); currently no method exists of analytically finding the global optimal M'.

The BW algorithm works by using the forward and backward algorithm, which are two computational methods using recursion (see Rabiner, 1989 for more information). The BW algorithm is given by:

1   (Initialization): using observation data O and initial values of M', calculate $p(O|M')$ by using the forward algorithm. (If initial values of M' do not exist then randomly assign values).

2   Estimate new values of M:

   a   By using the forward and backward algorithm and current M' calculate the forward variable

$$\kappa_t(i) = p(O_1 O_2 \ldots O_t, q_t = i | M) \tag{3.18}$$

   and backward variable

$$\rho_{t+1}(j) = p(O_{t+2} O_{t+3} \ldots O_T | q_{t+1} = j, M) \tag{3.19}$$

   Using above $\kappa_t(i)$ and $\rho_{t+1}(\mathbf{j})$ calculations, calculate $\psi_t(i,j)$ by equation:

$$\psi_t(i,j) = \kappa_t(i) a_{ij} b_j(O_{t+1}) \rho_{t+1}(j) / p(O|M') \tag{3.20}$$

   b   Using calculated $\psi_t(i,j)$ in (a), determine new estimate of M' (where $\mathbf{A}$ is obtained from a'_{ij}, $\mathbf{B}$ is obtained from $b'_j(s)$ and $p(q_1 = i)$ from p' $(q_1 = i)$) using equations:

   (I) $a'_{ij} \displaystyle\sum_{t=1,2,\ldots,T-1} \psi_t(i,j) / \chi(i)$ $\tag{3.21}$

   where

   $\chi(i) \displaystyle\sum_{t=1,2,\ldots,T-1} \Gamma_t(i)$

   and

   $\Gamma_t(i) = \displaystyle\sum_{j=1,\ldots,R} \psi_t(i,j)$

   where R is the total number of states.

   (II) $p'(q_1 = i) = \Gamma_1(i)$ $\tag{3.22}$

   (III) $b'_j(s) = \displaystyle\sum_{t=1,2,\ldots,T} \Gamma_t(j,s) / v(j)$ $\tag{3.23}$

where $\Gamma_t(j,s)$ is $\Gamma_t(j)$ with condition $O_t = s$ (where s is some specific observation signal), and

$$v(i) \sum_{t=1,2,\ldots,T} \Gamma_t(i) \tag{3.24}$$

c   Calculate $p(O|M')$ with new M' (obtained from (b)) by using the forward algorithm.

3   End algorithm if two consecutive calculations of $p(O|M')$ converge within a specified range. Otherwise repeat iteration: go to step 2.

The BW algorithm is started with initial estimates of M'; these estimates in turn are used to calculate (I)–(III) in (b), which give the next new estimate of M'. We consider the new estimate M_n to be a better estimate than the previous estimate M_p if $p(O|M_n) > p(O|M_p)$, with both probabilities calculated via the forward algorithm. In other words, we prefer the M that increases the probability of observation O occurring.

If $p(O|M_n) > p(O|M_p)$ then the BW algorithm is re-iterated with M_n as the new input to the algorithm. On the other hand, the iteration will be stopped when $p(O|M_n) = p(O|M_p)$ or is arbitrarily close enough. Since the BW algorithm has been proven to always converge to the local optimum, the BW will always provide an answer (and not continue calculating indefinitely) and output the local optimal values of M'.

In addition to determining M, the BW method (unlike the Hamilton filter) has the additional advantage of being able to make full use of the forward algorithm. Therefore the BW can calculate the probability of observing some data, given the HMM parameters, that is $p(O|M)$. For instance, we may wish to know the probability of observing six quarters of GDP growth, given M models the economy.

The straightforward method of calculating $p(O|M)$ is

$$p(O \mid M) = \sum_{all Q} p(O, Q \mid M) \tag{3.25}$$

where '*all Q*' means all possible state sequences $q_1 q_2 \ldots q_T$ that could account for observation sequence O. We must sum this equation over all possible Q state sequences, requiring R^T computations; this is computationally infeasible even for small R and T. To overcome this computational difficulty, we apply the forward algorithm (which uses dynamic programming). The forward algorithm only requires computations of the order $R^2 T$ and so is significantly faster for large R and T.

3.3 Advantages of the Baum–Welch method

Although the Hamilton filter method has some advantages over the BW method (for instance, fewer parameters to estimate and simpler to understand), the BW algorithm has significant advantages. We will now explain them.

First, the BW algorithm is a complete HMM parameter estimation method, unlike the Hamilton filter. The BW algorithm is an estimation method for all the HMM parameters because it estimates **A**, **B** and $p(q_1 = i)$, whereas the Hamilton method only estimates **A** and **B**. Furthermore, the BW method specifies a computational optimization algorithm that guarantees finding the locally optimal parameter solutions. However, Hamilton's method provides no method or guidance as to the computational optimization algorithm to apply for finding the parameters using the Hamilton filter. Moreover, the parameter estimates found using the (non-linear) Hamilton filter can be significantly influenced by the optimization algorithm applied.

Second, the Hamilton filter has no method of estimating the initial state probabilities $p(q_1 = i)$ (unlike the BW method). This has a number of important consequences:

1   Using the Hamilton filter we cannot determine the probability of observation sequences $p(O|M)$, since this requires the initial state probabilities. The ability to estimate $p(O|M)$ is important to evaluating the possibility of various trading strategies and is possible under BW.

2   Using the Hamilton filter we cannot determine the most likely state sequence that accounts for a given observation sequence; such state sequences are useful for trading strategies. The state sequences requires the initial state probabilities (and applying the Viterbi algorithm) and this can be achieved using the BW.

3   Without the initial state probabilities we cannot simulate state sequences, since the initial state radically alters the state sequence generation and its influence on the state sequence increases as the sequence size decreases. Hence the Hamilton filter limits our simulation options compared to using the BW method and simulation is a frequently used technique in trading.

Third, the Hamilton filter cannot be applied to modelling data with multivariate distributions nor complicated univariate distributions. In particular for financial applications, we use multivariate data to model portfolios and multivariate stochastic volatility is becoming an increasingly important area. Although Hamilton has proposed a calibration method for univariate mixture distributions (the Quasi-Bayesian MLE approach (Hamilton, 1991)), this requires some prior knowledge regarding the reliability of observations.

Finally, the Hamilton filter requires observation data to be taken from the invariant distribution in order to estimate the HMM parameters. To obtain observations from the invariant distribution implies the number of state transitions approaches a large number and so is not suited to HMMs that have run for a short period. Furthermore, the time to reach the invariant distribution increases with the number of states.

Psaradakis and Sola (1998) investigated the finite sample properties of the Hamilton filter for financial data. They concluded that samples of at least 400 observations are required for a simple two-state HMM when each state's observation is modelled by a normal distribution. Therefore we require a large amount of observation data before we can apply the Hamilton filter, unlike the BW method. Therefore the Hamilton filter is not suitable for trading applications that have short time series data; this is a limiting property as many trading strategies are based on limited data.

4 Application of the Baum–Welch method and Hamilton filter to financial markets

4.1 Introduction

In this section we undertake a detailed and practical study of the Baum–Welch and Hamilton filter applied to two financial markets: equity and fixed-income markets. The aim of the section is to see an application and understanding of the use of the calibration methods of HMM to practical financial applications. It will also provide an opportunity to compare the two calibration methods.

4.2 Equity markets application

Equities form a significant part of trading strategies and investment portfolios, hence modelling equities is of particular interest. Consequently, the ability to understand bull and bear market cycles is a fundamental preoccupation as it is frequently cited that market timing is one of the most important aspects of trading. In this section we model bull and bear market cycles using HMM; we apply both the Hamilton filter and the BW calibration method.

The bull and bear phases of markets are never directly observed, they are 'hidden' from investors; for instance, stocks can rise or fall for significant periods in bull or bear markets, so one cannot determine the phase by stock returns alone. Using a two-state HMM we can model the market phases, with one state corresponding to a bull and another state corresponding to a bear market, since we do not need to observe the states to use HMM. Moreover, one can use stock returns as our observation signals for the states as we would expect a statistical dependency between the phases and the stock returns.

In our study we will model the bull and bear phases for two stock markets over 1976–1996 using annual return data for: S&P 500 index and the Nikkei 225 index. We assume the state transitions occur at yearly time intervals to coincide with the yearly data used for calibration. We take the index returns as our observation signals and model them using a Gaussian mixture distribution as equity return distributions tend to follow non-normal distributions.

We now present the results for each market and from each calibration method (note that the original results are taken from Mitra and Date (2010). The results are given in Figures 3.2–3.3 and the transition matrices are given below:

S&P 500 index:
BW method:

$$\begin{bmatrix} 0.78 & 0.22 \\ 0.82 & 0.18 \end{bmatrix}$$

Hamilton method:

$$\begin{bmatrix} 0.60 & 0.40 \\ 0.03 & 0.97 \end{bmatrix}$$

Nikkei 225 index:
BW method:

$$\begin{bmatrix} 0.87 & 0.13 \\ 0.41 & 0.59 \end{bmatrix}$$

Hamilton method:

$$\begin{bmatrix} 0.93 & 0.07 \\ 0.08 & 0.92 \end{bmatrix}$$

We notice from the empirical returns graphs (Figures 3.2 and 3.3) that one cannot easily classify the years that correspond to bull or bear markets, since we can have positive returns in bull or bear markets. Therefore, the HMM enables us to detect the bull and bear markets. In this study we denote state 1 as the bull market and state 2 as the bear market.

In Figures 3.2–3.3 we can see the states classified by each calibration method for each market. There is general agreement between both calibration methods for states in each year in both markets, although the BW method seems to identify bear markets more successfully. This is because the BW method appears to be identifying market states that correspond to movements in annual return changes, unlike those identified by the Hamilton filter.

The transition probabilities provide useful information for investors about the stock markets. For instance, there is a tendency for the market to remain in its current market phase (bull or bear) rather than switch between states (although this would not be the case according to the BW results for the Nikkei index, as there is the 0.41 probability). Hence the current market state is a good indicator for the future state of the market. Therefore investors should determine the market state before considering investment or trading positions; this is consistent with market practise, where industry professionals spend considerable time determining the current state of the market.

As can be seen from the transition matrix results, there is general agreement between both calibration methods for both markets, although there are some differences. For instance, both calibration methods give high probabilities for the

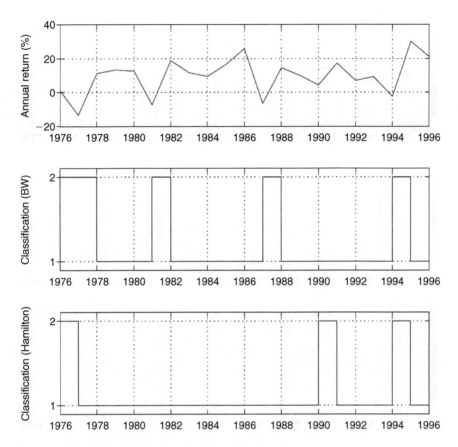

Figure 3.2 Graphs for the S&P 500 index 1976–1996.

Notes
Top: empirical annual returns of the S&P 500 index
Middle: state classifications for each year by the BW method
Bottom: state classifications for each year by the Hamilton filter

diagonal entries. For the S&P 500 the BW method estimates the probability of remaining in state 2 is quite unlikely, whereas under the Hamilton filter the probability is quite high. However, if we look at the empirical returns in Figure 3.2, this suggests that state 2 is generally a transient state and does not remain in that state; hence it would appear the BW results are more correct.

The usage of HMM for modelling markets enables us determine other useful information about the market phases. For instance, we can determine the average frequency of a bear market; for instance, for the S&P 500 this is approximately every 3–6 years, which is consistent with other research. Overall, the markets tend to be more in the bull phase rather than the bear phase.

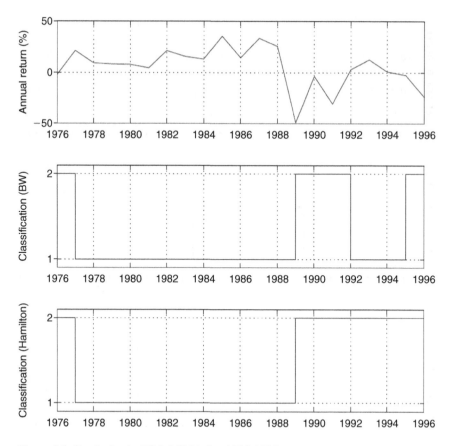

Figure 3.3 Graphs for the Nikkei 225 index 1976–1996.

Notes
Top: empirical annual returns of the Nikkei 225 index
Middle: state classifications for each year by the BW method
Bottom: state classifications for each year by the Hamilton filter

4.3 Fixed-income markets application

Fixed-income products (such as bonds) are important investment and trading assets for a number of reasons. First, bonds have always represented a significant component of a balanced portfolio. Second, traders can make speculative profits from the changing price of fixed-income products. Furthermore, trading in the bond market has increased due to speculation of a 'bond bubble' forming in government bonds across international markets.

As the price of fixed income products are influenced by interest rates, the ability to model and understand interest rate dynamics is important to any fixed income trading strategy. This has been particularly important to understand since the advent of the credit crunch, which has drastically influenced interest rate dynamics. One way to model interest rate dynamics is to use HMMs.

Using HMMs we model UK Bank of England interest rates. To model interest rate dynamics, we note in Figure 3.4 that there is no obvious relation over time with interest rates; however, one can see that interest rate *changes* appear to be in two distinct states: in one state interest rates change rapidly and in another state the rates change at a slower rate. One could therefore capture interest rate dynamics by using a two-state HMM, where each state relates to the rate of change of interest rates. Furthermore, as the state of fast or slow change is hidden from the observer, the application is even more suited to HMM.

Using the BW method we determine the parameters for a two-state HMM to model interest rate changes. We achieve this by using Bank of England monthly interest rate data (October 1980 to December 2008) as our observation data. We assume our HMM transitions states at monthly intervals to coincide with interest rate changes in the empirical data. We also assume the data can be modelled by a Gaussian mixture distribution.

The results of BW calibration are given below for the transition matrix and in Figure 3.5, where state 1 denotes a fast interest rate change phase and state 2 denotes the slow interest rate change phase.

$$\begin{bmatrix} 0.7697 & 0.2303 \\ 0.0820 & 0.9180 \end{bmatrix}$$

As one can see from the transition matrix, the interest rates have a tendency to remain in their current states, since the diagonal entries have high probabilities. Hence state changes are not frequent and when transitions occur, it is

Figure 3.4 Graph of Bank of England interest rates (%) for each month from October 1980 to December 2008.

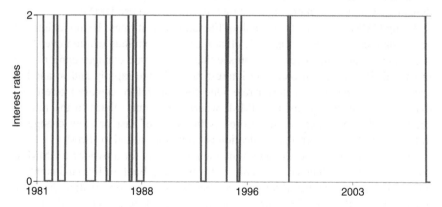

Figure 3.5 Graph of interest rates states for each month from October 1980 to December 2008.

difficult for the interest rates to change states. This is also reflected in Figures 3.4–3.5: when interest rates begin to move from a slow change to a large change phase, the large change phase persists for some time before reverting back to the slow change phase.

From Figure 3.5 we can see that state 1 occurs for relatively short time periods compared to state 2, hence we should expect interest rates to be relatively stable for the majority of the time and rapid changes in interest rates to be short-term effects. We also note that the latter period of interest rate states in Figure 3.5 show an unusually extended period of remaining in the slow change phase; this is consistent with the interest rate data but also other literature on interest rates. This suggests our HMM has successfully captured the interest rate dynamics.

The two-state HMM information is useful for fixed-income trading strategies for a number of reasons. First, our results show that high interest rate changes can be sustained for some period of time (due to the 0.9180 probability), but also can be short-lived. Therefore, it may be prudent to hedge out interest rate risk during times of high interest rate changes as the phase will last for some time, but also to remove the hedge once the high state is over (as the slow state is likely to persist for some time). Second, the 0.7697 and 0.9180 probabilities tell us that interest rate states are highly likely to remain in their current state. Therefore, the current state is an important indicator of the future state, which is important to forecasting interest rates for trading strategies and risk management.

5 Survey of current applications of hidden Markov models in finance

HMMs have been used in a range of financial and economic applications; their usage is becoming more popular but has not reached the same popularity as other modelling methods in finance yet (e.g. stochastic differential equations). In the finance/economics literature HMMs are commonly referred to as 'regime switching' models rather than HMMs. We now provide an up-to-date survey of current applications of HMMs in finance; their wide range of applications is evidence of the HMM's versatility.

A fundamental aspect of asset price modelling is volatility. One method of modelling volatility is as a stochastic process (commonly called stochastic volatility) and this is typically achieved using some stochastic differential equation. The advantage of stochastic volatility is its theoretical and empirical consistency with asset price moves. However, stochastic volatility causes a number of problems, e.g. derivation of analytical solutions, calibration and computational implementation. Consequently, such models have been less attractive.

One method of modelling volatility as stochastic without incurring the previously mentioned problems is to model it using an HMM. The volatility's value changes depending on the current (hidden) state. An additional key advantage of such a model is that it can capture the dependency of volatility on unobservable variables and the behaviour of such variables (e.g. bull or bear market phases).

Examples of stochastic volatility models using HMMs include: Vo (2009), who uses HMMs in stochastic volatility to explain the behaviour of oil prices; Carvalho and Lopes (2007), who use HMM volatility to model the returns of the Ibovespa stock index; and Rossi and Gallo (2006), who use it for the S&P 500 stock index. Flavin and Panopoulou (2009) model volatility as an HMM to model the advantages of international diversification in portfolio construction.

HMMs have been used in portfolio selection. Portfolio selection has been an important problem in financial modelling since the seminal paper of Markowitz (1952). However, many portfolio selection methods involve single-period, rather than multi-period or dynamic, modelling of asset price changes, as it facilitates optimization and analytical implementation. This is typically unsatisfactory as portfolio managers wish to manage portfolios over many periods, taking into account changes in portfolio value.

Using HMM one can model portfolio value changes, while still enabling one to use common portfolio selection techniques to optimize portfolios. Moreover, portfolio values tend to depend on hidden variables (such as the business cycle of the economy) which the HMM is able to capture; the HMM can also model the behaviour of the hidden variables themselves with time, e.g. the dependencies between the different phases in cycles.

Liu (2011) uses HMMs to model risky US stocks, which enables the author to choose optimal portfolios in a multi-period setting. Wu and Li (2012) are able to optimize portfolios in a multi-period setting when cashflows follow a stochastic process governed by an HMM. Frauendorfer *et al.* (2007) model volatility and correlations with an HMM and this enables portfolio management in a multi-period setting that takes account of more realistic volatility and correlation dynamics.

HMMs have been used in option pricing applications. Option pricing is an important area in finance; since the derivation of the Black–Scholes option pricing equation (Black and Scholes, 1973) this area has grown significantly. The interest in options has arisen because they can be used for risk management (such as hedging) and trading positions with heavy leverage. Since the Black–Scholes equation makes a number of assumptions to price options, the model has been developed to be more realistic. However, these have resulted in intractable models with no analytical solutions or feasible computational implementation e.g. Johnson and Shanno's option model (Johnson and Shanno, 1987) has no analytical equation and answers must be obtained by Monte Carlo simulation.

Using HMMs one can formulate option pricing models that take into account more realistic modelling effects, but also enable one to derive analytical solutions and other advantages, e.g. computational implementations. Examples of such models include an option pricing model that takes into account economic states affecting option prices, which is consistent with empirical observations, (see, for instance, Zhu et al., 2012; Elliot et al., 2011). In Liu and Siu (2010) a method to price options is developed with key parameters varying with time (unlike the Black–Scholes model) specifically with the interest rates, growth rates of the assets and their volatilities. Bo et al. (2010) price currency options, but unlike many option models they take into account modulated exchange rate jumps. This enables option pricing that takes into account jump risk.

HMMs have been used in credit risk modelling; credit risk modelling had been an area of growing interest prior to the credit crunch. The quantitative modelling in credit risk was primarily developed by Merton (1974) and Jarrow and Turnbull (1995). HMMs have become especially appealing to credit risk modelling because the hidden Markov process is able to capture particular factors of credit risk and credit rating behaviour. For instance, credit rating migrations (e.g. AAA to AA) tend to follow a Markov process. Also, factors that influence credit risk (such as interest rates, GDP and inflation) tend to follow a hidden Markov process.

Examples of credit risk models using HMM include Liang and Wang (2012), who model credit risk with default shocks modelled by an HMM. Their model also enables them to derive closed form expressions for default times and to price basket default swaps, which are important for credit risk hedging. Huang and Hu (2012) model CDS (credit default swaps) prices using a two-state HMM, where each state reflects a high or low state of CDS pricing. Guo et al. (2011) investigate market contagion in a range of markets (including the credit market) using an HMM approach.

HMM have been used in modelling macroeconomic variables and was one of the first applications of HMM in finance and economics. This has been primarily initiated by Hamilton (1989). HMM are now used to model a number of macroeconomic variables, ranging from inflation, interest rates to exchange rates and business cycles.

Kerekes (2012) uses HMM to classify the GDP growth rate of 84 countries over the period 1962–2003; Mittnik and Semmler (2012) model fiscal multipliers using HMMs. Zhou and Mamon (2012) are able to model short-term interest rate fluctuations as a function of economic cycles using HMMs; this enables them to capture various characteristics of the yield curve. Cologni and Manera (2009) model the relation between economic output and oil shocks through HMMs.

HMMs have also been used for other financial and economic applications. Sotomayor and Cadenillas (2011) determine optimal dividend policies using HMM to model stock dividends; the HMM enables the dividends to capture their dependency on the economy. Boyle and Draviam (2007) are able to price exotic derivatives using HMMs. Finally, Guo *et al.* (2010) used HMMs to model IPO (initial public offering) cycles in China.

6 Concluding remarks

In this chapter we have discussed HMMs for financial applications, specifically with respect to trading and investing applications. HMMs are highly flexible models that have a range of applications in finance, without requiring demanding modelling assumptions, and are consistent with important theories in finance, such as the EMH.

In this chapter we have discussed the advantages of using HMMs for financial modelling, such as the EMH, and their computational implementation using empirical data. Specifically, we have introduced the calibration method that is most frequently applied in economic and financial research literature (Hamilton filter), but also a less well-known method – the BW method. Moreover, we have shown the superior advantages the BW method has to offer and the trading or investment advantages it offers compared to the Hamilton filter.

The future developments of HMMs include developing them to take into account more features of financial markets. In particular, we would like to introduce stochastic transition matrices whereby transition probabilities are not constant but change with time. We would also like to develop portfolio models of HMMs to increase their applications to portfolios. We would also like to see HMMs developed for other areas of finance, such as operational risk modelling, exotic derivative modelling and modelling emerging markets.

In conclusion, HMMs offer a rich scope for quantitative modelling in finance and there exists much scope for development in the future. It is anticipated that HMM will become a key quantitative tool for finance as other methods have become in finance (such as stochastic differential equations), but will be more accessible to a wider audience. Such models will be used for enhancing trading and investment strategies.

References

Bates, D., 'Jumps and stochastic volatility: exchange rate processes implicit in Deutsche Mark options', *Review of Financial Studies* 9(1), 1996, 69–107.

Baum, L., 'An equality and associated maximization technique in statistical estimation for probabilistic functions of Markov processes', *Inequalities* 3, 1972, 1–8.

Baum, L. and J. Eagon, 'An inequality with applications to statistical estimation for probabilistic functions of Markov processes and to a model for ecology', *Bulletin of the American Mathematics Society* 73(3), 1967, 360–363.

Baum, L. and T. Petrie, 'Statistical inference for probabilistic functions of finite state Markov chains', *The Annals of Mathematical Statistics* 37(6), 1966, 1554–1563.

Baum, L. and G. Sell, 'Growth transformations for functions on manifolds', *Pacific Journal of Mathematics* 27(2), 1968, 211–227.

Black, F. and M. Scholes, 'The pricing of options and corporate liabilities', *The Journal of Political Economy*, 1973, 637–654.

Bo, L.Y. Wang and X. Yang, 'Markov-modulated jump-diffusions for currency option pricing', *Insurance: Mathematics and Economics* 46(3), 2010, 461–469.

Boyle, P. and T. Draviam, 'Pricing exotic options under regime switching', *Insurance: Mathematics and Economics* 40(2), 2007, 267–282.

Carvalho, C. and H. Lopes, 'Simulation-based sequential analysis of Markov switching stochastic volatility models', *Computational Statistics & Data Analysis* 51(9), 2007, 4526–4542.

Cologni, A. and M. Manera, 'The asymmetric effects of oil shocks on output growth: a Markov-switching analysis for the G-7 countries', *Economic Modelling* 26(1), 2009, 1–29.

Elliott, R., T. Siu and A. Badescu, 'On pricing and hedging options in regime-switching models with feedback effect', *Journal of Economic Dynamics and Control* 35(5), 2011, 694–713.

Fama, E., 'The behavior of stock-market prices', *Journal of Business*, 38, 1965, 34–105.

Flavin, T. and E. Panopoulou, 'On the robustness of international portfolio diversification benefits to regime-switching volatility', *Journal of International Financial Markets, Institutions and Money* 19(1), 2009, 140–156.

Frauendorfer, K., U. Jacoby and A. Schwendener, 'Regime switching based portfolio selection for pension funds', *Journal of Banking & Finance* 31(8), 2007, 2265–2280.

Guo, F., C. Chen and Y. Huang, 'Markets contagion during financial crisis: a regime-switching approach', *International Review of Economics & Finance* 20(1), 2011, 95–109.

Guo, H., R. Brooks and R. Shami, 'Detecting hot and cold cycles using a Markov regime switching model: evidence from the Chinese A-share IPO market', *International Review of Economics & Finance* 19(2), 2010, 196–210.

Hamilton, J., 'A new approach to the economic analysis of nonstationary time series and the business cycle', *Econometrica: Journal of the Econometric Society*, 57(2), 1989, 357–384.

Hamilton, J., 'A quasi-Bayesian approach to estimating parameters for mixtures of normal distributions', *Journal of Business & Economic Statistics* 9(1), 1991, 27–39.

Heston, S., 'A closed-form solution for options with stochastic volatility with applications to bond and currency options', *Review of Financial Studies* 6(2), 1993, 327–343.

Huang, A. and W. Hu, 'Regime switching dynamics in credit default swaps: evidence from smooth transition autoregressive model', *Physica A: Statistical Mechanics and its Applications* 391(4), 2012, 1497–1508.

Jarrow, R. and S. Turrnbull, 'Pricing derivatives on financial securities subject to credit risk', *The Journal of Finance* 50(1), 1995, 53–85.

Johnson, H. and D. Shanno, 'Option pricing when the variance is changing', *Journal of Financial and Quantitative Analysis* 22(2), 1987, 143–151.

Kerekes, M., 'Growth miracles and failures in a Markov switching classification model of growth', *Journal of Development Economics* 98(2), 2012, 167–177.

Liang, X. and G. Wang, 'On a reduced form credit risk model with common shock and regime switching', *Insurance: Mathematics and Economics* 51(3), 2012, 567–575.

Liu, C. and T. Siu, 'A hidden Markov regime-switching model for option valuation', *Insurance: Mathematics and Economics* 47(3), 2010, 374–384.

Liu, H., 'Dynamic portfolio choice under ambiguity and regime switching mean returns', *Journal of Economic Dynamics and Control* 35(4), 2011, 623–640.

Markowitz, H., 'Portfolio selection', *The Journal of Finance* 7(1), 1952, 77–91.

Merton, R., 'On the pricing of corporate debt: the risk structure of interest rates', *Journal of Finance* 29(2), 1974, 449–470.

Mitra, S. and P. Date, 'Regime switching volatility calibration by the Baum–Welch method', *Journal of Computational and Applied Mathematics* 234(12), 2010, 3243–3260.

Mittnik, S. and W. Semmler, 'Regime dependence of the fiscal multiplier', *Journal of Economic Behavior & Organization* 83(3), 2012, 502–522.

Psaradakis, Z. and M. Sola, 'Finite-sample properties of the maximum likelihood estimator in autoregressive models with Markov switching', *Journal of Econometrics* 86(2), 1998, 369–386.

Rabiner, L., 'A tutorial on hidden Markov models and selected applications in speech recognition', *Proceedings of the IEEE* 77(2), 1989, 257–286.

Rossi, A. and G. Gallo, 'Volatility estimation via hidden Markov models', *Journal of Empirical Finance* 13(2), 2006, 203–230.

Scott, L., 'Option pricing when the variance changes randomly: theory, estimation, and an application', *Journal of Financial and Quantitative analysis* 22(4), 1987, 419–438.

Sotomayor, L. and A. Cadenillas, 'Classical and singular stochastic control for the optimal dividend policy when there is regime switching', *Insurance: Mathematics and Economics* 48(3), 2011, 344–354.

Vo, M., 'Regime-switching stochastic volatility: evidence from the crude oil market', *Energy Economics* 31(5), 2009, 779–788.

Wu, H. and Z. Li, 'Multi-period mean-variance portfolio selection with regime switching and a stochastic cash flow', *Insurance: Mathematics and Economics* 50(3), 2012, 371–384.

Zhou, N. and R. Mamon, 'An accessible implementation of interest rate models with Markov-switching', *Expert Systems with Applications* 39(5), 2012, 4679–4689.

Zhu, S., A. Badran and X. Lu, 'A new exact solution for pricing European options in a two-state regime-switching economy', *Computers & Mathematics with Applications* 64(8), 2012, 2744–2755.

4 Adaptive filtering on forecasting financial derivatives indices

Christos Dimitrakopoulos, Andreas Karathanasopoulos, Georgios Sermpinis and Spiros Likothanassis

1 Introduction

The application of machine learning techniques for market predictions has been broadly established in the scientific community. Developing high-performance techniques for predicting financial time series is a crucial problem for economists, investigators and analysts. The traditional statistical methods used by economists in the past years seem to fail to capture the discontinuities, non-linearities and high complexity of the financial time series. Complex machine learning techniques have been used so far to predict the trends of the financial time series. Three major examples are the artificial neural networks (Holland *et al.*, 1995), the random forests (Breiman *et al.*, 2001) and the support vector machines (SVMs) (Vapnik and Cortes, 1995). They provide enough learning capacity and are more likely to capture the complex non-linear models which are dominant in the financial markets. Although machine learning techniques have been widely used in financial indexes forecasting, adaptive filtering techniques have rarely been used.

In the present chapter, we achieved high-performance predictions of the trends of the three indexes of DAX30, CAC40 and Euronext with classifiers built based on adaptive filtering techniques. Adaptive filtering techniques do not require previous knowledge of the signal statistics, have a small computational complexity per iteration and converge to a neighbourhood of the optimal solution. Moreover, adaptive filtering techniques are suitable for non-stationary signals and systems, and the trend of a financial index can be characterized as such. Three classical parameter estimation algorithms (least mean squares (LMS), recursive least squares (RLS) and Kalman filter) and one gain adaptation algorithm (incremental delta-bar-delta (IDBD)) were considered. The gain adaptation algorithms have been shown to perform comparably to the best algorithms (Kalman and RLS), but they have a lower complexity (Diniz, 2002). Overall, the adaptive filtering techniques used in this survey are the LMS (Widrow and Hoff, 1960), the RLS (Goodwin and Payne, 1977), the extended Kalman filtering method (EKF) (Welch and Bishop, 1995) and the IDBD (Sutton, 1992). We use as benchmark/comparative methods the well-known naive strategy, buy and hold strategy, ARMA model and MACD model. The adaptive filtering techniques have proved to perform significantly better that the classical benchmark techniques. Four different evaluation criteria are used to confirm this superiority (annualized return, information gain, maximal draw-down and correct bidirectional change).

The rest of the chapter is organized as follows: In Section 2 a description of the three financial indices is given, and all the traditional and machine learning techniques used are briefly described. In Section 3 the comparative results of the methods are presented and discussed, and in Section 4 some future research directions are proposed.

2 Adaptive filtering in finance

Although machine learning techniques have been widely used in financial index forecasting, adaptive filtering techniques have rarely been used. Maridakis and Wheelwright (1977) extended the applicability of a heuristic filtering technique, adaptive filtering, by dealing with a number of practical considerations in time series forecasting. These are problems that have been raised by other researchers examining this technique and by practitioners using it for time series analysis. These modifications make adaptive filtering much more comparable to the Box-Jenkins methodology for autoregressive/moving-average processes. A specific application of adaptive filtering is provided.

Huang and Tsai (2007) hybridized support vector regression with the self-organizing feature map (SOFM) technique and a filter-based feature selection to reduce the cost of training time and to improve prediction accuracies. The hybrid system conducts the following processes: filter-based feature selection to choose important input attributes; SOFM algorithm to cluster the training samples; and SVR to predict the stock market price index. The proposed model was demon-strated using a real future dataset – Taiwan index futures (FITX) to predict the next day's price index. The experiment results show that the proposed SOFM SVR is an improvement over the traditional single SVR in average prediction accuracy and training time.

Gencay *et al.* (2001) focused on the basic premise of wavelet filtering, which provides insight into the dynamics of economic/financial time series beyond that of current methodology. Wavelet filtering provides a natural platform to deal with the time-varying characteristics found in most real-world time series, and thus the assumption of stationarity may be avoided. They state that a transform that decomposes a process into different time horizons is appealing as it differ-entiates seasonalities, reveals structural breaks and volatility clusters and identi-fies local and global dynamic properties of a process at these timescales. Moreover, they claim that wavelet filters provide a convenient way of dissolving the correlation structure of a process across timescales. This indicates that the wavelet coefficients at one level are not much associated with coefficients at dif-ferent scales or within their scale. This is convenient when performing tasks such as simulations, estimation and testing since it is always easier to deal with an uncorrelated process as opposed to one with unknown correlation structure.

3　Materials and methods

3.1　Datasets

In the current survey we focus on predicting three noisy derivative financial signals: CAC40, DAX30 and the Euronext.

The DAX30 (German stock index) is a stock market index consisting of the 30 major German companies trading on the Frankfurt Stock Exchange. Prices are retrieved from the electronic Xetra trading system. DAX actually measures the performance of the Prime Standard's 30 largest German companies in terms of order-book volume and market capitalization. It is the equivalent of the FT30 and the Dow Jones Industrial Average, and because of its small selection it does not necessarily represent the vitality of the economy as a whole. We use data for the index close prices for 1,779 consecutive days starting from 4 November 2004 until 1 October 2010.

The CAC40 is a benchmark French stock market index and it represents a capitalization-weighted measure of the 40 most significant values among the 100 highest market caps on the Paris Bourse (now Euronext Paris). It is one of the main national indices of the pan-European stock exchange group Euronext, alongside Brussels' BEL20, Lisbon's PSI-20 and Amsterdam's AEX. We use data for the index close prices for 3,159 consecutive days, starting from 21 February 2000 until 1 October 2010.

Euronext N.V. is a European electronic stock exchange based in Amsterdam, Netherlands and with subsidiaries in Belgium, France, Netherlands, Portugal and the United Kingdom. In addition to equities and derivatives markets, the Euronext group provides clearing and information services. As of December 2010, markets run by Euronext had a market capitalization of US$2.93 trillion, making it the fifth largest exchange in the world. We use data for the index close prices for 2,508 consecutive days starting from 5 November 2002 until 1 October 2010.

For all three indices we use the last two years as a validation set. Table 4.1 shows the proportion of the datasets used as in-sample and out-of-sample.

3.2　Computational methods

The main goal of this chapter is to benchmark the performance of four state-of-the-art adaptive filtering techniques with four traditional strategies, namely an

Table 4.1 Proportion of the datasets used for in-sample or out-of-sample

Name of period	Trading days	Beginning	End
Total dataset	3,102	2 April 2001	17 May 2013
In-sample dataset	2,494	2 April 2001	31 December 2010
Out-of-sample dataset (validation set)	608	3 January 2011	17 May 2013

autoregressive moving average model (ARMA), a moving average convergence/divergence technical model (MACD), a naive strategy and buy and hold strategy. The adaptive filtering techniques examined are the LMS, the RLS, the Kalman filter and the gain adaptation filtering; they are described in Section 2.2.2.

3.2.1 Benchmark models

3.2.1.1 NAIVE STRATEGY

The naive strategy simply takes the most recent period change as the best prediction of the future change. The model is defined by:

$$Y_{t+1} = Y_t \tag{4.1}$$

where Y_t is the actual rate of return at period t and Y_{t+1} is the forecast rate of return for the next period. The performance of the strategy is evaluated in terms of trading performance via a simulated trading strategy.

3.2.1.2 BUY AND HOLD STRATEGY

Buy and hold is a long-term investment strategy based on the view that in the long run financial markets give a good rate of return despite periods of volatility or decline. This viewpoint also holds that short-term market timing, i.e. the concept that one can enter the market on the lows and sell on the highs, does not work; attempting timing gives negative results, at least for small or unsophisticated investors, so it is better for them to simply *buy and hold*.

3.2.1.3 SIMPLE ARMA MODEL

ARMA models assume that the value of a time series depends on its previous values (the autoregressive component) and on previous residual values (the moving average component)

The ARMA model takes the form:

$$Y_t = \varphi_0 + \varphi_1 Y_{t-1} + \varphi_2 Y_{t-2} + \ldots + \varphi_p Y_{t-p} + \varepsilon_t - w_1 \varepsilon_{t-1} - w_2 \varepsilon_{t-2} - \ldots - w_q \varepsilon_{t-q} \tag{4.2}$$

where:

Y_t is the dependent variable at time t
Y_{t-1}, Y_{t-2} and Y_{t-p} are the lagged dependent variables
$\varphi_0, \varphi_1, \varphi_2$, and φ_p are regression coefficients
ε_t is the residual term
$\varepsilon_{t-1}, \varepsilon_{t-2}$ and ε_{t-p} are previous values of the residual
w_1, w_2 and w_q are weights.

Using as a guide the correlogram in the training and the test sub-periods we have chosen a restricted ARMA (1,6) model for CAC index, a restricted ARMA (1,7) for Euronext and a restricted ARMA (1,3) for DAX index. All of its coefficients are significant at the 99 per cent confidence interval. The null hypothesis that all coefficients (except the constant) are not significantly different from zero is rejected at the 99 per cent confidence interval

The model selected was retained for out-of-sample estimation. The performance of the strategy is evaluated in terms of traditional forecasting accuracy and in terms of trading performance

3.2.1.4 MACD

The moving average model is defined as:

$$M_t = \frac{\left(Y_t + Y_{t-1} + Y_{t-2} + \ldots + Y_{t-n+1}\right)}{n} \tag{4.3}$$

where:

M_t is the moving average at time t
n is the number of terms in the moving average
Y_t is the actual rate of return at period t.

The MACD strategy used is quite simple. Two moving average series are created with different moving average lengths. The decision rule for taking positions in the market is straightforward. Positions are taken if the moving averages intersect. If the short-term moving average intersects the long-term moving average from below, a 'long' position is taken. Conversely, if the long-term moving average is intersected from above a 'short' position is taken.

The forecaster must use judgement when determining the number of periods n on which to base the moving averages. The combination that performed best over the in-sample sub-period was retained for out-of-sample evaluation. The first model selected was a combination of the DAX and its nine-day moving average, namely $n=1$ and 9, respectively, or a (1,9) combination. The second model selected was a combination of the Euronext and its eight-day moving average, namely $n=1$ and 8, respectively, or a (1,8) combination, and the third model selected was a combination of the CAC and its ten-day moving average, namely $n=1$ and 10, respectively, or a (1,10) combination. The performance of this strategy is evaluated solely in terms of trading performance.

3.2.2 *Adaptive filtering prediction techniques*

3.2.2.1 LMS

The LMS is a search algorithm in which a simplification of the gradient vector computation is made possible by appropriately modifying the objective function.

The LMS algorithm, as well as others related to it, is widely used in various applications of adaptive filtering due to its computational simplicity. The convergence characteristics of the LMS algorithm are examined in order to establish a range for the convergence factor that will guarantee stability.

The convergence speed of the LMS is shown to be dependent on the eigenvalue spread of the input signal correlation matrix. In this chapter, several properties of the LMS algorithm are discussed, including the misadjustment in stationary and non-stationary environments and tracking performance. The analysis results are verified by a large number of simulation examples.

The LMS algorithm (Widrow and Hoff, 1960) is by far the most widely used algorithm in adaptive filtering, for several reasons. The main features that promoted the use of the LMS algorithm are its low computational complexity, proof of convergence in stationary environment and stable behaviour when implemented with finite-precision arithmetic. To guarantee the convergence of LMS it is good practice to set the learning rate in the range,

$$0 < \mu < \frac{1}{\lambda_{\max}} \tag{4.4}$$

where $\lambda_{\max}$ is the largest eigenvalue of $R = E[x(k)x^T(k)]$, where $x(k)$ is the vector of the input variables. The resulting gradient-based algorithm is known as the LMS algorithm, whose updating equation is

$$w(k+1) = w(k) + 2\mu e(k)x(k) \tag{4.5}$$

where the convergence factor μ should be chosen in a range to guarantee convergence. In particular, learning rate parameter controls the final convergence value of the mean square error (MSE) and the speed of convergence of the MSE.

3.2.2.2 RLS

Least-squares algorithms aim at the minimization of the sum of the squares of the difference between the desired signal and the model filter output. When new samples of the incoming signals are received in every iteration, the solution for the least-squares problem can be computed in recursive form resulting in the RLS algorithms. The conventional version of these algorithms will be the topic of the present chapter.

The RLS (Goodwin and Payne, 1977) algorithms are known to pursue fast convergence even when the eigenvalue spread of the input signal correlation matrix is large. These algorithms have excellent performance when working in time-varying environments. All these advantages come at the cost of an increased computational complexity and some stability problems, which are not as critical in LMS-based algorithms. Several properties related to the RLS algorithms are discussed, including misadjustment and tracking behaviour, which are verified through a number of simulation results.

The objective here is to choose the coefficients of the adaptive filter such that the output signal $y(k)$, during the period of observation, will match the desired signal as closely as possible in the least-squares sense. The minimization process requires the information of the input signal available so far. Also, the objective function we seek to minimize is deterministic.

3.2.2.3 KALMAN FILTER

This section provides a brief description of the Kalman filter, which can be considered an extension of the Wiener filtering concept. The Kalman filter has as its objective the minimization of the estimation square error of a non-stationary signal buried in noise. The estimated signal itself is modelled utilizing the state-space formulation describing its dynamical behaviour. In summary, Kalman filtering deals with random processes described using state-space modelling, which generate signals that can be measured and processed utilizing time recursive estimation formulas.

In general, the Kalman filter (Welch and Bishop, 1995) addresses the problem of trying to estimate the state of a discrete-time controlled process that is governed by a linear stochastic difference equation. The Kalman filter is a set of mathematical equations which constitutes an efficient means to estimate the state of a process by minimizing the mean of the square error. The EKF is the non-linear version of the Kalman filter, and its goal is to approach the situation where the process to be estimated or the measurement relationship to the process is non-linear. Its purpose is to use measurements observed over time, containing noise (random variations) and other inaccuracies, and produce values that tend to be closer to the true values of the measurements and their associated calculated values.

The specific equations for the time and measurement updates are divided into two groups. The time update equations

$$x_k^- = f(x_{k-1}, u_{k-1}, 0) \tag{4.6}$$

$$P_k^- = A_k P_{k-1} A_k^T + W_k Q_{k-1} W_k^T \tag{4.7}$$

and the measurement update equations

$$K_k = P_k^- H_k^T (H_k P_k^- H_k^T + V_k R_k V_k^T)^{-1} \tag{4.8}$$

$$x_k = x_k^- + K_k(z_k - H_k^T x_k^-) \tag{4.9}$$

$$P_k = (I - K_k H_k)P_k^- \tag{4.10}$$

In our case, we assume that the time update equations produce no difference. The first task during the measurement update is to compute the Kalman gain. The next step is to actually measure the process to obtain, and then to generate an a posteriori state estimate by incorporating the measurement. The final step is to obtain an a posteriori error covariance estimate.

The Kalman filter has numerous applications in technology. A common application is for guidance, navigation and control of vehicles, particularly aircraft and spacecraft. Furthermore, the Kalman filter is a widely applied concept in time series analysis used in fields such as signal processing and econometrics.

The algorithm works in a two-step process. In the prediction step, the Kalman filter produces estimates of the current state variables, along with their uncertainties. Once the outcome of the next measurement (necessarily corrupted with some amount of error, including random noise) is observed, these estimates are updated using a weighted average, with more weight being given to estimates with higher certainty. Because of the algorithm's recursive nature, it can run in real time using only the present input measurements and the previously calculated state; no additional past information is required.

From a theoretical standpoint, the main assumption of the Kalman filter is that the underlying system is a linear dynamical system and that all error terms and measurements have a Gaussian distribution (often a multivariate Gaussian distribution).

Extensions and generalizations to the method have also been developed, such as the EKF and the unscented Kalman filter, which work on non-linear systems. The underlying model is a Bayesian model similar to a hidden Markov model, but where the state space of the latent variables is continuous and where all latent and observed variables have Gaussian distributions.

The Kalman filter uses a system's dynamics model (e.g. physical laws of motion), known control inputs to that system and multiple sequential measurements (such as from sensors) to form an estimate of the system's varying quantities (its state) that is better than the estimate obtained by using any one measurement alone. As such, it is a common sensor fusion and data fusion algorithm.

All measurements and calculations based on models are estimates to some degree. Noisy sensor data, approximations in the equations that describe how a system changes, and external factors that are not accounted for introduce some uncertainty about the inferred values for a system's state. The Kalman filter averages a prediction of a system's state with a new measurement using a weighted average. The purpose of the weights is that values with better (i.e. smaller) estimated uncertainty are 'trusted' more. The weights are calculated from the covariance, a measure of the estimated uncertainty of the prediction of the system's state. The result of the weighted average is a new state estimate that lies between the predicted and measured state, and has a better estimated uncertainty than either alone. This process is repeated every time step, with the new estimate and its covariance informing the prediction used in the following iteration. This means that the Kalman filter works recursively and requires only the last 'best guess', rather than the entire history, of a system's state to calculate a new state.

Because the certainty of the measurements is often difficult to measure precisely, it is common to discuss the filter's behaviour in terms of gain. The Kalman gain is a function of the relative certainty of the measurements and current state estimate, and can be 'tuned' to achieve particular performance. With a high gain, the filter places more weight on the measurements, and thus follows them more closely. With a low gain, the filter follows the model predictions more closely, smoothing out noise but decreasing the responsiveness. At the extremes, a gain of one causes the filter to ignore the state estimate entirely, while a gain of zero causes the measurements to be ignored.

When performing the actual calculations for the filter (as discussed below), the state estimate and covariances are coded into matrices to handle the multiple dimensions involved in a single set of calculations. This allows for representation of linear relationships between different state variables (such as position, velocity and acceleration) in any of the transition models or covariances.

3.2.2.4 GAIN ADAPTATION: IDBD FILTERING

Gain adaptation algorithms (Sutton, 1992) implement a sort of meta-learning in that the learning rate is adapted based on the current inputs and on the trace of previous modifications (Lanzi *et al.*, 2006). The IDBD uses a different adaptive learning rate for each input. This action can lead to the improvement of the system when some of the inputs are irrelevant or when noise affects the inputs in different ways. In IDBD, each element of the $k_i(t)$ of the gain vector $k(t)$ is computed separately as,

$$k_i(t) = e^{\beta_i(t)} \varphi_i(t) \tag{4.11}$$

$$\beta_i(t+1) = \beta_i(t) + n\delta(t)\varphi_i(t)h_i(t) \tag{4.12}$$

$$h_i(t+1) = h_i(t)[1 - k_i(t)\varphi_i(t)] + k_i(t)\delta(t) \tag{4.13}$$

where $\delta(t)$ is the error computed as $y(t) - \theta(t)^T \varphi(t)$, n is the meta-learning rate and the function $[x]+$ returns x if $x > 0$, zero otherwise.

4 Evaluation metrics, results and discussion

4.1 Evaluation metrics

In order to evaluate the performance of each algorithm/technique we used some state-of-the-art performance measures.

Annualized return: the average amount of money earned by an investment each year over a given time period. An annualized total return provides only a snapshot of an investment's performance and does not give investors any indication of its volatility. Annualized total return merely provides a geometric average, rather than an arithmetic average:

$$R^A = 252 * \frac{1}{N} \sum_{t=1}^{N} R_t \tag{4.14}$$

Information ratio: a ratio of portfolio returns above the returns of a bench-mark (usually an index) to the volatility of those returns. The information ratio (IR) measures a portfolio manager's ability to generate excess returns relative to a benchmark, but also attempts to identify the consistency of the investor. This ratio will identify whether a manager has beaten the benchmark by a lot in a few months or a little every month. The higher the IR the more consistent a manager is; consistency is an ideal trait:

$$IR = \frac{R^A}{\sigma^A} \tag{4.15}$$

Maximum drawdown: a drawdown is measured from the time a retrenchment begins to when a new high is reached. This method is used because a valley can't be measured until a new high occurs. Once the new high is reached, the percentage change from the old high to the smallest trough is recorded. Draw-downs help determine an investment's financial risk:

$$MDD(T) = \max_{\tau \in (0,T)} [\max_{t \in (0,\tau)} X(t) - X(\tau)] \tag{4.16}$$

Correct directional change: a measure for the accuracy of the predictions, this computes the percentage of the correct predictions compared to the full number of attempted predictions:

$$CDC = \frac{\# \text{ correct predictions}}{\# \text{ all predictions}} \tag{4.17}$$

4.2 Results and discussion

In Table 4.2, the performance measures for the different techniques on predict-ing the three financial index trends are reported.

As is clear from Tables 4.2 and 4.3, the Kalman filtering algorithm achieves the highest correct bidirectional change. According to the annualized return measure as well as the correct bidirectional change, adaptive filtering techniques can be generally ranked from the best to the worst as Kalman, RLS, IBDB and LMS. Kalman and RLS perform almost the same (they are theoretically identical (Diniz, 2002)), but Kalman achieves a slightly higher annualized return.

The LMS algorithm is known for its computational simplicity, but the RLS algorithm and Kalman filter have higher performance as they focus on the mini-mization of the MSE between the desired return and the predicted return of the filter. IDBD, which is a gain adaptation algorithm, performs better than the LMS algorithm and very close to the Kalman filter. IDBD is generally more unstable than the other algorithms and this is proven by its largest percentage in the maximal drawdown. This fact can be attributed to the fact that the learning rate of the IDBD algorithm is optimized within the algorithm itself (meta-learning parameter).

Table 4.2 Comparative results for classical benchmark methods predicting the DAX30, CAC40 and Euronext financial indices

	Buy and hold	Naive	MACD	ARMA
CAC40 Daily				
Information ratio	−0.25	0.69	0.35	0.45
Annualized return (including costs) (%)	−12.16	14.98	12.65	3.45
Maximum drawdown (%)	−45.24	−42.27	−42.26	−38.92
Correct directional change (%)	49.11	51.02	50.45	50.13
Euronext Daily				
Information ratio	0.38	0.95	0.41	0.19
Annualized return (including costs) (%)	7.05	17.35	7.64	2.87
Maximum drawdown (%)	−31.49	−35.10	−13.68	−16.83
Correct directional change (%)	50.01	49.97	51.92	52.17
DAX30 Daily				
Information ratio	0.49	0.64	0.40	0.14
Annualized return (including costs) (%)	4.85	14.82	10.88	1.08
Maximum drawdown (%)	−37.79	−45.49	−19.48	−27.32
Correct directional change (%)	52.08	47.99	51.74	48.22

Table 4.3 Comparative results for adaptive filtering methods predicting the DAX30, CAC40 and Euronext financial indices

	LMS	RLS	Kalman	IDBD
CAC40 daily				
Information ratio	0.71	0.73	0.73	0.70
Annualized return (including costs) (%)	40.56	33.82	52.39	39.47
Maximum drawdown (%)	−17.3	−12.4	−12.4	−12.6
Correct directional change (%)	50.73	50.35	51.87	49.34
Euronext daily				
Information ratio	0.39	0.93	0.93	0.46
Annualized return (including costs) (%)	14.69	21.73	23.74	20.53
Maximum drawdown (%)	−21.5	−23.7	−23.7	−25.8
Correct directional change (%)	51.29	53.20	53.20	52.45
DAX30 daily				
Information ratio	0.70	0.70	0.74	0.61
Annualized return (including costs) (%)	11.84	18.92	18.5	12.38
Maximum drawdown (%)	−22.2	−28.4	−11.1	−29.3
Correct directional change (%)	52.95	52.35	53.84	51.49

Thus, among the local search algorithms explored in the present chapter, the EKF algorithm is the best solution. The RLS, LMS and IDBD algorithms use parameters that should have been optimized in order to permit the algorithms to achieve their highest performance. However, Kalman does not use any parameters and has a smoother convergence. Moreover, IBDB optimizes its meta-learning parameter, which potentially is the main reason that leads to its superior performance compared to the LMS algorithm.

Apart from comparing the adaptive filtering techniques with each other, it is obvious that they clearly overcome the classical measures in all performance measures. The mathematical model used within the Kalman algorithm is a non-linear exponential one. Even if simple linear models gave acceptable results for the problem of predicting the DAX30, CAC40 and Euronext financial indexes (MACD, ARMA), we demonstrated how the daily returns could be alternatively combined in a non-linear way in order to achieve better forecasting performances.

5 Conclusion

We have focused on the influence of different adaptive filtering techniques on the problem of efficiently predicting three well-known financial indexes which are DAX30, CAC40 and Euronext. Adaptive filtering techniques have been proved to outperform the forecasting performance of four classical techniques (naive, buy and hold, MACD and ARMA). Adaptive filtering techniques like LMS, RLS and IBDB are more unstable and less accurate than the Kalman filter-ing technique, which proves to be an innate stable and robust algorithm. In this chapter we examined the performance of some state-of the-art adaptive filtering techniques in the prediction of the trends of financial indexes and, to our know-ledge, this is the first time that adaptive filtering techniques have been used in financial index prediction.

In the future, we plan to compare the performance of the adaptive filtering techniques proposed in the current article with other well-known machine learn-ing techniques like SVMs (Cao and Tay, 2003; Ince and Trafalis, 2008), random forests (Manish and Thenmozhi, 2005) and artificial neural networks (Andreou *et al.*, 2008; Panda and Narasimhan (2007) that have been extensively tested in the problem of forecasting financial indexes.

References

Andreou, P., C. Charalampous and S. Martzoukos (2008). Pricing and trading European options by combining artificial neural networks and parametric models with implied parameters. *European Journal of Operational Research* 185(3): 1415–1433.

Breiman, L. (2001) Random forests, *Machine Learning* 45(1): 5–32.

Cao, L. and F. Tay (2003) Support vector machine with adaptive parameters in financial time series forecasting. *IEEE Transactions on Neural Networks* 14(6): 1506–1518.

Diniz, P.S. (2002) *Adaptive Filtering: Algorithms and Practical Implementation*, New York: Springer.

Gençay, R., F. Selçuk, and B.J. Whitcher (2001) *An Introduction to Wavelets and Other Filtering Methods in Finance and Economics*, San Diego, CA: Academic Press.

Goodwin, G.C. and R.L. Payne (1977) *Dynamic System Identification: Experiment Design and Data Analysis*, New York: Academic Press.

Holland, J. (1995) *Adaptation in Natural and Artificial Systems: An Introductory Analysis with Applications to Biology, Control, and Artificial Intelligence*, Cambridge, MA: MIT Press.

78   *C. Dimitrakopoulos* et al.

Huang, C. and C. Tsai (2009) A hybrid SOFM-SVR with a filter-based feature selection for stock market forecasting. *Expert Systems with Applications* 36(2): Part 1: 1529–1539.

Ince, H. and T. Trafalis (2008) Short term forecasting with support vector machines and application to stock price prediction. *International Journal of General Systems* 37(6): 677–687.

Lanzi, P.L., D. Loiacono, S.W. Wilson, D.E. Goldberg (2006) Prediction update algorithms for XCSF: RLS, Kalman filter, and gain adaptation, *Ninth International Workshop on Learning Classifier Systems (IWLCS 2006)*.

Manish, K. and M. Thenmozhi (2005) Forecasting stock index movement: a comparison of support vector machines and random forest. In *Proceedings of the Ninth Indian Institute of Capital Markets Conference*, Mumbai, India.

Maridakis, S. and S.C. Wheelwright (1977) Adaptive filtering: an integrated autoregressive/moving average filter for time series forecasting. *Journal of the Operational Research Society* 28: 425–437.

Panda, C. and V. Narasimhan (2007) Forecasting exchange rate better with artificial neural network. *Journal of Policy Modelling* 29(2): 227–236.

Sutton, R.S. (1992) Adapting bias by gradient descent: an incremental version of delta-bar-delta. In *Proceedings of the Tenth National Conference on Artificial Intelligence*, Cambridge, MA: MIT Press, pp. 171–176.

Vapnik, V. and C. Cortes (1995) Support-vector networks, *Machine Learning* 20(3): 273–297.

Welch, G. and G. Bishop (1995) An introduction to the Kalman filter, University of North Carolina at Chapel Hill, Department of Computer Science.

Widrow, B. and M.E. Hoff (1960) Adaptive switching circuits, in *WESCOM Convention Record* pt. 4, pp. 96–140.

Part III

Trading and investments with artificial neural networks

5 Modelling and trading the corn–ethanol crush spread with neural networks

Christian L. Dunis, Jason Laws,
Peter W. Middleton and
Andreas Karathanasopoulos

1 Introduction

The motivation behind this chapter derives from the recent surge in prices for agricultural commodities. Arguably, this is only the beginning of drastically rising and volatile prices to be experienced in the agricultural industry. For the most part this is due to rising global populations, with the improving economies of China and India exerting the most pressure on an upward trend in world food prices. With this in mind, a whole new tier of the middle class is beginning to emerge in these developing economies, consuming greater quantities of meats and grains. Other factors, such as the impact of climate change on agriculture, are also considered to be key reasons for previously unseen price swings. In addition, the use of ethanol as an alternative fuel has also had its effect on food prices. These influential forces have a global impact, affecting both developing and developed economies.

Rising volatile commodity prices have also lead to an increase in the number of market participants in these agricultural markets. For instance, farmers, commodity processors and grain elevators all use these financial markets to manage risk and hedge against adverse price movements. On the other hand, speculators are also drawn to these markets, primarily to make profits and to take advantage of diversified investment strategies. These opportunities present themselves as a result of growing world populations and climate change, as mentioned above, as well as technological advances in bio fuels. Ultimately, the increase in demand for agricultural commodities coupled with an uncertainty of supply and ever-increasing investment opportunities are all to blame for the most recent surges in prices across agricultural commodities markets.

This investigation aims to rigorously evaluate the profitability of the corn–ethanol spread. The profit margin created from the corn–ethanol spread is achieved from the process of converting corn into ethanol. This procedure involves extracting the carbohydrates stored in corn to create simple sugars in order to produce the valuable by-product known as ethanol. As a consequence, the ethanol industry is one of the fastest-growing industries in the United States, with production growing from 175 million gallons in the 1980s to almost 6.2 billion gallons in 2007.[1] The future prospects of the ethanol market appear to be extremely prosperous, with the Energy Independence and Security Act (EISA) of 2007 being passed and encouraging the additional construction of ethanol plants to accommodate the sharp rise in demand for ethanol as an alternative bio fuel. Furthermore, this act sets forth a mandate that gasoline consumption must include 15 billion gallons of ethanol to be produced in the United States by 2015. The underlying stimuli behind increasing the production of ethanol include lessening US dependence on foreign oil imports as well as efforts to quell pressures from environmental activists who call for the use of alternative, cleaner renewable energy. Moreover, with US crude oil prices reaching an all-time high in July 2008 at US\$147.27[2] per barrel, it has become apparent that alternative, cheaper bio fuels are essential.

Although corn-based ethanol as a bio fuel has many virtues, its efficiency as a renewable energy source has also been open to widespread criticism. Many feel it is not as efficient as other sources such as soy biodiesel and sugar cane-based bio fuels (Shapouri *et al.*, 2002). In particular, sugar cane-based bio fuels are widely produced in Brazil; however, the United States has imposed high tax levies on these imports to make them less attractive in an effort to suppress international competition. As a result of widespread production, ethanol as a bio fuel has also become highly controversial within the United States, creating a 'tug of war' scenario. On one side, cattle farmers are arguing that corn is more valuable as feed for livestock, while on the other ethanol manufacturers and politicians are steadfast in their promotion of corn as feed for bio fuel mass production. This has developed into what is now known as the 'food for fuel' debate. At the heart of this dispute is the fact that increasing ethanol production induces a higher demand for corn and hence increases the average price of corn, as highlighted by Shapouri *et al.* (1995). In effect, this then makes it more expensive for farmers to feed their livestock as corn is one of the main grains used in the feed process. As a knock-on effect this is also reflected in the prices of meats, dairies and various other related products. Additional mandates such as those set out by the Environmental Protection Agency (EPA) currently dictate regulations that require oil producers to maintain a 'blend' of 90 per cent gasoline/10 per cent ethanol mix. As long as these types of mandates are in place it seems only sensible to assume that the agricultural industry will experience ever-increasing feed prices as fuel is now competing with food for cropland. For instance, this issue recently surfaced in the 2006–2007 harvest when unprecedented high grain prices were experienced, in part due to the pressure for additional corn acres to meet the growing needs of the ethanol industry.

The main objective of this chapter is to develop profitable trading simulations from speculatively trade the corn/ethanol 'crush' spread. The analysis covers a five-year horizon commencing when the ethanol futures contract was first traded on the Chicago Board of Trade (CBOT) exchange (23 March 2005). The relationship between the two commodities is investigated by analysing the spread created from their daily closing prices with the application of optimal neural network forecasting architectures. The objective is to exploit and evaluate the relationship between the two underlying commodities in order to model, forecast and profitably trade the crush. In addition, this investigation also aims to build on earlier work carried out by Dunis *et al.* (2006b), who investigate the soybean–oil crush spread, comparing the effectiveness of various neural network architectures to more conventional forecasting techniques. With the motivations for carrying out this research reviewed above, further investigation into the mentioned commodity futures is warranted.

The remainder of this chapter is organized as follows. Section 2 provides a review of past and current literature. Section 3 discusses the descriptive statistics behind the 'crush' spread. Section 4 details the various methodologies employed for this investigation. Section 5 presents the empirical results. Finally, Section 6 concludes with a summary of observations and limitations.

2 Literature review

Numerous studies test the application of technical trading rules to trading financial assets and provide evidence that they are valuable tools for manipulation of financial time series. For instance, and perhaps most specific to this chapter, studies carried out by Kaastra and Boyd (1995), Trippi and De Sieno (1992) and Dunis (1989) all justify the use of technical trading rules as effective avenues to trading financial futures markets. Bessimber and Chan (1995) and Beja and Goldman (1980) also provide justification for the use of technical trading rules, especially during times when the market is experiencing 'informational inefficiencies'. During these times savvy investors have a limited window of opportunity in which to benefit from econometric analysis. Moreover, due to their effectiveness, trading strategies have been around for decades, with some proving to be more rewarding at times than others. However, the scope of this chapter is primarily focused on a trading strategy that has become increasingly popular due to the emergence of a wider range of financial products. This trading strategy is commonly referred to as spread trading and now commodity processors and farmers can directly hedge risks associated with processing margins.

The earliest literature on spread trading is by Working (1949). In his research, inter-temporal price relationships of futures contracts are evaluated with the application of a spread trading system. From this analysis, he uncovers numerous opportunities for traders to speculate on price irregularities between different futures contracts. In effect, this provided an insight into the strategy's initial purpose, which involves speculating on the 'cost of carry' between different futures contracts.

More recently, however, there have been subsequent studies which have uncovered additional benefits of the strategy. Most notably, Meland (1981) provides evidence that spread trading is also a valuable way of creating market liquidity. He indicates that spread trading not only provides speculative opportunities, but can also be utilized by arbitrageurs and hedgers alike. Peterson (1977) discusses the benefits of spread trading further by highlighting the fact that it also increases the amount of investment opportunities. Dunis *et al.* (2006a) discuss that spreads offer an 'affordable alternative approach' to investing.

Additionally, they also explain that spreads are less likely to suffer from information shocks with the movement of the two participating legs acting to effectively eliminate this by offsetting each other in such circumstances. With this in mind, 'speculative bubbles', as explained by Sweeney (1988), tend not to be associated with investment strategies such as spread trading.

2.1 Spread trading agricultural futures

Historically, agricultural futures markets were primarily used as platforms in which one could hedge against price risk exposures associated with price movements in the cash market. This view was first established by Working (1953, 1954, 1960, 1962), who argued that agricultural futures markets are used mainly for hedging purposes and that speculation is dictated by the volume of this hedging activity. However, with increased participants and technological advances, speculation plays a more prominent role in today's agricultural futures markets.

On review of the existing literature it becomes apparent that the virtues offered from hedging a corn crush spread over short-term horizons are investigated by some; however, there is limited literature regarding spread trading of agricultural commodity markets as a vehicle to hedge or speculate in the longer run. For one, Dahlgran (2009) investigates the effectiveness of one-through-eight-week hedges over a three-year horizon. In particular, part of his investigation examines the effectiveness of corn crush hedging as a risk management vehicle covering the period of 23 March 2005 to 31 December 2008. Dahlgran (2009) concludes that the effectiveness of hedging a corn crush is comparable to results yielded from a soybean crush. Hence, as a risk management tool, the corn crush hedge offers ethanol producers similar price risk protection as experienced by soybean processors who utilize the soybean crush hedge. Finally, he implies that the corn crush hedge may cater for more widespread use other than hedging. In support of his findings, the CBOT (2007) also promotes the 'corn crush' hedge as analogous to the soybean crush hedge. The limited literature review regarding speculation of the corn crush spread can perhaps be attributed to the fact that ethanol has only been traded on the CBOT as a futures contract since early 2005. Franken and Parcell (2003) explain that prior to the availability of ethanol futures contracts on the CBOT, ethanol price risk was cross-hedged with unleaded gasoline futures. However, with the recent creation of an ethanol-specific futures contract, opportunities have arisen that enable direct hedging. One can now hedge against the price risk associated with holding ethanol stock as well as safeguarding against price adversities linked with processing corn into ethanol.

Dunis *et al.* (2006b) explore agricultural spreads in the form of the soybean–oil crush spread. They investigate the profitability of spread trading a soybean–oil spread over a horizon of ten years, spanning from 1 January 1995 to 1 January 2005. The effectiveness of various neural network architectures is benchmarked against more conventional forecasting techniques such as the fair value co-integration model. The analysis concludes that profitability is present when trading such a spread, with higher order neural networks (HONNs) proving to produce the highest annualized out-of-sample returns. Hence, HONNs possess superior forecasting abilities to those of recurrent neural networks (RNNs), multilayer perceptron (MLP) and fair value co-integration when tasked with forecasting next-day returns for the soybean–oil spread.

2.2 Seasonality of agricultural futures

Weather uncertainty is a fundamental aspect in commodity trading as significant weather events can dramatically impact the supply of a commodity. Such seasonal behaviour is inherent in the grain market and pricing is dictated by factors such as when the commodity is planted, pollinated and harvested. Due to the nature of agricultural commodities, seasonal behaviour is experienced in annual cycles with markets tending to move in given directions throughout certain times of the year.

Corn as an agricultural grain commodity is broken down into three periods over a typical year, as shown in Table 5.1.

Till and Eagleeye (2004) discuss the nature of corn futures prices and the price pressure effect that is prevalent in commodity futures contracts. Their investigation uncovers the nature of commodity contracts, such as corn, discovering that a fear premium is commonly added into their pricing. This is particularly common in the build-up to a harvest season in circumstances when adverse weather conditions are forecasted. It is common for grain markets to assume a rather pessimistic view which creates this 'premium' during times when real or perceived threats to food supply are forecasted. With this in mind, the seasonality of corn is such that grain futures prices are inclusive of this 'premium', especially when approaching the US harvest season in the months before July. However, as the harvest season progresses, and providing adverse weather does not occur, then the 'weather premium' in corn gradually diminishes from the fair value price of the contract and this is reflected by a gradual decrease in the futures price of corn. For instance, at the end of July the weather conditions

Table 5.1 Typical corn cycle: seasonal sub-periods

Period	Months	General market sentiment
Late spring to mid-summer	March–June	Bullish (weather premium)
Mid-summer harvest	July–September	Bearish (supply is plentiful and major threats to crop supply have now passed)
Post harvest	October–February	Bearish (a sharp decline during the 'February break'[1] is often experienced in corn prices)

Note

1 One of the most common seasonal patterns experienced in grains and soybeans. Usually follows a short rally which occurs during the post-harvest months of December and January.

affecting the corresponding year's harvest would have either already occurred or may not have been present at all. Therefore, late July futures prices are less inclined to include a weather premium. Furthermore, in months following July the crop is entering its harvest season, where seasonal lows are prevalent as a result of supplies being plentiful. This bolsters confidence and perceived security in the commodity.

Till and Eagleeye (2004) discuss various methods for trading commodities. However, they highlight that by using futures spreads the risks of experiencing large losses are limited. Spread trading allows market participants to hedge for 'first-order' or exogenous risk. For example, when certain events occur, such as Hurricane Katrina, then both legs of the spread will be affected. As a result, a loss in one position is offset by a gain in the other due to the different views being taken on each leg. Generally this is when one leg is long and the other is short. Spread trading does, however, run the risk of experiencing timing differences when inventory cycles between the two participating commodities are not the same.

A full explanation into how seasonality is accounted for can be seen in Section 3.4.

2.3 Application of neural network architectures

Neural networks are computationally powerful and intuitive modelling tools that can be applied to financial time series in order to rationalize masses of data into knowledge useful for making investment decisions. As a consequence, the forecasting of time series' future trends has been analysed by many in the academic world. Fama and French (1986) determined that market prices exhibit, to some extent, a form of memory pattern within them and as a result future price trends do in fact contain an element of predictability based on historic prices. In recognition of this, a variety of forecasting techniques have been applied throughout the years. In more recent years, however, there has been a noticeable increase in popularity for artificial intelligence, and its rapid growth in financial time series analysis and forecasting. In particular, there has been a resurgence of neural networks in a variety of architectures such as MLP (Lisi and Schiavo, 1999; Faraway and Chatfield, 1998; Hill *et al.*, 1996; Lachtermacher and Fuller, 1995; Jayawardena and Fernando, 1995); RNNs (Freedman, 1994); radial basis functions (RBFs) (Jayawardena and Fernando, 1998; Hutchinson, 1994); and a comparative analysis of MLP and RBF (Jayawardena and Fernando, 1998; Jayawardena *et al.*, 1996). Neural networks have become particularly popular in finance because they are a fairly robust computing tool with learning and adaptive capabilities. These characteristics have been utilized to accurately predict financial assets by successfully capturing and interpreting non-linear relationships between explanatory variables and target outputs. Traditional statistical methods have proven to be less accurate due to the fact that in most cases they fail to disseminate non-linear data and discontinuities which are both common in financial time series.

3 The corn–ethanol spread and related financial data

The daily closing prices for each of the commodities' contract months were obtained from Datastream for the period covering 23 March 2005 to 31 December 2009. Corn futures[3] are the most heavily traded agricultural commodity and have been traded on the CBOT exchange since the mid-1800s. On the other hand, ethanol futures are a more recent addition to the CBOT exchange, having only been traded as a futures contract since 23 March 2005. As a result, ethanol is not traded as frequently as corn and is therefore less liquid. Both contracts are traded from 09:30 a.m. to 13:15 p.m. and 18:00 p.m. to 7:15 a.m. CST (Central Standard Time). As a result, the issue of non-synchronous pricing that plagues many other investigations does not affect the construction of a reliable trading dataset.

The corn 'crush' spread is calculated taking the fact that both commodity futures contracts are priced and traded in different units into consideration. Corn is priced in cents per bushel, whereas ethanol is traded in dollars per gallon. Therefore, a conversion of prices into equal units is required. Currently, one bushel of corn yields approximately 2.8 gallons of ethanol (CME, 2010). To create a tradable spread between the two contracts the price of ethanol must be multiplied by 2.8 in order to convert it into dollars per bushel. Lastly, to calculate the corn 'crush' spread, the price of corn is subtracted from the price of ethanol (in dollars per bushel). This calculation is mathematically depicted in equation (5.1).

$$C_t = P_C - [(2.8 * P_E) / 100] \tag{5.1}$$

where:

C_t = price of the crush spread at time t (in cents per bushel)

P_C = price of the corn contract at time t (in cents per bushel)

P_E = price of the ethanol contract at time t (in dollars per gallon).

There are various other ways to calculate the spread, depending on what the market participant is attempting to achieve. Other corn crush spread combinations may include distillers' dried grains (another by-product of corn) and natural gas, as this is consumed during the 'crushing' process. However, for the purpose of this investigation the analysis is solely focused on the relationship between corn and ethanol.

The methodology applied throughout this investigation to calculate the returns of the corn crush spread can be seen in equation (5.2) as also used by Butterworth and Holmes (2002) and more recently by Dunis *et al.* (2006b):

$$\Delta S_t = \left[\frac{\left(P_{C(t)} - P_{C(t-1)} \right)}{\left(P_{C(t-1)} \right)} - \frac{\left(P_{E(t)} - P_{E(t-1)} \right)}{\left(P_{E(t-1)} \right)} \right] \tag{5.2}$$

where:

ΔS_t = percentage change in the spread at time t

$P_{C(t)}$ = is the price of corn at time t (in cents per bushel)

$P_{C(t-1)}$ = is the price of corn at time $t-1$ (in cents per bushel)

$P_{E(t)}$ = is the price of ethanol at time t (in cents per bushel)

$P_{E(t-1)}$ = is the price of ethanol at time $t-1$ (in cents per bushel).

3.1 Statistical behaviour of commodity prices

The spread time series for the full sample period can be seen in Figure 5.1.

By observation of Figure 5.1 it is apparent that post-2007 the spread displays mean reversion around 100 ¢/bushel. However, previous years are characterized by large deviations which are experienced in 2005 and 2006. These large deviations are as a result of shocks to both the demand for and supply of each commodity during the period 2005–2006. Most notably, there are two major spikes in the spread occurring during the 'in-sample' period. The first occurred on 29 August 2005 as a result of Hurricane Katrina, which devastated the harvest in the South and Midwest of the United States. The second spike occurred as a result of a US government mandate which phased out MTBE (methyl tertiary butyl ether) oxygenates. Furthermore, this mandate called for ethanol refiners to increase their capacities in order to produce four billion gallons of ethanol in 2006 (McKay, 2006).

The price behaviours of commodities have been observed and analysed by many over the past few decades. For one, Deaton and Laroque (1992) observe yearly prices for 13 of the most popular commodities (including corn) over a period spanning from 1900 to 1987. Findings identify a number of common pricing attributes associated with commodities. Most notably, even though commodity prices appear to be inherently volatile, they still remain mean reverting. Furthermore, the prices also display high degrees of autocorrelation even in normal times, perhaps explained by seasonal patterns. In addition, Sorensen (2002) analyses the price behaviour associated with agricultural commodities between the periods of 1972 through to 1997. In this analysis the prices of soybean, corn and wheat are observed, focusing primarily on permanent trend shifts, seasonality and mean reversion. Conclusions also reveal that commodity prices are generally mean reverting.

More recently, however, Geman (2005) observes that on average commodity prices neither grow nor decline. As a result, Geman (2005) concludes that prices tend to mean-revert due to the marginal cost of production. Hence, mean-reversion is one of the main properties that has been systematically incorporated in the literature surrounding commodity price modelling.

3.2 Descriptive statistics

Statistical analysis is based on the change in daily closing prices,[4] and from the histogram shown in Figure 5.2 it can be observed that the corn–ethanol spread

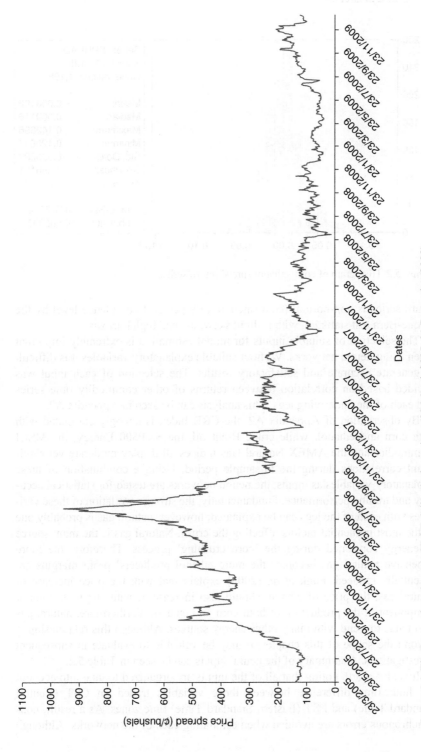

Figure 5.1 The corn–ethanol crush CBOT daily closing prices (23 March 2005–31 December 2009).

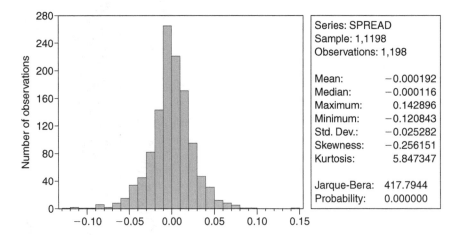

Figure 5.2 Histogram of corn–ethanol spread return series.

return series is non-normal (confirmed at a 99 per cent confidence level by the Jarque-Bera test statistic), with a slight skewness and high kurtosis.

The selection of suitable inputs for model estimation is extremely important when using neural networks. Without suitable explanatory variables it is difficult to generate accurate and satisfactory results. The selection of each input was decided based on correlation between returns of other commodity time series and each of the underlying legs. This analysis can be seen in Appendix A2.

By observation of Appendix A2, the CRB Index is strongly correlated with both corn and ethanol, while crude Brent oil, the S&P500 Energy, the MSCI Commodity and the AMEX Natural Gas indices all display moderate yet significant correlations during the in-sample period. Using a combination of these explanatory variables as inputs, the neural networks are tested for statistical accuracy and trading performance. Fundamentally, the strong correlation of these variables with each of the legs can be explained; however, natural gas is probably one of the most influential factors affecting the crush. Natural gas is the main source of energy consumed during the 'corn crushing' process. Therefore, the more expensive natural gas becomes the more ethanol producers' profit margins are potentially reduced. Funk *et al.* (2008) explain that with the price increase of natural gas, the price of ethanol should also increase as natural gas is a major component in the production of both corn and ethanol. Furthermore, natural gas also tends to trend with many other energy sources. Although this relationship is beyond the scope of this chapter, it may be valuable to evaluate in subsequent investigations. A summary of the neural inputs can be seen in Table 5.2.

It is also worth noting that all of the inputs are organized to take into account the hour time difference between those variables traded on CST (Central Standard Time) and EST (Eastern Standard Time) time zones. As a result, non-synchronous errors are avoided when estimating each of the networks. Although

Table 5.2 Explanatory variables

Number	Explanatory variable	Lags (days)
1	Corn crush spread returns	1
2	Corn crush spread returns	2
3	Corn crush spread returns	3
4	AMEX Natural Gas Index returns	1
5	Thomson Reuters/Jefferies CRB Index returns	1
6	NYMEX Brent Crude Oil returns	1
7	1-Day Risk Metrics Volatility of spread returns	1
8	S&P500 Energy Index returns	1
9	MSCI Commodity Index returns	1
10	CBOT corn Returns	1
11	CBOT ethanol Returns	1
12	Moving average of the corn crush spread returns	14
13	Moving average of the corn crush spread returns	21

a full investigation into the determination of lag structures is beyond the scope of this chapter, the lag structure displayed in Table 5.2 is retained as it produced the most satisfactory returns and forecasting accuracy during the training and test periods.

The observed data period spanning from 23 March 2005 to 31 December 2009 has been segregated into in-sample and out-of-sample datasets, as used during the modelling process.

As an inference it should be noted that the reasoning behind further segmentation of the in-sample dataset into sub-samples is to avoid 'overfitting' when modelling the neural networks. This is discussed in more detail in Section 4.2.

3.3 Rolling forward procedure

A number of implications arise when applying analysis to a non-continuous time series as any valuable long-term study of financial information requires scrutiny of continuous data. One of the biggest implications is the process of rolling a position forward from a contract that is nearing maturity to a new contract month in the future. As a result, a 'rollover day' is used by traders to start trading the new contract by switching, on this day, from the old contract before it reaches maturity to the new contract in order to maintain a continuous data series.

Table 5.3 Data segregation for the full sample period

Period	Trading days	Beginning	End
Total dataset	1,199	23 March 2005	31 December 2009
Training dataset (in sample)	664	23 March 2005	19 November 2007
Test dataset (in sample)	167	20 November 2007	21 July 2008
Validation set (out of sample)	368	22 July 2008	31 December 2009

As some commodity contracts have longer lives than others the implications of creating a realistic, accurate and continuous spread series can be numerous. For example, grain contracts tend to be traded on average for a year or two while financial markets can be traded up to as much as five to ten years into the distant future. Therefore, agricultural traders and hedgers have to roll their positions more frequently.

For the purpose of this application all of these aspects were taken into consideration and it was decided to use the same rollover days for both the corn and ethanol contracts. As a result, the spread is simultaneously rolled forward for each of the underlying legs on the last Thursday of the month preceding maturity months. While it is accepted that this may not be the 'optimal' rollover procedure, it is recognized that the optimization of rolling forward procedures might be another interesting topic to examine in future analysis. Despite this, the procedure is fairly pragmatic as it still enables the construction of an accurate and tradable time series which avoids both the risk of physical delivery and increasing volatility associated with illiquid periods.

3.4 Discounting the existence of seasonality

In the initial analysis of seasonality each of the legs are individually assessed. From this analysis it appears that both corn and ethanol are stationary when integrated of order 1. Regardless, it is apparent that in both the corn and ethanol series autocorrelation is present between lags 1–5. This is revealed by significant spikes indicating that both data series are not random. Results from a correlogram of the spread are displayed in more detail in Appendix A3. This observation is in line with those made by Klement (2005), Corsi (2003) and Anderson *et al.* (2003), who have all found that seasonality does in fact exist in the daily returns of various agricultural commodities.

Analysis of the spread, however, reveals that the data series is actually random, with no evidence of significant spikes. Furthermore, as there is nothing to support autocorrelation between any of the lags it can be assumed that by combining both corn and ethanol daily return series, in a spread trading system, the series is in fact random and free of seasonality. Pindyck and Rubinfeld (1998) highlight that a time series is only seasonal in circumstances when the autocorrelation function displays regular and frequent peaks. Ultimately, 'deseasonalization' techniques are not deemed necessary as autocorrelation is not identified between any of the lags.

4 Methodology

This section provides details for each of the different models, trading strategies and filters implemented to successfully establish parameters for modelling the corn/ethanol spread. The particulars with regard to the forecasting of each time series are also discussed to include various benchmark models and a number of different neural network architectures.

4.1 Benchmark models

In this investigation three architecturally different neural network models are benchmarked against popular linear models. These benchmark models include trading signals produced by naive and MACD (moving average convergence/ divergence) trading strategies and a traditional ARMA (autoregressive moving average) model. Co-integration was not deemed to be a suitable benchmark model due to the fact that the underlying legs (corn and ethanol) were not found to be co-integrated during the observed period. Co-integration between multiple non-stationary variables occurs when the linear combination of the variables results in a stationary series (Engle and Granger 1987). Taking this into consideration, the linear combination of ethanol and corn was not found to be stationary during the in-sample period. For this reason, co-integration has not been included as a benchmark model to forecast the crush. For brevity, the I(1) test results and the trace statistics are not reported in the Appendix.[5] However, all of the results and parameters for in-sample models can be found in Appendices A6 and A4, respectively.

4.1.1 Naive trading strategy

This strategy is known as 'naive' due to its simplistic nature: the forecasted returns for today are simply the returns generated from the previous day. In other words, a forecasted time series is generated based on a one-day regressive linear method. The naive model is mathematically depicted in equation (5.3).

$$\hat{Y}_{t+1} = Y_t \qquad (5.3)$$

where: Y_t is the actual rate of return at period t
$\hat{Y}_{t+1}$ is the forecast rate of return for the next period.

4.1.2 MACD model

Introduced by Appel (1979), the MACD indicator is one of the most widely used indicators in technical analysis and has since established itself as a prominent benchmark in forecasting. As a result, this has been included as a benchmark model for a comparative analysis. The MACD model is mathematically defined in equation (5.4).

$$M_t = \frac{\left(Y_t + Y_{t-1} + Y_{t-2} + ... + Y_{t-n+1}\right)}{n} \qquad (5.4)$$

where:

M_t is the moving average at time t
n is the number of terms in the moving average
Y_t is the actual rate of return at period t.

The MACD strategy used is also fairly straightforward as two moving average series are created with different moving average lengths. One of the moving averages is considered to be a short-term moving average, while the other is a longer-term moving average. These moving averages are determined based on which combination performed best over the in-sample period in terms of annualized returns. This combination is then retained for out-of-sample evaluation. In this case a one-day moving average (hence the daily return of the crush) for the shorter term and a 27-day moving average for the longer term were used. Therefore, a (1,27) combination was deemed to be the most profitable in terms of trading performance with $n=1$ and 27, respectively. Trading signals are triggered when the two moving averages intersect. For instance, a long position is taken when the short-term moving average intersects the long-term moving average from below and a short position is adopted when the long-term moving average is intersected from above.

4.1.3 ARMA model

ARMA models assume that the value of a time series depends on its previous values (the autoregressive component) and on previous residual values (the moving average component). A typical ARMA model takes the form:

$$Y_t = \phi_0 + \phi_1 Y_{t-1} + \phi_2 Y_{t-2} + \ldots + \phi_p Y_{t-p} + \varepsilon_t - w_1 \varepsilon_{t-1} - w_2 \varepsilon_{t-2} - \ldots - w_q \varepsilon_{t-q} \quad (5.5)$$

where:

Y_t is the dependent variable at time t
Y_{t-1}, Y_{t-2} and Y_{t-p} are the lagged dependent variables
ϕ_0, ϕ_1, ϕ_2 and ϕ_p are regression coefficients
ε_t is the residual term
$\varepsilon_{t-1}, \varepsilon_{t-2}$ and ε_{t-p} are previous values of the residual
w_1, w_2 and w_q are weights.

Using the correlogram as a guide in the training and the test sub-periods, a restricted ARMA (11,11) model is determine to be the most suitable. All of its coefficients are significant at the 99 per cent confidence interval. The null hypothesis that all coefficients (except the constant) are not significantly different from zero is rejected at the 99 per cent confidence interval (see Appendix A5).

The model estimated during the in-sample period was retained for out-of-sample trading. The performance of the strategy is evaluated in terms of forecasting accuracy and trading performance.

The specific ARMA model is presented in equation (5.6):

$$Y_t = -4.04 * 10^{-4} + 0.321 Y_{t-1} + 0.288 Y_{t-2} - 0.379 Y_{t-8} + 0.548 Y_{t-11} +$$
$$0.283 \varepsilon_{t-1} + 0.261 \varepsilon_{t-2} - 0.437 \varepsilon_{t-8} + 0.585 \varepsilon_{t-11} \quad (5.6)$$

4.2 Neural networks

Neural networks exist in a variety of different architectures and have been implemented in numerous financial applications. However, the architecture that is most widely used for the analysis of stock markets is known as the MLP neural network.

A generic neural network is built with at least three layers comprising an input, hidden and output layer. The structure of the input layer is determined by the number of explanatory variables depicted as nodes in the architecture. The hidden layer represents the capacity of complexity in which the model can support or 'fit'. Moreover, both the input and hidden layers contain what is known as a bias node. The value attributed to this node is a fixed value and is equal to one. Its purpose is similar to the functionality of which the intercept serves in more traditional regression models. The final and third layer of a standard neural network, the output layer, is governed by a structure of nodes corresponding to a number of response variables. Furthermore, each of these layers is linked via a node-to-node interconnecting system enabling a functional network of 'neurons'.

On the whole, neural networks learn the relationships in data using neurons, similar to how the human brain works. They are a non-parametric tool and use a series of waves and neurons to capture even very complex relationships between the predictor inputs and the target variables.[6] They can overcome messy data such as noise and imprecision in the measurement system. Neural networks are appropriate for regression as well as classification, time series analysis and clustering.

The functionality of a simple network can be surmised as a step-by-step process as follows:

1   Inputs are determined and entered into the network for analysis. Target outputs (variables) are also set to enable the network to proceed and develop a learning ability.
2   The input data are then processed by the input nodes, which contain a value of explanatory variables.
3   Furthermore, due to the fact that each node connection represents a weight factor, the information then reaches a hidden layer node as a weighted calculation of its inputs.
4   The nodes of the hidden layer then pass the processed data through a non-linear activation function.
5   This is then processed by the output layer, providing the calculated value is above the threshold (determined by the backpropagation of errors algorithm).
6   Finally, the processed outputs are then validated to measure whether the network needs to be retrained in order to better fit the data series.

4.2.1 The MLP

The MLP allows the user to select a set of activation functions to explore, including identity, logistic, hyperbolic tangent, negative exponential and sine.[7] These activation functions can be used for both hidden and output neurons. MLP also trains networks using a variety of algorithms such as gradient descent, conjugant descent and BFGS (Broyden, Fletcher, Goldfarb and Shanno). Here the logistic activation function and gradient descent algorithm are used.

The network architecture of a conventional MLP network can best be illustrated as shown in Figure 5.3.

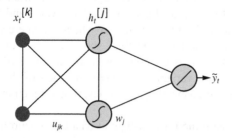

Figure 5.3 A single output, inter-connected MLP model (two neurons/nodes).

Where:

$x_t^{[n]}(n = 1, 2, \ldots, k+1)$ model inputs (including the input bias node) at time t
$h_t^{[m]}(m = 1, 2, \ldots, j+1)$ hidden node outputs (including the hidden bias node)
$\tilde{y}_t$ = MLP model output
u_{jk} and w_j = network weights.

transfer sigmoid function: $S(x) = \dfrac{1}{1+e^{-x}}$ (5.7)

linear function: $F(x) = \sum_i x_i$ (5.8)

The error function to be minimized is:

$$E\left(u_{jk}, w_j\right) = \frac{1}{T} \sum_{t=1}^{T} \left(y_t - \tilde{y}_t\left(u_{jk}, w_j\right)\right)^2$$ (5.9)

with y_t being the target value.

The training and selection of a network was halted once profit (in the form of an annualized return) was at a satisfactory level during in-sample back testing.

4.2.2 The recurrent network

RNNs are adaptive neural networks with asymmetric connections that are related to the 'Hopfield network'. While a complete review of RNNs is beyond the scope of this study, the architecture that was adopted for this investigation can be seen in Figure 5.4. It is, however, important to understand its differences when compared to the other two networks (MLP and HONN). RNNs consist of both feedforward and feedback connections which enable them to retain information for later use (Draye *et al.*, 1996). As a consequence, a standard RNN comprises a greater amount of neuron connections compared to the other two models, implying longer computational times during the training process. Each of the neurons are graded using an activation feedback function to create forecasts (see Tenti, 1996). Furthermore, forecasts are created by adaptively modifying the synaptic weights within this model, utilizing the generalization of the delta rule introduced by Rumelhart *et al.* (1986).

Past papers have evaluated the effectiveness of RNNs and discovered that, due to their additional memory inputs, they can sometimes yield better annualized returns in comparison to simple MLP networks. Additive neural networks have been extensively studied in both their continuous-time and discrete-time versions. More recently, Tino *et al.* (2001) and Haschke and Steil (2005) elaborate further on the benefits of using RNNs.

A simple illustration of the architecture of an Elman (1990) RNN is presented in Figure 5.4.

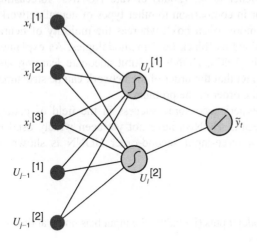

Figure 5.4 Elman RNN architecture with two neurons/nodes for the hidden layer.

Where:

$x_t^{[n]}(n=1, 2, \ldots, k+1)$, $u_t^{[1]}$, $u_t^{[2]}$ model inputs (including the input bias node) at time t

$\tilde{y}_t$ = recurrent model output

$d_t^{[f]}(f=1, 2)$ and $w_t^{[n]}$ $(n=1, 2, \ldots, k+1)$ = network weights

$U_t^{[f]}(f=1, 2)$ = output of the hidden nodes at time t.

$\bigcirc$ transfer sigmoid function: $S(x) = \dfrac{1}{1+e^{-x}}$ (5.10)

$\bigcirc$ linear output function: $F(x) = \sum_i x_i$ (5.11)

The error function to be minimized is:

$$E(d_t, w_t) = \frac{1}{T} \sum_{t=1}^{T} \left(y_t - \tilde{y}_t(d_t, w_t) \right)^2$$ (5.12)

In summary, the RNN architecture has the potential to provide more accurate outputs because the inputs are (potentially) taken from all previous values (see inputs $U_{j-1}^{[1]}$ and $U_{j-1}^{[2]}$ in Figure 5.4).

4.2.3 The HONNs

HONNs were first introduced by Giles and Maxwell (1987) and were called 'tensor networks'. Although the extent of their use in finance has so far been limited, Knowles *et al.* (2009: 54) show that with shorter computational times and limited input variables, 'the best HONN models show a profit increase over the MLP of around 8%'. Fulcher *et al.* (2006) elevate HONNs' forecasting ability to be distinctly superior in comparison to other types of neural networks as they are considered to be more 'open box', whereas the majority of neural networks are commonly classified as 'black box' methodologies. As explained further by Giles and Maxwell (1987), HONNs exhibit adequate learning and storage capabilities due to the fact that the order of the network can be structured in a manner which resembles the order of the problem.

While they have already experienced some success in the field of pattern recognition and associative recall,[8] HONNs have not yet been widely used in finance. The architecture of a three-input second-order HONN is shown in Figure 5.5.

Where:

$x_t^{[n]}(n=1, 2, \ldots, k+1) = $ model inputs (including the input bias node) at time t
$\tilde{y}_t = $ HONNs model outputs
$u_{jk} = $ network weights
$\bullet = $ model inputs.

$\bigcirc$ transfer sigmoid function: $S(x) = \dfrac{1}{1+e^{-x}}$ (5.13)

$\bigcirc$ a linear function: $F(x) = \sum_i x_i$ (5.14)

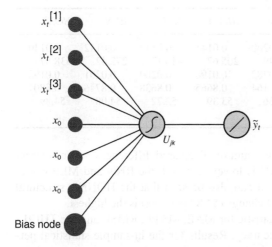

$x_t^{[1]}$

$x_t^{[2]}$

$x_t^{[3]}$

x_0

x_0

x_0

Bias node

U_{jk}

$\tilde{y}_t$

Figure 5.5 Second order HONN with three inputs (1 neuron/node).

The error function to be minimized is:

$$E\left(u_{jk}, w_j\right) = \frac{1}{T} \sum_{t=1}^{T} \left(y_t - \tilde{y}_t\left(u_{jk}\right)\right)^2 \qquad (5.15)$$

with y_t being the target value.

HONNs use joint activation functions to reduce the need to establish the relationships between inputs when training. Furthermore, this function also reduces the number of free weights and as a consequence the training procedure for HONNs is less time consuming compared to other neural networks. Due to the nature of HONNs and the fact that the number of inputs can be numerous, orders of four and over are rarely used. Another benefit of reducing free weights is that issues of 'over fitting' and local optima which are known to affect neural network results can be largely avoided. For a more comprehensive and thorough investigation into HONNs, refer to Knowles *et al.* (2009) and Zhang and Qi (2005).

The HONN methodology was estimated in line with parameters also used for both MLP and RNN networks. Therefore the training process was stopped once satisfactory annualized returns were produced during the in-sample simulation. Empirical results are presented in the following section with the parameters for the HONN network also being included in Appendix A4.

5 Empirical results

5.1 Statistical performance

Table 5.4 reveals that the HONN model is the most accurate and statistically superior, with leading statistics for three out of the five measures. For the most

Table 5.4 Out-of-sample statistical performance

	Naive	ARMA	MLP	RNN	HONN
MAE	0.0200	0.0141	0.0142	0.0142	0.0140
MAPE (%)	991.49	205.67	446.17	272.42	438.57
RMSE	0.0282	0.0198	0.0200	0.0201	0.0198
THEIL-U	0.7164	0.8665	0.8638	0.8746	0.8801
Correct directional change (CDC) (%)	51.36	53.39	52.72	54.08	54.89

part, this is due to the fact that the sum of all squared differences between target and actual values for the HONN is lower than both the RNN and MLP neural models and the ARMA model. It can also be seen that the HONN's structural ability to predict the direction of change (54.89 per cent) is the highest.

In summary, the lower the statistic for MAE, MAPE, RMSE and the THEIL-U, the better the forecasting accuracy. Results for the in-sample statistical performance can be seen in Appendix A6.

5.2 Trading performance

Results obtained from the out-of-sample unfiltered trading simulation can be seen in Table 5.5. The models used for out-of-sample trading were retained from the test sub-period. These were the models which produced attractive returns over the test sub-period. The same trading strategy was employed across all of the unfiltered models with the exception of the MACD model. In the MACD model trading signals were generated when the long-term moving average either converged or diverged on the daily closing prices, as discussed in Section 4.1.2. The trading strategy that was used for the remaining models is to go long on the spread when the forecasted returns are greater than zero and short when the forecast proves negative returns. In circumstances where consecutive upward or downward spread movements are experienced the previous day's position is held.

Further observation of Table 5.5 reveals that the best-performing model is the HONN as it generates the highest annualized returns and the lowest maximum drawdowns. In addition, the HONN model performs marginally better than the other neural networks when considering its return/risk tradeoff represented by the information ratio (1.19). As mentioned previously, the maximum drawdown is also at its lowest (−15.09 per cent), which improves the return/maximum drawdown yield captured by the calmar ratio (2.45). For the remaining neural network models the trading performance for the MLP model, in terms of annualized returns, were slightly lower than the HONN model, yet significantly higher when compared to the RNN model. However, there was little difference between the two when comparing information and calmar ratios, although the RNN model did produces slightly lower maximum drawdowns.

As the crush spread is evidently volatile a market timing threshold filter similar to that used by Dunis and Miao (2006) is applied. The idea of this filter is

Table 5.5 Out-of-sample trading performance results (unfiltered)

	Naive	MACD	ARMA	MLP	RNN	HONN
Annualised return (excluding costs) (%)	22.40	10.67	30.62	36.59	36.88	37.02
Annualised volatility (excluding costs) (%)	31.25	31.30	31.25	31.23	31.22	31.22
Maximum drawdown (excluding costs) (%)	−23.26	−19.82	−31.42	−22.31	−18.45	−15.09
Calmar ratio (excluding costs)	0.96	0.54	0.97	1.64	2.00	2.45
Information ratio (excluding costs)	0.72	0.34	0.98	1.17	1.18	1.19
Number of transactions (annualized)	122	24	82	72	108	67
Trading days	368	368	368	368	368	368
Transaction costs (%)	17.8	3.4	8.13	10.5	15.7	9.7
Annualized return (including costs) (%)[1]	4.6	7.27	22.49	26.09	21.18	27.32

Note
1 Calculated using five basis points per contract (round trip) as used by King and Zulauf (2010) for the electronic trading of agricultural futures. In this case every transaction consists of one corn contract and one ethanol contract.

to avoid entering the market during times of high volatility. A volatility time series is calculated using the risk metrics formula derived from JP Morgan (1997). The risk metrics formula used to calculate volatility is displayed in equation (5.16).

$$\sigma^2(t+1/t) = \mu * \sigma^2(t/t-1) + (1-\mu) * r^r(t) \tag{5.16}$$

where:

σ^2 is the volatility forecast of spread returns
r^2 is the squared return of the spread
μ is 0.94 for daily data as computed by JP Morgan (1997).

The trading strategy is to stop trading the spread once an optimized level of volatility[9] (derived from the above risk metrics formula) is breached. This strategy is depicted in equation (5.17).

$$\sigma^2_{(t+1/t)} > T \tag{5.17}$$

where:

σ^2 is the risk metrics volatility of the spread returns
t is the dependent variable at time t
T is the optimized threshold of volatility.

From the results generated by the filtered models displayed in Table 5.6 it is apparent that the market timing filter generates higher annualized returns while also decreasing each model's overall volatility. As a result, the risk metrics filter offers an improved risk–return tradeoff by increasing information ratios. Furthermore, the maximum drawdowns are also improved relative to the gross annualized returns. This can be seen in each of the calmar ratios.

6 Concluding remarks

From the outset the aim of this investigation was to model and forecast the corn–ethanol spread in a trading simulation from 22 July 2008 to 31 December 2009, the out-of-sample period. Results produced by each of the unfiltered models were for the most part satisfactory. The HONN generated the highest unfiltered set of results compared to the RNN and MLP neural network models, as well as the naive, MACD and ARMA linear methodologies. This is in line with current literature, as Dunis *et al.* (2006b), who forecast the soybean crush, also arrive at the same conclusion. It is also worth noting that the HONN model achieved the highest annualized returns and the most attractive risk–return profile over both the training and validation sample periods. However, each model's volatility and maximum drawdown can be improved by applying a trading filter.

Table 5.6 Out of sample trading performance results (filtered)

	Naive	MACD	ARMA	MLP	RNN	HONN
Annualized return (excluding costs) (%)	25.69	20.96	36.34	41.26	40.68	42.76
Annualized volatility (excluding costs) (%)	25.94	27.44	29.57	27.24	26.78	27.81
Maximum drawdown (excluding costs) (%)	−21.22	−19.35	−29.99	−16.34	−14.61	−16.61
Calmar ratio	1.21	1.08	1.21	2.53	2.78	2.60
Information ratio	1.15	0.76	1.23	1.51	1.52	1.54
Number of transactions (annualized)	128	44	79	87	107	85
Trading days	368	368	368	368	368	368
Transaction costs (%)	18.6	6.30	7.82	12.60	15.60	12.30
Annualized return (including costs) (%)	7.09	14.66	28.52	28.66	25.08	30.46

During a filtered trading simulation the HONN maintained its position as the most accurate and profitable trading model. On the whole, trading performance was enhanced by the application of the risk metrics market timing filter. This trading filter is similar to that used by Dunis and Miao (2006), who also achieve improved results when employing a risk metrics market timing strategy. During the out-of-sample, filtered trading returns are significantly improved, maximum drawdowns are reduced and overall model volatility is decreased.

With ethanol manufacturers improving processing efficiencies and expanding capacity, the future profitability of the crush spread appears to be a prosperous one. The crushing process yielded 2.4 gallons per bushel a few years ago; however, due to technological improvements the current yield has been increased to 2.8 gallons per bushel. Furthermore, as demand for ethanol continues to grow this should, in theory, push supply/demand in favour of the stronger ethanol producers and perhaps lessen the fragmentation of the ethanol market. This may also encourage the acceleration of mergers and acquisitions, improving 'economies of scale' and as a result lessening the cost of production further. Currently, large producers only occupy 40 per cent of the market, with the remaining 60 per cent being filled by smaller family producers and farmers.

Limitations found within the research are numerous. For instance, future research could expand and provide more robust selection criteria for inputs. Different training algorithms could also be investigated to improve results. Lastly, the spread could include distillers' dried grains (DDGs) in the computation; however, due to the current lack of historical data for DDG this is not possible in a long-term study.

For the most part, this investigation offers an example of forecasting the spread between corn and ethanol futures providing ethanol plants, fund managers, grain elevators, processors and other market participants with an insight into artificial intelligence as a methodology to capture and forecast non-linear relationships. All of the mentioned market participants are able to use alternative forecasting methods such as neural networks in order to manage price risk and profit margins of producing ethanol. Furthermore, some ethanol plants may opt to expand this spread trading strategy to included DDGs, as this is another by-product of 'corn crushing', as well as natural gas as this is the main energy consumed in the production process. Finally, it can be concluded that the corn–ethanol spread can also be traded successfully by speculators to benefit from arbitrage opportunities and diversified investment strategies.

Appendix

A1 Contract specifications

Table 5.7 Contract specifications

Contract specifics	Corn	Ethanol
Product code (ticker)	ZC	EH
Contract size	5,000 bushels	29,000 gallons
Contract months	March, May, July, September, December	All
Trading venue	CME Globex	CME Globex
Last trading day	The business day prior to the fifteenth calendar day of the contract month.	Third business day of delivery month.
Tick size	One-quarter of 1 cent per bushel ($12.50 per contract).	$0.001 per gallon ($29 per contract)
Trading times	6:00 p.m. to 7:15 a.m. and 9:30 a.m. to 1:15 p.m. (CST)	6:00 p.m. to 7:15 a.m. and 9:30 a.m. to 1:15 p.m. (CST)

A2 Network input criteria and selection

Table 5.8 Correlation matrix of neural inputs (in-sample correlation of returns)

	CORN	AMEX Natural Gas	CRB Index	Crude Brent Oil	ETHANOL	MSCI Commodity	S&P500 Energy IG
CORN	1.00	0.43	0.86	0.46	0.74	0.55	0.31
AMEX Natural Gas	0.43	1.00	0.35	0.35	0.53	0.93	0.96
CRB Index	0.86	0.35	1.00	0.44	0.71	0.37	0.33
Crude Brent Oil	0.46	0.35	0.44	1.00	0.56	0.38	0.34
ETHANOL	0.74	0.53	0.71	0.56	1.00	0.51	0.51
MSCI Commodity	0.55	0.93	0.37	0.38	0.51	1.00	0.94
S&P500 Energy IG	0.31	0.96	0.33	0.34	0.51	0.94	1.00

Where the following correlation criteria were retained:

- 0.0 to 0.2: very weak to negligible correlation
- 0.2 to 0.4: weak, low correlation (not very significant)
- 0.4 to 0.7: moderate correlation
- 0.7 to 0.9: strong, high correlation
- 0.9 to 1.0: very strong correlation

A3 Correlogram of spread returns

Table 5.9 Correlogram of crush returns

Date: 22 May 2013 Time: 15:47							
Sample: 1 1,199							
Included observations: 1199							

Autocorrelation	*Partial Correlation*		*AC*	*PAC*	*Q-Stat*	*Prob*
||	||	1	0.041	0.041	2.0432	0.153
||	||	2	0.033	0.032	3.3753	0.185
||	||	3	0.037	0.035	5.0633	0.167
||	||	4	0.010	0.006	5.1823	0.269
||	||	5	−0.010	−0.013	5.2935	0.381
||	||	6	0.018	0.017	5.6870	0.459
||	||	7	0.020	0.019	6.1779	0.519
||	||	8	0.008	0.006	6.2564	0.619
||	||	9	−0.050	−0.053	9.2544	0.414
||	||	10	−0.019	−0.017	9.6731	0.470
||	||	11	−0.008	−0.004	9.7529	0.553
||	||	12	−0.003	0.002	9.7662	0.636
||	||	13	0.030	0.032	10.858	0.623
||	||	14	0.020	0.017	11.358	0.658
||	||	15	0.019	0.017	11.791	0.695
||	||	16	0.002	−0.000	11.797	0.758
||	||	17	0.035	0.034	13.270	0.718
||	||	18	−0.033	−0.039	14.602	0.689

Observation 1: serial correlation is not present as none of the terms are considered to be significant. All are greater than 0.05.

A4 Network characteristics

Parameters for each of the neural networks are displayed in Table 5.10.

Table 5.10 Network characteristics

Parameters	*MLP*	*RNN*	*HONNs*
Learning algorithm	Gradient descent	Gradient descent	Gradient descent
Learning rate	0.001	0.001	0.001
Momentum	0.003	0.003	0.003
Iteration steps	1,500	1,500	1,000
Initialization of weights	$N(0,1)$	$N(0,1)$	$N(0,1)$
Input nodes	13	13	13
Hidden nodes (1 layer)	6	5	0
Output node	1	1	1

A5 ARMA modelling

Estimation output from the ARMA modelling is shown in Table 5.11

Table 5.11 ARMA output

Dependent Variable: RETURNS				
Method: Least Squares				
Sample (adjusted): 12 831				
Included observations: 820 after adjustments				
Convergence achieved after 27 iterations				
MA Backcast: 1 11				
Variable	*Coefficient*	*Std. Error*	*t-statistic*	*Prob.*
C	−0.000404	0.001344	−0.300557	0.7638
AR(1)	0.321385	0.062300	5.158709	0.0000
AR(2)	0.287610	0.064725	4.443539	0.0000
AR(8)	−0.379210	0.044733	−8.477207	0.0000
AR(11)	0.547661	0.029768	18.39757	0.0000
MA(1)	−0.282525	0.050096	−5.639677	0.0000
MA(2)	−0.260749	0.054168	−4.813708	0.0000
MA(8)	0.436688	0.041548	10.51045	0.0000
MA(11)	−0.584663	0.023774	−24.59253	0.0000
R-squared	0.025820	Mean dependent var		−0.000365
Adjusted R-squared	0.016211	S.D. dependent var		0.027505
S.E. of regression	0.027281	Akaike info criterion		−4.354347
Sum squared resid	0.603583	Schwarz criterion		−4.302660
Log likelihood	1,794.282	Hannan–Quinn criterion		−4.334514
F-statistic	2.686931	Durbin–Watson stat		1.992264
Prob(F-statistic)	0.006407			
Inverted AR Roots	0.96	0.89 − 0.44i	0.89 + 0.44i	0.44 + 0.87i
	0.44 − 0.87i	−0.16 + 0.89i	−0.16 − 0.89i	−0.56 − 0.68i
	−0.56 + 0.68i	−0.93 + 0.30i	−0.93 − 0.30i	
Inverted MA Roots	0.94	0.89 + 0.44i	0.89 − 0.44i	0.44 + 0.89i
	0.44 − 0.89i	−0.17 + 0.90i	−0.17 − 0.90i	−0.56 − 0.69i
	−0.56 + 0.69i	−0.94 + 0.30i	−0.94 − 0.30i	

A6 Empirical results in the training and test sub-periods

Table 5.12 In-sample statistical accuracy

	Naive	*ARMA*	*MLP*	*RNN*	*HONN*
MAE	0.0284	0.0200	0.0201	0.0203	0.0201
MAPE (%)	500.35	178.31	164.81	163.56	141.96
RMSE	0.0376	0.0270	0.0274	0.0274	0.0273
THEIL-U	0.6867	0.8444	0.8864	0.8571	0.8705
Correct Directional Change (CDC) (%)	48.80	52.28	54.03	51.74	54.15

Table 5.13 In-sample trading performance (unfiltered)

	Naive	MACD	ARMA	MLP	RNN	HONN
Annualized return (excluding costs) (%)	30.06	34.87	55.41	67.32	66.04	68.82
Annualized volatility (excluding costs) (%)	43.35	43.31	43.23	43.15	43.16	43.14
Maximum drawdown (excluding costs) (%)	−39.47	−33.24	−36.76	−28.08	−34.75	−27.43
Calmar ratio	0.76	1.05	1.51	2.40	1.90	2.51
Information ratio	0.69	0.81	1.28	1.56	1.53	1.60
Number of transactions (annualized)	131	19	87	93	103	98
Trading days	831	831	831	831	831	831

Table 5.14 In-sample trading performance results (filtered)

	Naïve	MACD	ARMA	MLP	RNN	HONN
Annualised return (excluding costs) (%)	33.56	41.39	58.08	71.72	72.70	75.69
Annualised volatility (excluding costs) (%)	33.19	32.43	35.39	33.05	34.80	34.41
Maximum drawdown (excluding costs) (%)	−31.46	−25.56	−32.44	−24.19	−28.80	−24.39
Calmar ratio	1.07	1.62	1.79	2.96	2.52	3.10
Information ratio	1.01	1.28	1.64	2.17	2.09	2.20
Number of transactions (annualized)	150	42	58	90	85	83
Trading days	831	831	831	831	831	831

A7 Performance measures

The performance measures are calculated as follows shown in Table 5.15.

Table 5.15 Performance measures

Root mean squared error (RMSE)	$RMSE = \sqrt{\dfrac{1}{N}\displaystyle\sum_{t=1}^{t+N}\left(\bar{\sigma}_t - \sigma_t\right)^2}$
Mean absolute error (MAE)	$MAE = \dfrac{1}{N}\displaystyle\sum_{t=1}^{t+N}\left|\bar{\sigma}_t - \sigma_t\right|$
Mean absolute percentage error (MAPE)	$MAPE = \dfrac{1}{N}\displaystyle\sum_{t=1}^{t+N}\left|\dfrac{\bar{\sigma}_t - \sigma_t}{\sigma_t}\right|$
Theils-U statistic	$THEIL-U = \dfrac{\sqrt{\dfrac{1}{N}\displaystyle\sum_{t=1}^{t+N}\left(\bar{\sigma}_t - \sigma_t\right)^2}}{\left[\sqrt{\dfrac{1}{N}\displaystyle\sum_{t=1}^{t+N}\left(\bar{\sigma}_t\right)^2} + \sqrt{\dfrac{1}{N}\displaystyle\sum_{t=1}^{t+N}\left(\sigma_t\right)^2}\right]}$
Correct directional change (CDC)	$CDC = \dfrac{100}{N}\displaystyle\sum_{t=1}^{t+N} D_t$ Where $D_t=1$ if $(\sigma_t - \sigma_{t-1})*(\bar{\sigma}_t - \sigma_{t-1})>0$, Else $D_t=0$
Annualized return	$R^A = 252*\dfrac{1}{N}\displaystyle\sum_{t=1}^{N} R_t$ with R_t being the daily return
Cumulative return	$R^C = \displaystyle\sum_{t=1}^{N} R_t$ with R_t being the daily return
Annualized volatility	$\sigma^A = \sqrt{252}*\sqrt{\dfrac{1}{N-1}*\displaystyle\sum_{t=1}^{N}\left(R_t - \bar{R}\right)^2}$
Information ratio	$IR = \dfrac{R^A}{\sigma^A}$
Maximum drawdown	Maximum negative value of $\sum(R_t^C)$ over the period $Max\,DD = Min\left[R_t - Max\left(\displaystyle\sum_{t=1}^{N} R_t\right)\right]$
Calmar ratio	$CR = \dfrac{R^A}{\left|Max\,DD\right|}$

Notes

1 Ethanol facilities: US *Ethanol Production*, American Coalition for Ethanol, www. ethanol.org/index.php?id=37&parentid=8 (accessed 25 November 2009).
2 *Financial Times*: Commodity markets in worst annual fall. 31 December 2008. www. ft.com/cms/s/0/52ea3658-d72d-11dd-8c5c-000077b07658.html (accessed 13 November 2009).
3 CBOT corn contract specifications can be found in Appendix A1.
4 In the analysis arithmetic returns are used rather than logarithmic returns due to the fact that the latter are not linearly additive across portfolio components. As a result, log returns can prove to be problematic and furthermore market participants have a tendency to look more at discrete returns in their daily trading activity. On this basis alone the use of arithmetic returns is deemed to be more realistic and more suitable for the purpose of this investigation.
5 These form part of the author's final PhD thesis and can be provided on request.
6 As such, neural networks are often considered 'black box' as they fail to show the significance of each input. The way the network weights independent variables to form the forecasted outputs is also unclear.
7 This activation function is considered to be non-monotonic in that it is difficult to make weights vary sufficiently from their initial position. Therefore, this can result in much larger number of local minima in the error surface (Sopena *et al.*, 1999).
8 Associative recall is the act of associating two seemingly unrelated entities, such as smell and colour. For more information see Karayiannis and Venetsanopoulos (1994).
9 All of the models were optimized in-sample. The optimal volatility thresholds were then selected for out-of-sample trading.

References

Andersen, T., T. Bollerslev and F. Diebold, 'Some Like It Smooth, and Some Like It Rough: Untangling Continuous and Jump Components in Measuring, Modelling and Forecasting Asset Return Volatility', Manuscript, Northwestern University, Duke University and University of Pennsylvania, 2003.

Appel, G., *The Moving Average Convergence: Divergence Method.* Great Neck, NY: Signalert, 1979.

Beja, A. and M. Goldman, 'On the Dynamic Behaviour of Prices in Disequilibrium', *Journal of Finance* 34, 1980, 235–247.

Bessimber, H. and K. Chan, 'The Profitability of Trading Rules in the Asian Stock Markets', *Pacific Basin Finance Journal* 3, 1995, 257–284.

Butterworth, D. and P. Holmes, 'Inter-Market Spread Trading: Evidence from UK Index Futures Markets', *Applied Financial Economics* 12(11), 2002, 783–791.

CBOT, 'Ethanol Futures: Corn Crush Reference Guide'. Online. Available at www.cbot. com/cbot/docs/73511.pdf (accessed April 2010), 2007.

CME, 'Commodity Products: Trading The Corn for Ethanol Crush', Online. Available at www.cmegroup.com/trading/agricultural/files/AC-406_DDG_CornCrush_042010.pdf (accessed April 2010), 2010.

Corsi, F., 'A Simple Long Memory Model of Realized Volatility', Manuscript, University of Southern Switzerland, 2003.

Dahlgran, R., 'Inventory and Transformation Hedging Effectiveness in Corn Crushing', *Journal of Agricultural and Resource Economics* 34(1), 2009, 154–171.

Deaton, A. and G. Laroque, 'On the Behaviour of Commodity Prices', *Review of Economic Studies* 59, 1992, 1–23.

Draye, J., D. Pavisic, G. Cheron and G. Libert, 'Dynamic Recurrent Neural Networks: A Dynamic Analysis', *IEEE Transactions SMC – Part B* 26(5), 1996, 692–706.

Dunis, C., 'Computerised Technical Systems and Exchange Rate Movements', in C. Dunis and M. Feeny (eds), *Exchange Rate Forecasting*. Probus Publishing Company, Cambridge, 1989, 165–205.

Dunis, C. and J. Miao, 'Volatility Filters for Asset Management: An Application to Managed Futures', *Journal of Asset Management* 7(3–4), 2006, 179–189.

Dunis, C., J. Laws and B. Evans, 'Modelling and Trading the Soybean-Oil Crush Spread with Recurrent and Higher Order Networks: A Comparative Analysis', *Neural Network World* 13(3/6), 2006a, 193–213.

Dunis, C., J. Laws and B. Evans, 'Trading Futures Spreads: An Application of Correlation and Threshold Filters', *Applied Financial Economics* 16(12), 2006b, 903–914.

Elman, J., 'Finding Structure in Time', *Cognitive Science* 14, 1990 179–211.

Engle, R. and C. Granger, 'Co-integration and Error-Correction: Representation, Estimation and Testing', *Econometrica* 55, 1987, 251–276.

Fama, E. and K. French, 'Permanent and Temporary Components of Stock Prices', *Journal of Political Economy* 98, 1986, 246–274.

Faraway, J. and C. Chatfield, 'Time Series Forecasting with Neural Networks: A Case Study', *Applied Statistics*, 47, 1998, 231–250.

Franken, J. and J. Parcell, 'Cash Ethanol Cross-Hedging Opportunities', *Journal of Agricultural and Applied Economics* 35(3), 2003, 1–19.

Freeman, J., *Simulating Neural Networks with Mathematica*, Addison-Wesley, Reading, MA, 1994.

Fulcher, J., M. Zhang and S. Xu, 'The Application of Higher-Order Neural Networks to Financial Time Series', *Artificial Neural Networks in Finance and Manufacturing*, Idea Group, London, 2006.

Funk, S., J. Zook and A. Featherstone, 'Chicago board of trade ethanol contract efficiency'. Selected paper prepared for a presentation at the Southern Agricultural Economics Association Annual Meeting, Dallas, TX, 2–6 February 2008. Online. Available at: http://age-consearch.umm/bitstream/6811/2/sp08fu01.pdf (accessed 15 September 2012).

Geman, H., *Commodities and Commodity Derivatives*, John Wiley & Sons, Chichester, 2005.

Giles, L. and T. Maxwell, 'Learning, Invariance and Generalization in Higher Order Neural Networks' *Applied Optics* 26, 1987, 4972–4978.

Haschke, R. and J. Steil, 'Input Space Bifurcation Manifolds of Recurrent Neural Networks', *Neurocomputing* 64C, 2005, 25–38.

Hill, T., M. O'Conner and W. Remus, 'Neural Network Models for Time Series Forecasts', *Management Science* 42(7), 1996, 1082–1092.

Hutchinson, J., 'A Radial Basis Function Approach to Financial Time Series Analysis' PhD dissertation, Massachusetts Institute of Technology, Cambridge, MA, 1994.

Jayawardena, A. and D. Fernando, 'Artificial Neural Networks in Hydrometeorological Modelling', in: *Proceedings of the Fourth International Conference on the Application of Artificial Intelligence to Civil and Structural Engineering*, edited by B.H.V. Topping, Civil Comp Press, Cambridge, 1995, 115–120.

Jayawardena, A. and D. Fernando, 'Use of Radial Basis Function Type Artificial Neural Networks for Runoff Simulation', *Computer-Aided Civil and Infrastructure Engineering* 13(2), 1998, 91–99.

Jayawardena, A., D. Fernando and M. Zhou, 'Comparison of Multilayer Perceptron and Radial Basis Function Networks as Tools for Flood Forecasting', in: *Destructive*

Water: Water-Caused Natural Disaster, their Abatement and Control, International Association of Hydrological Sciences Press, Oxfordshire, 1996, 173–182.

JP Morgan, J., *Risk Metrics Technical Document*, Morgan Guaranty Trust Company, New York, 1997.

Kaastra, I. and M. Boyd, 'Forecasting Futures Trading Volume Using Neural Networks', *The Journal of Futures Markets* 16(8), 1995, 953–970.

Karayiannis, N. and A. Venetsanopoulos, 'On the Training and Performance of High-Order Neural Networks', *Mathematical Biosciences* 129, 1994, 143–168.

King, K. and C. Zulauf, 'Are New Crop Futures and Option Prices for Corn and Soybeans Biased? An Updated Appraisal'. Paper presented at the NCCC-134 Conference on Applied Commodity Price Analysis, Forecasting, and Market Risk Management St. Louis, Missouri, 2010, 19–20.

Klement, J., 'Riding the Waves of Investment Returns', *UBS Wealth Management Research Working Paper 01-2005*, 2005.

Knowles, A., A. Hussein, W. Deredy, P. Lisboa and C. Dunis, 'Higher-Order Neural Networks with Bayesian Confidence Measure for Prediction of EUR/USD Exchange Rate', in: M. Zhang (ed.), *Artificial Higher Order Neural Networks for Economics and Business*, Information Science Reference, Hershey, PA, 2009, 48–59.

Lachtermacher, G. and J. Fuller, 'Backpropagation in Time Series Forecasting', *Journal of Forecasting* 14(26), 1995, 381–393.

Lisi, F. and R. Schiavo, 'A Comparison Between Neural Networks and Chaotic Models for Exchange Rate Predictions', *Computational Statistics and Data Analysis* 30, 1999, 87–201.

McKay, P., 'Demand for Ethanol Aggravates Pain at the Pump', *Wall Street Journal* (eastern edition), 19 June 2006.

Meland, L., 'Futures Market Liquidity and the Technique of Spreading', *Journal of Futures Markets* 1, 1981, 405–411.

Peterson, R., 'Investor Preferences for Futures Straddles', *Journal of Financial and Quantitative Analysis* 12, 1977, 105–120.

Pindyck, R. and D. Rubinfeld, *Econometric Models and Economic Forecasts*, 4th edition, McGraw-Hill, New York, 1998.

Rumelhart, D., G. Hinton and R. Williams, 'Parallel Distributed Processing: Explorations in the Microstructure of Cognition', in: D.E. Rumelbart and J.L. McClelland (eds), *Parallel Distributed Processing*, MIT Press, Cambridge, MA, 1986, 318–362.

Shapouri, H., J. Duffield and M. Graboski, *Estimating the Net Energy Balance of Corn Ethanol*, USDA/Economic Research Service, Office of Energy, Washington, DC, 1995. Online. Available at: www.ers.usda.gov/publication/aer721/AER721.PDF (accessed 18 February 2010).

Shapouri, H., J. Duffield and M. Wang, *The Energy Balance of Corn Ethanol: An Update*, US Department of Agriculture, Economic Research Service, Washington, DC, 2002.

Sopena, J., E. Romero and R. Alquezar, 'Neural Networks with Periodic and Monotonic Activation Functions: A Comparative Study in Classification Problems', in *Proceedings of the 9th International Conference on Artificial Neural Networks*, 1999, 323–328.

Sorensen, C., 'Modelling Seasonality in Agricultural Commodity Futures', *Journal of Futures Markets* 22(5), 2002, 393–426.

Sweeney, R., 'Some New Filter Rule Tests: Methods and Results', *Journal of Financial and Quantitative Analysis* 23, 1988, 285–300.

Tenti, P., 'Forecasting foreign exchange rates using recurrent neural networks', *Applied Artificial Intelligence* 10, 1996, 567–581.

Till, H. and J. Eagleeye, 'How to Design a Commodity Futures Trading Program', in: G. Gregoriou, V. Karavas, F.-S. L'habitant and F.D. Rouah (eds), *Commodity Trading Advisors: Risk, Performance Analysis and Selection*, Wiley Finance, Hoboken, NJ, 2004.

Tino, P., B. Horne and C. Giles, 'Attractive Periodic Sets in Discrete-Time Recurrent Neural Networks (with Emphasis on Fixed-Point Stability and Bifurcations in Two-Neuron Networks)', *Neural Computation* 13, 2001, 1379–1414.

Trippi, R. and D. DeSieno, 'Trading Equity Index Futures with a Neural Network', *Journal of Portfolio Management* 19, 1992, 27–34.

Working, H., 'The Theory of Price of Storage', *American Economic Review* 39, 1949, 1254–1262.

Working, H., 'Futures Trading and Hedging', *American Economic Review* 43, 1953, 314–343.

Working, H., 'Whose Markets? Evidence on Some Aspects of Futures Trading', *Journal of Marketing* 29, 1954, 1–11.

Working, H., 'Speculation on Hedging Markets', *Food Research Institute Studies* 1, 1960, 185–220.

Working, H., 'New Concepts Concerning Futures Markets and Prices' *American Economic Review* 62, 1962, 432–459.

Zhang, G. and M. Qi, 'Neural Network Forecasting for Seasonal and Trend Time Series', *European Journal of Operational Research* 160(2), 2005, 501–514.

6 Trading decision support with historically consistent neural networks

Hans-Jörg von Mettenheim

1 Introduction

It is a salient feature of today's markets that they are highly interconnected. This leads to challenges for the financial modeller. Financial time series may depend mutually on each other without clear lead–lag relationships. Additionally, we can assume that financial markets exhibit non-linear behaviour. This naturally leads to a wish-list for the financial modeller:

- model several markets at once, all markets being equally important;
- incorporate non-linearity;
- provide a distribution of possible outcomes to avoid a single point forecast;
- allow for an analysis of several time steps.

The historically consistent neural network (HCNN) combines the abovementioned points.

2 Historically consistent neural networks

The basic idea is to model a dynamic system which forecasts every component of the system as a whole. Simply put, the system produces its own forecast. As we cannot assume that we are able to observe *everything* that is important for the system, we add hidden states which absorb the unknowns. Think about it: just because we consider something is *meaningful* it does not follow that other variables are *not meaningful*. Just look into your world: which variables do *you* see? A few thousand, perhaps a few million? And how many variables are relevant to the world? We cannot account for all these variables in the model. And we cannot measure them with arbitrary accuracy. This is not the goal. But we can build a model that at least acknowledges hidden influences and does not ignore them. To be specific: just because one takes an interest in forecasting exchange rates, they will not suddenly become something special. They continue to move, together with equity indices, interest rates, commodities, economic indicators, market actors, other humans, molecules, atoms and elementary particles. We have a coherent system.

HCNNs were first introduced by Zimmermann (2009). In the following several studies we analyse HCNNs in more detail (see Zimmermann, 2010; Mettenheim and Breitner, 2010; Breitner *et al.*, 2010; Mettenheim and Breitner, 2011; Mettenheim, 2009; Zimmerman *et al.*, 2013 for a selection of follow-up literature). Zimmermann (2010) also provides a compact introduction to HCNNs.

We can model such a system with a $D \times W$ matrix of weights W which encodes the dynamics. At every time t one has a D-dimensional state vector $\mathbf{s}^t$. The first N elements are the observables. These are the variables one can measure, deem especially important for the system and want to predict as a whole. The next $D-N$ elements are hidden states. For state transitions one uses the following simple neural network formulation:

$$\mathbf{s}^{t+1} = \mathbf{f}(\mathbf{s}_t) \tag{6.1}$$

In the present case one has

$$\mathbf{s}^{t+1} = \tanh(W\mathbf{s}^t) \tag{6.2}$$

Note that tanh is applied element-wise to the vector $W\mathbf{s}^t$. Figure 6.1 illustrates the HCNN.

3 Data

We approximate a world market with the financial time series in Table 6.1. The time series are chosen to provide a balance between different asset classes like equities, interest rates, exchange rates and commodities. Additionally, the dataset represents different regions of the world. Care has to be taken to account for different time zones. Interest rate series are combined to give a crude yield curve. Finally, to get a stationary time series, we take simple returns or differences (in the case of interest rates) of the time series.

The portfolio comprises 2,609 daily observations in a time span of ten years from July 1999 to July 2009. The first 330 days are used for training, the following 110 days for validation.

4 Trading strategy

Here the focus lies on finding an adequate investment strategy. This is in its most basic form equivalent to correctly forecasting the sign of tomorrow's rate of return. We benchmark the neural network against two other technical strategies (see also Dunis *et al.*, 2008). The first is the naive strategy, which simply states:

$$r_{t+1} = r_t \tag{6.3}$$

i.e. tomorrow's return equals today's. If today's price already reflects all available information then the best bet is that the return remains unchanged. In an efficient market the naive strategy should be a tough benchmark to beat. This

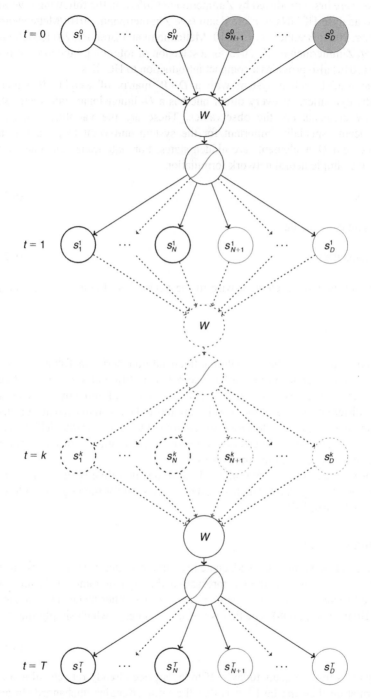

Figure 6.1 Modelling with the HCNN. The initial hidden states can also be trained.

Table 6.1 The time series used in the following examples, ordered by instrument type. The given region indicates not necessarily where the instrument is quoted, but rather that it's important and widely followed in the given area

Name	Instrument	Region	Datastream
FTSE 100 Index	Equities	United Kingdom	FTSE100
DAX 30 Index	Equities	Germany	DAXINDX
CAC 40 Index	Equities	France	FRCAC40
FTSE MIB	Equities	Italy	FTSEMIB
Dow Jones Euro Stoxx 50	Equities	Europe	DJES50I
S&P 500 Index	Equities	United States	S&PCOMP
NASDAQ 100 Index	Equities	United States	NASA100
Nikkei 225 Index	Equities	Japan	JAPDOWA
Kospi Index	Equities	South Korea	KORCOMP
3 months LIBOR	Interest rate	United Kingdom	ECUK£3M
12 months LIBOR	Interest rate	United Kingdom	BBGBP12
Germany 3 months	Interest rate	Germany	ECWGM3M
France 3 months	Interest rate	France	ECFFR3M
Italy 3 months	Interest rate	Italy	ECITL3M
EURIBOR 3 months	Interest rate	Euro area	ECEUR3M
Eurodollars 3 months	Interest rate	United States (Europe)	ECUS$3M
Benchmark Bond 3 months	Interest rate	Japan	ECJAP3M
Benchmark Bond 10 years	Interest rate	United Kingdom	UKMBRYD
Bund Future 10 years	Interest rate	Germany	BDBRYLD
Benchmark Bond 10 years	Interest rate	France	FRBRYLD
Benchmark Bond 10 years	Interest rate	Italy	IBRYLD
US Treasuries 10 years	Interest rate	United States	USBD10Y
Benchmark Bond 10 years	Interest rate	Japan	JPBRYLD
US Dollar to Great British Pound	Exchange rate	United Kingdom	USDOLLR
US Dollar to Swiss Franc	Exchange rate	Switzerland	SWISFUS
US Dollar to Euro	Exchange rate	Euro area	USEURSP
Yen to US Dollar	Exchange rate	Japan	JAPAYE$
Gold Bullion	Commodity	United Kingdom (world)	GOLDBLN
Brent Crude Oil	Commodity	Europe (world)	OILBREN
CRB Index	Commodities	United States (world)	NYFECRB
Baltic Exchange Dry Index	Commodities	World	BALTICF

also provides us with an efficiency measure. The excess return, if any, of the neural network over the naive strategy indicates how efficient or rather inefficient markets are.

The second strategy is a typical technical strategy using moving averages. The *n*-day moving average is

$$MA_n(t) = \frac{1}{n} \sum_{i=t-n+1}^{t} X_i \qquad (6.4)$$

where X_i is the value of the examined financial index and not its return value. One now looks at two moving averages of different periods. The rule is to buy when the shorter moving average moves through the longer one from below.

One sells when the reverse happens: i.e. the shorter moving average intersects the longer one from above. This strategy is abbreviated MA in Table 6.2, which presents an overview of all results.

The basic neural network strategy is straightforward: one takes the forecasted rate of return, r_{t+1}. If $r_{t+1} > 0$ one goes or stays long. If $r_{t+1} < 0$ one goes or stays short. The basic neural network strategy is abbreviated NN.

This strategy is tentatively augmented by a threshold filter. If the forecast is not decisive enough one goes or stays flat. For the subsequent analysis one only trades, if $|r_{t+1}| > 0.005$. This is mostly intended to avoid trading when the probability to cover transaction costs is only low (Dunis et al., 2008). This strategy is abbreviated NNthr. One should expect this strategy to produce better risk measures. To be specific, it should improve Sharpe ratio and maximum drawdown.

Finally, one would like to trade only if one expects the trend to go on. The multi-step forecast offers the possibility to select only those trades where

$$\operatorname{sgn} r_{t+1} = \operatorname{sgn} r_{t+2} \tag{6.5}$$

i.e. one wants the two-day ahead forecast to go in the same direction as the one-day ahead forecast. This double forecast strategy is abbreviated NNdbl. Again, one expects this strategy to show improved risk measures over the basic strategy.

Results for all assets and strategies are shown in Table 6.2. From an investing point of view one is first interested in the annualized return,

$$r_a = 252 \cdot \frac{1}{T} \sum_{t=1}^{T} r_t \tag{6.6}$$

for all relevant times. Of course, one excludes the training and validation data, i.e. the first 440 days. r_{atc} refers to annualized return with transaction costs subtracted. Here, 0.033 per cent are taken for a round-trip. Transaction costs, of course, differ in various markets. But these costs are realistic for a market maker or a financial institution (Dunis et al., 2008).

The Sharpe ratio is a risk-adjusted measure of return. It compares annualized return with incurred volatility:

$$\text{Sharpe} = \frac{r_a}{\sigma_a} \tag{6.7}$$

where the annualized volatility is given by

$$\sigma_a = \sqrt{252} \cdot \sqrt{\frac{1}{T-1} \sum_{t=1}^{T} (r_r - \bar{r})^2} \tag{6.8}$$

The Sharpe ratio may be interpreted as follows: a Sharpe ratio inferior to zero signifies a negative return; a Sharpe ratio greater than zero signifies positive returns with higher Sharpe ratios being better.

Table 6.2 Comparison of different strategies; the naive and moving average or MA strategy are the benchmark strategies; NN refers to a basic neural network strategy, whereas NNthr uses a threshold filter

FTSE100						
*Naive	0.437	0.421	2.55	−0.034	0.171	49
	−0.129	−0.494	−0.61	−0.870	0.213	1,106
MA	−0.364	−0.368	−2.12	−0.154	0.172	13
	−0.057	−0.139	−0.27	−0.539	0.215	249
NN	0.124	0.106	0.71	−0.133	0.175	54
	0.047	−0.247	0.22	−0.438	0.215	891
NNthr	0.155	0.140	1.17	−0.100	0.132	44
	−0.047	−0.288	−0.26	−0.655	0.176	731
NNdbl	0.117	0.105	1.03	−0.078	0.113	35
	0.003	−0.181	0.02	−0.519	0.164	558
DAXINDX						
*Naive	0.491	0.475	2.42	−0.065	0.203	49
	−0.127	−0.487	−0.48	−0.839	0.265	1,091
MA	0.007	0.003	0.03	−0.104	0.206	13
	0.119	0.054	0.44	−0.372	0.269	197
NN	0.278	0.260	1.34	−0.151	0.207	53
	0.011	−0.315	0.04	−0.502	0.269	987
NNthr	0.111	0.095	0.65	−0.142	0.171	47
	−0.025	−0.315	−0.11	−0.569	0.234	881
NNdbl	0.204	0.193	1.39	−0.072	0.147	34
	−0.047	−0.240	−0.23	−0.595	0.199	586
FRCAC40						
*Naive	0.262	0.244	1.34	−0.087	0.196	54
	−0.130	−0.504	−0.52	−0.875	0.250	1,134
MA	−0.028	−0.031	−0.14	−0.121	0.200	9
	−0.011	−0.078	−0.04	−0.566	0.252	205
NN	0.176	0.156	0.88	−0.117	0.200	61
	−0.002	−0.321	−0.01	−0.592	0.252	965
NNthr	0.181	0.166	1.09	−0.113	0.167	45
	0.039	−0.247	0.19	−0.375	0.210	867
NNdbl	0.022	0.012	0.17	−0.103	0.133	33
	−0.051	−0.234	−0.28	−0.626	0.184	556
FTSEMIB						
* Naive	0.276	0.258	1.71	−0.096	0.161	53
	−0.105	−0.474	−0.46	−0.840	0.230	1,117
MA	−0.393	−0.400	−2.40	−0.170	0.164	21
	0.091	0.017	0.39	−0.437	0.233	223
NN	0.249	0.231	1.55	−0.062	0.161	57
	0.053	−0.277	0.23	−0.516	0.233	1,002
NNthr	0.244	0.226	1.94	−0.046	0.126	53
	−0.004	−0.287	−0.02	−0.596	0.197	857
NNdbl	0.036	0.026	0.31	−0.094	0.113	28
	−0.030	−0.220	−0.17	−0.569	0.174	576

continued

Table 6.2 Continued

DJES50I						
*Naive	0.409	0.390	2.08	−0.076	0.197	55
	−0.162	−0.533	−0.64	−0.902	0.254	1,124
MA	0.020	0.016	0.10	−0.093	0.201	13
	−0.012	−0.088	−0.05	−0.640	0.257	229
NN	0.318	0.298	1.60	−0.119	0.199	61
	0.113	−0.212	0.44	−0.363	0.256	985
NNthr	0.173	0.158	1.04	−0.077	0.167	46
	−0.019	−0.308	−0.09	−0.661	0.220	875
NNdbl	0.129	0.118	0.93	−0.083	0.138	32
	0.003	−0.179	0.01	−0.398	0.189	550
SPCOMP						
* Naive	−0.085	−0.105	−0.45	−0.124	0.191	58
	−0.306	−0.693	−1.43	−0.946	0.214	1,171
MA	0.051	0.047	0.26	−0.074	0.192	13
	−0.010	−0.080	−0.05	−0.619	0.220	213
NN	0.405	0.388	2.12	−0.076	0.191	50
	0.004	−0.325	0.02	−0.478	0.220	995
NNthr	0.146	0.133	1.11	−0.046	0.131	42
	−0.008	−0.293	−0.05	−0.444	0.184	863
NNdbl	0.239	0.228	1.70	−0.057	0.140	32
	0.005	−0.171	0.03	−0.303	0.159	535
NASA100						
*Naive	0.370	0.350	0.74	−0.189	0.503	60
	−0.178	−0.549	−0.60	−0.924	0.294	1,126
MA	−0.196	−0.201	−0.38	−0.321	0.513	13
	0.001	−0.080	0.00	−0.550	0.303	244
NN	0.512	0.494	1.00	−0.237	0.512	54
	−0.119	−0.473	−0.39	−0.824	0.303	1,073
NNthr	0.101	0.084	0.23	−0.244	0.443	51
	−0.130	−0.475	−0.47	−0.798	0.279	1,044
NNdbl	0.173	0.163	0.44	−0.227	0.393	32
	−0.063	−0.237	−0.30	−0.574	0.209	529
JAPDOWA						
*Naive	−0.376	−0.394	−1.50	−0.250	0.251	56
	−0.084	−0.446	−0.35	−0.646	0.242	1,097
MA	−0.046	−0.050	−0.18	−0.166	0.261	10
	−0.018	−0.090	−0.07	−0.560	0.257	217
NN	1.107	1.090	4.39	−0.089	0.252	50
	0.211	−0.136	0.82	−0.448	0.256	1,053
NNthr	1.034	1.018	4.97	−0.050	0.208	47
	0.203	−0.082	0.95	−0.364	0.213	864
NNdbl	0.524	0.513	2.81	−0.070	0.187	33
	0.027	−0.167	0.15	−0.413	0.179	589

Table 6.2 Continued

KORCOMP						
*Naive	0.155	0.136	0.62	−0.144	0.249	58
	0.118	−0.228	0.46	−0.463	0.257	1,049
MA	0.289	0.287	1.14	−0.114	0.254	6
	0.142	0.076	0.53	−0.355	0.266	201
NN	0.480	0.467	1.91	−0.085	0.252	41
	0.201	−0.091	0.76	−0.416	0.266	885
NNthr	0.407	0.394	1.66	−0.092	0.244	39
	0.129	−0.161	0.53	−0.474	0.244	880
NNdbl	0.182	0.172	0.91	−0.085	0.200	29
	0.142	−0.036	0.68	−0.510	0.208	540
BBGBP12						
*Naive	−0.027	−0.044	−0.23	−0.068	0.122	51
	0.272	−0.019	2.02	−0.264	0.135	883
MA	0.259	0.256	2.12	−0.039	0.122	9
	0.277	0.227	2.03	−0.273	0.136	151
NN	0.157	0.142	1.28	−0.068	0.123	47
	0.069	−0.221	0.50	−0.202	0.137	877
NNthr	−0.037	−0.039	−1.13	−0.022	0.033	7
	−0.006	−0.055	−0.17	−0.111	0.033	148
NNdbl	0.283	0.274	2.57	−0.029	0.110	26
	0.093	−0.090	0.81	−0.128	0.114	554
ECEUR3M						
*Naive	−0.116	−0.134	−1.05	−0.129	0.111	54
	−0.133	−0.396	−0.89	−0.879	0.149	795
MA	−0.035	−0.037	−0.28	−0.060	0.124	5
	0.134	0.074	0.74	−0.671	0.181	181
NN	−0.191	−0.207	−1.54	−0.184	0.124	47
	0.057	−0.237	0.32	−0.318	0.181	893
NNthr	−0.040	−0.054	−0.38	−0.104	0.106	44
	0.064	−0.193	0.45	−0.232	0.143	779
NNdbl	−0.213	−0.221	−2.05	−0.145	0.104	26
	−0.004	−0.164	−0.03	−0.406	0.131	484
UKyc						
*Naive	−3.285	−3.305	−3.78	−0.842	0.869	62
	−1.125	−1.511	−1.07	−1.000	1.056	1,171
MA	−2.244	−2.251	−2.55	−0.838	0.881	21
	−0.316	−0.406	−0.30	−1.000	1.061	270
NN	1.419	1.399	1.59	−0.436	0.893	61
	0.435	0.056	0.41	−1.374	1.061	1,148
NNthr	1.814	1.795	2.11	−0.336	0.859	59
	0.386	0.011	0.37	−1.302	1.041	1,137
NNdbl	1.537	1.528	2.61	−0.220	0.589	29
	0.359	0.165	0.45	−2.374	0.796	587

continued

Table 6.2 Continued

GERyc						
*Naive	0.885	0.868	1.35	−0.252	0.656	51
	−0.391	−0.751	−0.51	−0.999	0.771	1,093
MA	−0.174	−0.178	−0.26	−0.437	0.657	13
	0.367	0.297	0.48	−0.869	0.772	212
NN	−0.127	−0.147	−0.19	−0.464	0.658	59
	0.003	−0.306	0.00	−0.987	0.772	937
NNthr	−0.119	−0.138	−0.19	−0.487	0.643	58
	0.153	−0.154	0.21	−0.952	0.745	930
NNdbl	−0.033	−0.042	−0.07	−0.260	0.457	25
	0.047	−0.124	0.08	−0.801	0.561	520
FRyc						
*Naive	0.548	0.531	0.81	−0.326	0.680	51
	−0.370	−0.732	−0.48	−0.999	0.764	1,096
MA	−0.255	−0.259	−0.38	−0.422	0.679	11
	0.262	0.186	0.34	−0.952	0.765	230
NN	−1.087	−1.106	−1.61	−0.567	0.677	57
	−0.126	−0.447	−0.16	−0.986	0.765	973
NNthr	−0.309	−0.328	−0.52	−0.399	0.599	56
	−0.126	−0.448	−0.17	−0.982	0.733	971
NNdbl	−0.848	−0.858	−1.71	−0.403	0.496	29
	−0.116	−0.301	−0.21	−0.947	0.542	560
ITyc						
*Naive	−0.452	−0.473	−0.71	−0.572	0.639	65
	−0.169	−0.533	−0.23	−0.997	0.743	1,101
MA	−0.777	−0.784	−1.21	−0.484	0.641	21
	0.308	0.233	0.41	−0.903	0.749	229
NN	−1.069	−1.088	−1.67	−0.604	0.640	59
	−0.069	−0.364	−0.09	−0.996	0.749	895
NNthr	−1.159	−1.177	−1.87	−0.627	0.619	56
	0.082	−0.209	0.11	−0.988	0.722	883
NNdbl	−0.481	−0.490	−1.03	−0.353	0.466	26
	−0.036	−0.201	−0.06	−0.947	0.562	501
USyc						
*Naive	−2.252	−2.272	−1.97	−0.791	1.144	61
	−0.850	−1.213	−0.66	−1.000	1.279	1,100
MA	0.210	0.204	0.18	−0.816	1.172	18
	0.647	0.579	0.50	−0.989	1.287	208
NN	0.126	0.107	0.11	−0.655	1.168	57
	−0.048	−0.392	−0.04	−1.000	1.288	1,043
NNthr	−0.871	−0.889	−0.79	−0.671	1.097	54
	0.208	−0.135	0.17	−1.000	1.246	1,040
NNdbl	0.041	0.030	0.05	−0.392	0.800	32
	0.159	−0.026	0.17	−0.997	0.928	559

Table 6.2 Continued

JAPyc						
*Naive	0.048	0.030	0.10	−0.244	0.476	55
	−0.655	−1.027	−1.03	−1.000	0.635	1,127
MA	0.336	0.334	0.66	−0.231	0.512	8
	−0.283	−0.366	−0.44	−0.991	0.649	251
NN	−0.431	−0.452	−0.84	−0.306	0.511	62
	−0.015	−0.366	−0.02	−0.951	0.649	1,064
NNthr	−0.002	−0.023	−0.00	−0.264	0.478	61
	0.160	−0.189	0.26	−0.877	0.618	1,059
NNdbl	−0.632	−0.640	−1.87	−0.286	0.337	23
	0.033	−0.132	0.07	−0.873	0.483	501
USDOLLR						
*Naive	0.074	0.058	1.02	−0.031	0.072	48
	0.057	−0.289	0.58	−0.282	0.097	1,046
MA	−0.158	−0.164	−2.20	−0.090	0.072	18
	−0.007	−0.095	−0.07	−0.264	0.098	268
NN	0.014	−0.002	0.19	−0.049	0.073	49
	0.010	−0.310	0.11	−0.312	0.098	970
NNthr	0.043	0.039	2.28	−0.008	0.019	12
	0.005	−0.106	0.10	−0.111	0.048	335
NNdbl	−0.023	−0.033	−0.46	−0.022	0.050	30
	0.032	−0.155	0.42	−0.183	0.075	567
SWISFUS						
*Naive	0.124	0.106	1.32	−0.038	0.094	53
	−0.071	−0.455	−0.65	−0.546	0.109	1,165
MA	0.005	0.001	0.05	−0.078	0.098	12
	−0.062	−0.156	−0.56	−0.485	0.111	285
NN	0.144	0.125	1.47	−0.037	0.098	57
	−0.043	−0.368	−0.39	−0.461	0.111	984
NNthr	0.088	0.075	1.46	−0.040	0.060	39
	−0.032	−0.254	−0.45	−0.296	0.072	671
NNdbl	0.019	0.010	0.33	−0.038	0.059	29
	−0.033	−0.210	−0.42	−0.306	0.079	537
USEURSP						
*Naive	−0.019	−0.036	−0.18	−0.071	0.105	52
	0.002	−0.362	0.02	−0.253	0.099	1,102
MA	−0.051	−0.056	−0.48	−0.093	0.106	16
	0.026	−0.050	0.26	−0.212	0.100	229
NN	0.168	0.155	1.60	−0.033	0.105	39
	−0.011	−0.307	−0.11	−0.375	0.100	898
NNthr	0.080	0.071	1.32	−0.021	0.061	29
	−0.028	−0.225	−0.41	−0.346	0.067	598
NNdbl	0.207	0.199	2.42	−0.023	0.085	25
	0.001	−0.172	0.02	−0.243	0.077	524

continued

Table 6.2 Continued

JAPAYEUSD						
*Naive	0.069	0.050	0.73	−0.036	0.095	58
	0.036	−0.325	0.35	−0.230	0.103	1,093
MA	−0.056	−0.060	−0.58	−0.084	0.096	12
	0.014	−0.058	0.13	−0.192	0.104	219
NN	0.138	0.122	1.44	−0.073	0.096	50
	0.045	−0.272	0.43	−0.146	0.104	961
NNthr	0.137	0.128	2.43	−0.030	0.056	27
	0.036	−0.155	0.50	−0.166	0.072	579
NNdbl	0.092	0.084	1.22	−0.054	0.075	24
	0.001	−0.171	0.01	−0.189	0.079	520
GOLDBLN						
*Naive	0.107	0.091	0.96	−0.055	0.112	50
	−0.031	−0.395	−0.17	−0.433	0.183	1,104
MA	−0.117	−0.121	−1.00	−0.141	0.116	14
	0.008	−0.062	0.04	−0.384	0.190	211
NN	0.064	0.048	0.55	−0.084	0.116	47
	0.008	−0.289	0.04	−0.544	0.190	900
NNthr	−0.005	−0.017	−0.05	−0.060	0.097	38
	0.072	−0.151	0.51	−0.390	0.140	675
NNdbl	0.169	0.159	2.54	−0.020	0.067	31
	0.065	−0.127	0.43	−0.316	0.150	581
OILBREN						
*Naive	0.068	0.049	0.27	−0.121	0.256	58
	−0.083	−0.436	−0.23	−0.882	0.362	1,069
MA	0.447	0.444	1.72	−0.118	0.261	10
	0.140	0.066	0.38	−0.637	0.369	226
NN	−0.560	−0.579	−2.15	−0.250	0.260	57
	0.071	−0.270	0.19	−0.748	0.369	1,034
NNthr	−0.411	−0.431	−1.69	−0.203	0.243	56
	0.120	−0.210	0.36	−0.593	0.336	1,001
NNdbl	−0.122	−0.132	−0.63	−0.136	0.195	31
	0.048	−0.136	0.18	−0.447	0.265	557
NYFECRB						
*Naive	0.011	−0.007	0.14	−0.038	0.082	55
	0.083	−0.261	0.60	−0.202	0.139	1,044
MA	0.083	0.080	0.99	−0.038	0.084	9
	0.071	−0.000	0.50	−0.227	0.144	217
NN	0.062	0.044	0.74	−0.054	0.084	55
	0.007	−0.292	0.05	−0.349	0.144	906
NNthr	0.031	0.021	0.64	−0.022	0.049	31
	0.033	−0.164	0.35	−0.132	0.095	598
NNdbl	0.097	0.087	1.48	−0.028	0.065	30
	0.026	−0.169	0.23	−0.234	0.114	591

Table 6.2 Continued

BALTICF						
*Naive	1.343	1.337	16.12	−0.004	0.083	16
	2.474	2.371	10.54	−0.072	0.235	312
MA	0.960	0.959	9.39	−0.037	0.102	5
	1.507	1.485	5.62	−0.196	0.268	68
NN	1.126	1.121	11.79	−0.028	0.096	15
	1.876	1.773	7.26	−0.206	0.259	312
NNthr	0.805	0.801	9.16	−0.022	0.088	12
	1.686	1.599	6.99	−0.177	0.241	264
NNdbl	1.081	1.075	11.68	−0.022	0.093	14
	2.054	1.953	8.48	−0.107	0.242	304

Finally, the maximum drawdown, max DD, indicates which is the worst incurred loss before reaching new highs in equity. It is the smallest value of cumulated returns r_t, whichever happens during the life of the strategy. The author highly recommends reviewing further risk measures in Dunis *et al.* (2003, p. 33).

Additionally, for information purposes, the results table also shows the number of trades the strategy produces. A lower number of trades is generally preferred because of the transaction cost penalty. Each trade also involves the risk of slippage. However, with the advance of all-electronic trading, transaction costs are getting lower.

5 Discussion

The information contained in Table 6.2 is very dense. For this reason we start with a general overview of salient features:

- In most cases the basic neural network strategy delivers more consistent and stable results when comparing the shorter and longer timespans. It does not necessarily beat the benchmark strategies on the shorter timespan but generally beats them on the longer timespan.
- The naive strategy achieves impressive results in the short timespan. One may attribute this to the inherent ability of this strategy to exploit trends – in this case the consistent downtrend following the collapse of the new economy, which can be seen in most assets in the time interval under consideration. However, the neural network strategy either follows as a close second best or even beats the naive strategy.
- The moving average strategy is often disappointing, both for shorter and longer timespans. It, too, like the naive strategy, should work well in trending markets. But one sees that the strategy trades seldom. Trading activity is often only one-fifth of that of the other strategies. While this is good in respect of transaction costs, a closer look reveals that the moving average strategy simply misses out on important successful trades.

• Performance of the filtered neural network strategies compared to the basic neural network strategy is mixed. While they manage to reduce volatility, the improvement in Sharpe ratio, if any, if often only marginal. As trading activity is reduced to 60 per cent compared to the basic strategy, the filtered strategies, like the moving average strategy, miss out on too many good trades. On the longer timespan, however, the filtered strategies often perform better.

Let us now look in detail at strategy results for asset classes and individual assets. In the case of equity indices the naive strategy starts with very impressive results for the short timespan on FTSE 100, DAX 30, CAC 40, FTSE MIB, Dow Jones, NASDAQ and Kospi. It is, however, beaten by the neural network strategy in the case of NASDAQ and Kospi. In the other cases neural networks match the performance. Interestingly, the neural network strategies perform much better for S&P and Nikkei. In both cases the naive strategy fails to perform at all. This is surprising because both indices are perceived to represent very different markets.

Analysing the longer timespan one notes very bad results for the naive strategy and bad results for the moving average. This is due to the fact that the longer timespan of eight years encompasses very different market types which the simple strategies fail to adapt to. The neural networks, although not retrained, manage to at least break even in most cases. While this is, of course, not satisfactory, one should keep in mind that in quantitative trading models are recalibrated regularly to catch up with different market dynamics. However, the point of the present analysis is to look at the flexibility of neural networks. And from this point of view the author deems it a succès d'estime that the networks manage to perform at all. One also notes that before transaction costs neural networks feature quite impressive returns even on the longer timespan for Nikkei and Kospi.

Comparing filtered and unfiltered neural network strategies, one sees the threshold strategy sometimes leads to small improvements. This is especially the case for the FTSE 100 on the shorter timespan. In other cases returns are reduced. It is only with the benefit of hindsight that one would have been able to chose the better of the two strategies. The double neural network strategy that only invests on forecasted two-day moves generally produces inferior results than the basic strategy. However, it sometimes improves on the threshold strategy, e.g. for the NASDAQ. This improvement takes place with significantly fewer trades, e.g. 32 instead of 51. The incurred maximum drawdown is also reduced. Although this fails to improve the Sharpe ratio, the calmer trading style of the double strategy has its own merits. One concludes that it might be preferred by less active investors.

Performance on interest rates and yield curves is mixed for all time spans and strategies. To be more specific: neural networks decidedly outperform on 12 months LIBOR and the UK yield curve. The naive strategy delivers good short-term results on the German and French yield curves. Moving averages perform well on US and Japanese yield curves. However, three months EURIBOR fails to be forecast accurately by all strategies. Still, moving averages and neural networks realize marginal profits before transaction costs on the longer timespan.

Interestingly, filtered neural network strategies manage to improve the performance on the longer timespan. For example, the threshold strategy delivers satisfactory results on three months EURIBOR, the German, US and Japanese yield curve. Keep in mind that performance here is not measured in per cent of invested capital, but simply reflects basis points. The real performance depends on the kind of product one chooses to actually realize a view on interest rates.

Performance on currencies is clearly balanced towards neural networks. They outperform impressively on SFR|USD, EUR|USD and USD|JPY and come as a close second for GBP|USD. The naive strategy also achieves satisfactory performance on GBP|USD, SFR|USD and USD|JPY. It fails to perform completely on EUR|USD. On the longer timespan performance is low, sometimes slightly positive, sometimes slightly negative for all strategies.

Commodities perform with mixed results. On the Gold Bullion the naive strategy slightly outperforms neural networks for the short time span. On the other hand, all neural network strategies manage to produce positive returns before transaction costs on the longer timespan. In this case the filtered strategies clearly add value by reducing the number of trades significantly. Short-term directional oil trades accumulate losses while moving averages impressively outperform. However, the filtered threshold strategy manages to produce positive returns before transaction costs on the longer timespan. The CRB index is forecast best by the double neural network strategy in the short term. However, in the long term, the naive strategy slightly outperforms. Both strategies, which emphasize trends in their most basic form, gain from cyclical commodity markets which are indexed by the CRB. Finally, the Baltic Dry Index performs very well for all strategies and all time frames. Obviously, all strategies exploit the consistent trends in the index. From the point of view of quantitative investment the BDI might be an interesting asset to look at.

We may summarize the analysis as follows:

- By the consistency of their returns on short and long time frames, neural networks are especially suitable for forecasting financial time series.
- However, simple technical strategies might prove lucrative, too. One sees that these simple strategies do not produce consistent returns in the long term.
- A very interesting application – possibly with neural networks as it is a pattern-recognition problem – is therefore to determine which strategy to use. This is beyond the scope of this work.
- One can clearly recommend the use of neural networks for forecasting equity indices. They consistently produce very satisfying and often best returns for all indices. This is not the case for the naive and moving average strategies.

6 Conclusion

This chapter has briefly introduced a special class of recurrent neural networks, the HCNN. The main abilities of the HCNN are:

- model a coherent market portfolio;
- easy multi-step forecasts;
- network ensembles allow for a distribution.

While the mathematical formulation of the HCNN is quite simple, it delivers good results, which are consistent over time.

References

Breitner, M.H., C. Luedtke, H.-J. von Mettenheim, D. Rösch, P. Sibbertsen and G. Tymchenko, 'Modeling portfolio value at risk with statistical and neural network approaches'. In C. Dunis, M. Dempster, M.H. Breitner, D. Rösch and H.-J. von Mettenheim, (eds), *Proceedings of the 17th International Conference on Forecasting Financial Markets: Advances for Exchange Rates, Interest Rates and Asset Management*, Hannover, 26–28 May 2010.

Dunis, C., J. Laws and P. Naïm (eds), *Applied Quantitative Methods for Trading and Investment*. Wiley, Southern Gate, Chichester, 2003.

Dunis, C.L., J. Laws and G. Sermpinis, 'Modelling and trading the EUR/USD exchange rate at the ECB fixing', Liverpool Business School and CIBEF, June 2008. *CIBEF Working Papers*.

Mettenheim, H.-J. von 'Advanced neural networks: finance, forecast, and other applications'. PhD thesis, Faculty of Economics, Leibniz Universität Hannover, December 2009.

Mettenheim, H.-J. von and M.H. Breitner, 'Robust forecasts with shared layer perceptrons'. In C. Dunis, M. Dempster, M.H. Breitner, D. Rösch and H.-J. von Mettenheim (eds), *Proceedings of the 17th International Conference on Forecasting Financial Markets: Advances for Exchange Rates, Interest Rates and Asset Management*, Hannover, 26–28 May 2010.

Mettenheim, H.-J. von and M.H. Breitner, 'Neural network model building: a practical approach'. In C. Dunis, M. Dempster, E. Girardin and A. Péguin-Feissolle (eds), *Proceedings of the 18th International Conference on Forecasting Financial Markets: Advances for Exchange Rates, Interest Rates and Asset Management*, Marseille, 25–27 May 2011.

Zimmermann, H.G. 'Forecasting the Dow Jones with historical consistent neural networks'. In C. Dunis, M. Dempster and V. Terraza (eds), *Proceedings of the 16th International Conference on Forecasting Financial Markets: Advances for Exchange Rates, Interest Rates and Asset Management*, Luxembourg, 27–29 May 2009.

Zimmermann, H.G. 'Advanced forecasting with neural networks'. In C. Dunis, M. Dempster, M.H. Breitner, D. Rösch and H.-J. von Mettenheim (eds), *Proceedings of the 17th International Conference on Forecasting Financial Markets: Advances for Exchange Rates, Interest Rates and Asset Management*, Hannover, 26–28 May 2010.

Zimmermann, H.G., R. Grothmann and H.-J. von Mettenheim. 'Planning purchase decisions with advanced neural networks'. In *Business Intelligence and Performance Management*, Springer, New York, 2013, 125–141.

Part IV

Trading and investments with hybrid evolutionary methodologies

7 Advanced short-term forecasting and trading deploying neural networks optimized with an adaptive evolutionary algorithm

Konstantinos Theofilatos, Thomas Amorgianiotis,
Andreas Karathanasopoulos, Georgios Sermpinis,
Efstratios Georgopoulos and Spiros Likothanassis

1 Introduction

Stock market analysis is an area of growing quantitative financial applications. Modelling and trading financial indices is a very challenging open problem for the scientific community due to their chaotic non-linear nature. Forecasting financial time series is a difficult task because of their complexity and their non-linear, dynamic and noisy behaviour.

Traditional methods such as ARMA and MACD models fail to capture the complexity and the non-linearities that exist in financial time series. Neural network-based approaches have given satisfactory results, but they suffer from certain limitations such as overfitting, difficulties in parameters and convergence issues.

Multilayer perceptron (MLP) neural networks (NN) are used in the present chapter as they are the most famous among them. Additionally, wavelet neural networks (WNNs), a modern architecture which is believed to surpass the limitations of MLPs, such as slow convergence and training difficulties, are also deployed.

Both MLPs and WNNs have already been used for the modelling of financial time series. Specifically, Dunis *et al.* (2010) have applied the MLP NN to the problem of modelling and trading the ASE 20 index. Compared to classical models, such as ARMA models, MLPs are proven to perform better in terms of annualized return. Moreover, WNNs have also been applied to financial forecasting problems (Bozic *et al.*, 2011) and they have been proven to outperform simple MPL NNs.

Despite their high performance in many practical problems, including financial forecasting, NNs present some drawbacks that should be surpassed in order to establish them as reliable trading tools. Specifically, their performance is highly related to their structure and parameter values. The optimization of the structure and parameter values of NNs for financial forecasting and trading is an open problem, even if some initial approaches have been developed (Karathanasopoulos *et al.*, 2010; Tao, 2006). All of these approaches appear to be able to optimize the NNs structure and parameters, but include some extra parameters of the optimization technique which should in turn be optimized through experimentation.

In the present chapter, a novel evolutionary approach (adaptive genetic algorithms) is introduced, which adapts their parameters during the evolutionary process to achieve better convergence characteristics and to allow inexperienced users to handle them. These evolutionary techniques were used to optimize the structure and the parameters of MLP NNs and WNNs. The produced hybrid techniques were applied to the problem of modelling and trading the DJIA index. Experimental results have demonstrated that they present better trading performance than statistical trading techniques. From the proposed hybrid techniques, the one which combines the adaptive genetic algorithm method with WNNs outperformed all other examined models in terms of annualized returns, even when transactions costs and leveraging are taken into account.

The rest of the present chapter is organized as follows: in Section 2 the related work about financial forecasting and trading with neural networks and hybrid methodologies is described. In Section 3 the datasets used in the present study are presented, and in Section 4 the forecasting methods are described. In Section 5 the experimental results are presented and in Section 6 some useful conclusions are drawn.

2 Related work

Artificial NNs (ANNs) have been extensively used in many forecasting and trading tasks so far. Vahidinasab *et al.* (2008) successfully used an ANN with a modified Levenberg–Marquardt (LM) learning algorithm for forecasting the electricity day-ahead prices in the Pennsylvania–New Jersey–Maryland (PJM) market. Also, Pino *et al.* (2008) developed an MLP ANN for forecasting the next-day price of electricity in the Spanish energy market. They proposed a training method for artificial neural nets, which is based on making a previous selection for the MLP training samples using an ART-type NN, which are a category of ANNs that enables the addition of new inputs without the need to repeat the learning procedure. The MLP is then trained and finally used to calculate forecasts. Another MLP application in financial forecasting is the one of Tsai and Wu (2008), who used MLP ANN for bankruptcy prediction and credit scoring.

Yu *et al.* (2008) proposed a method for forecasting the foreign exchange rates using a multi-stage non-linear radial basis function (RBF) neural network ensemble. Moreover, WNNs were used by Kumar *et al.* (2008) for forecasting the cost of software development. For forecasting and trading the EUR/USD exchange rate, Dunis *et al.* (2011) deployed higher-order and recurrent neural architectures, proving the superiority of higher-order NNs among these two alternatives.

All the previous approaches face the aforementioned constraints and limitations of the ANN techniques. For this reason, a variety of NN-based hybrid methodologies have been proposed in the literature to overcome these limitations.

Khashei *et al.* (2008), based on the basic concepts of ANNs and fuzzy regression models, proposed a new hybrid method that yields more accurate results with incomplete datasets for time series forecasting. Tsenga *et al.* (2008) incorporated a novel hybrid asymmetric volatility approach into an artificial neural network (ANN) option-pricing model to upgrade the forecasting ability of the price of derivative securities. According to their work, the ANN option-pricing model reveals that Grey-EGARCH volatility provides greater predictability than other volatility approaches. EGARCH models are generalized autoregressive conditional heteroscedasticity (GARCH) models which allow positive and negative shocks to have different effects on the estimated variance. The Grey model is a system modelling approach using only a few data points. The Grey-EGARCH model is the GARCH model when the Grey model is used to model the error of EGARCH predictions. Ardalani-Farsa and Zolfaghari (2010) proposed a method for prediction of chaotic time series with a residual analysis method using hybrid Elman–NARX neural networks. The NARX neural networks are feedforward time delay neural networks without the feedback loop of delayed outputs.

One of the most contemporary trends is the combination of meta-heuristic algorithms to optimize the structure or the parameters of ANNs. In 2002, Andreou *et al.* demonstrated a hybrid technique which involved deploying a simple genetic algorithm to locate the structure of an MLP neural network and the localized extended Kalman filter algorithm to locate the optimal network weights. This algorithm was successfully applied in the task of forecasting four major exchange rate daily indexes. Chauhan *et al.* (2009) used differential evolution-trained WNNs in order to forecast bankruptcy at US banks, Turkish banks and Spanish banks. Sermpinis *et al.* (2013) introduced a hybrid NN architecture of particle swarm optimization and adaptive radial basis function (ARBF–PSO), a time varying leverage trading strategy based on Glosten, Jagannathan and Runkle (GJR) volatility forecasts and an NN fitness function for financial forecasting purposes. Their hybrid combination was applied to a variety of forecasting and trading tasks and it was proved to be able to extract highly profitable strategies. Shen *et al.* (2011) used an RBF NN optimized by artificial fish swarm algorithm for forecasting the Shanghai Stock Exchange. Furthermore, Hsieba *et al.* (2011) presented an integrated system (called ABC-RNN) in which wavelet transforms and recurrent neural networks (RNNs) optimized by the artificial bee colony (ABC) algorithm are combined for stock price forecast.

3 The examined financial indexes and related financial data

The Dow Jones Industrial Average (DJIA), also called the Industrial Average, the Dow Jones, the Dow 30 or simply the Dow, is a stock market index, and one of several indices created by *Wall Street Journal* editor and Dow Jones & Company co-founder Charles Dow. It was founded on 26 May 1896, and is now owned by Dow Jones Indexes, which is majority-owned by the CME Group. It is an index that shows how 30 large, publicly owned companies based in the United States have traded during a standard trading session in the stock market.

The FTSE100 index is weighted according to market capitalization and currently comprises 101 large cap constituents listed on the London Stock Exchange. For the purpose of our trading simulation the iShares FTSE100 exchange traded fund is traded to capture daily movements of the FTSE100 index. Positions are initiated at the opening of a trading day and closed at or around 16:30 GMT. The cash settlement of this index is simply determined by calculating the difference between the traded price on the open and the closing price of the index. When the model forecasts a negative return then a short position (sale) is assumed on the open and when it forecasts a positive return a long position (purchase) is taken. Profit/loss is realized on a daily basis and positions are not held overnight.

The DJIE and the FTSE100 daily time series are non-normal (Jarque–Bera statistics confirms this at the 99 per cent confidence interval), containing slight negative skewness and relatively high kurtosis. Arithmetic returns were used to calculate daily returns and they are estimated using equation (7.1). Given the price level $P_1, P_2, \ldots, P_t$, the arithmetic return at time t is formed by:

$$R_t = \frac{P_t - P_{t-1}}{P_{t-1}} = \tag{7.1}$$

In Table 7.1 the dataset and its subsets used for training the examined predictors and validating their performance are summarized. Fourteen autoregressive inputs were selected as inputs to our algorithms and our networks.

4 Forecasting models

Two novel hybrid methodologies, which we compare with two benchmark models (ARMA and MACD), are introduced in the present chapter.

4.1 Benchmark models

For comparison reasons two benchmark models were applied to the problem of modelling the DJIA and FTSE100 financial indexes. These are an ARMA model and a MACD model.

Table 7.1 Datasets summary

Name of period	Trading days	Beginning	End
Total dataset	3,597	27 October 1997	6 February 2012
Training set	2,157	27 October 1997	23 May 2006
Test set	720	24 May 2006	31 March 2009
Validation set	720	1 April 2009	6 February 2012

4.1.1 ARMA model

Autoregressive moving average (ARMA) models assume that the value of a time series depends on its previous values (the autoregressive component) and on previous residual values (the moving average component) (Dunis *et al.*, 2010). The ARMA model takes the form of equation (7.2)

$$Y_t = \varphi_0 + \varphi_1 Y_{t-1} + \varphi_2 Y_{t-2} + \ldots + \varphi_p Y_{t-p} + \varepsilon_t - w_1 \varepsilon_{t-1} - w_2 \varepsilon_{t-2} - \ldots - w_q \varepsilon_{t-q} \quad (7.2)$$

where:

Y_t is the dependent variable at time t
Y_{t-1}, Y_{t-2} and Y_{t-p} are the lagged dependent variables
$\varphi_0, \varphi_1, \varphi_2$ and φ_p are regression coefficients
ε_t is the residual term
$\varepsilon_{t-1}, \varepsilon_{t-2}$ and ε_{t-p} are previous values of the residual
w_1, w_2 and w_q are weights.

Using as a guide the correlogram in the training and the test sub-periods we have chosen a restricted ARMA (6,6) model. All of its coefficients are significant at the 99 per cent confidence interval. The null hypothesis that all coefficients (except the constant) are not significantly different from zero is rejected at the 99 per cent confidence interval.

4.1.2 MACD

The moving average model (Dunis *et al.*, 2010) is defined as:

$$M_t = \frac{\left(Y_t + Y_{t-1} + Y_{t-2} + \ldots + Y_{t-n+1}\right)}{n} \quad (7.3)$$

where:

M_t is the moving average at time t
n is the number of terms in the moving average
Y_t is the actual rate of return at period t.

The MACD strategy used is quite simple. Two moving average series are created with different moving average lengths. The decision rule for taking positions in the market is straightforward. Positions are taken if the moving averages intersect. If the short-term moving average intersects the long-term moving average from below, a 'long' position is taken. Conversely, if the long-term moving average is intersected from above, a 'short' position is taken.

The forecaster must use judgement when determining the number of periods n on which to base the moving averages. The combination that performed best over the in-sample sub-period for every one of the examined financial indexes was retained for out-of-sample evaluation. The model selected was a combination of every one of the examined indices and their eight-day moving average, namely $n=1$ and 8, respectively, or a (1,8) combination. The performance of this strategy is evaluated solely in terms of trading performance.

4.2 Proposed hybrid techniques

NNs exist in several forms in the literature. In the present study, MLP, which is one of the most famous architectures, was used in addition to WNNs, which consist of an alternative NN architecture designed to overcome convergence limitations of the MLP NNs.

4.2.1 Multilayer perceptron neural networks

A standard MLP NN has three layers; this structure is adapted in the present chapter. The first layer is called the input layer (the number of its nodes corresponds to the number of explanatory variables). The last layer is called the output layer (the number of its nodes corresponds to the number of response variables). An intermediary layer of nodes, the hidden layer, separates the input from the output layer. Its number of nodes defines the amount of complexity the model is capable of fitting. In addition, the input and hidden layer contain an extra node, called the bias node. This node has a fixed value of 1 and has the same function as the intercept in traditional regression models. Normally, each node of one layer has connections to all the other nodes of the next layer. The network processes information starting with the input nodes, which contain the value of the explanatory variables. Since each node connection represents a weight factor, the information reaches a single hidden layer node as the weighted sum of its inputs. Each node of the hidden layer transfers the information through a non-linear activation function and passes it on to the output layer if the calculated value is above a threshold. The training of the network (which is the adjustment of its weights in the way that the network maps the input value of the training data to the corresponding output value) starts with randomly chosen weights and proceeds by applying a learning algorithm called backpropagation of errors (Rumelhart *et al.*, 1986). The backpropagation algorithm simply tries to find those weights which minimize an error function. The most famous backpropagation variation is the LM backpropagation algorithm (Tummala *et al.*, 2011), which surpasses the classical backpropagation in terms of convergence speed and accuracy.

The parameters of the MLP that need to be tuned in every time-series modelling problem are the inputs that the MLP NNs should have, the number of nodes of the hidden layer, the activation functions which should be used for the hidden and output layers, the learning rate and the momentum parameter. Topologies with more than one hidden layer may be simplified to their equivalent topologies with a single hidden layer. For this reason in the present study the possibility of having an MLP neural network of more than one hidden layer was not examined.

4.2.2 Wavelet neural networks

WNNs are a generalized form of RBF feedforward NNs. Similar to simple MLPs they are three-layered architectures having only one hidden layer. In contrast to simple MLPs, WNNs use radial wavelets as activation functions to the hidden layer, while using the linear activation function in the output layer. The information processing of a WNN is performed as follows.

Suppose $x = [x_1, \ldots, x_d]$ to be the input signal, where d is the input's dimensionality, then the output of its jth hidden neuron is estimated using equation (7.4):

$$\psi_j(x) = \prod_{i=1}^{d} \varphi_{d_{ij}, t_{i,j}}(x_i) \tag{7.4}$$

where $\varphi_{d_{ij}, t_{i,j}}$ is the wavelet activation function (one among Mexican hat, Morlet and Gaussian wavelet) of the jth hidden node and $d_{i,j}$ and $t_{i,j}$ are the scaling and translational vectors, respectively. Then the output of the WNN is computed by estimating the weighted sum of the outputs of each hidden neuron using the weights that connect them with the output layer.

The learning process involves the approximation of the scaling and translational vectors which should be used for the hidden layer and of the weights that connect the hidden layer with the output. For the approximation of the scaling vector the methodology proposed by Zhang and Benveniste (1982) was used, and for the approximation of the translational vectors the k-means algorithm (Zainuddin and Pauline, 2010) with k being the number of hidden nodes, was deployed. The weight vector W can easily be computed analytically by computing the following equation:

$$W = (\Psi^T \Psi)^{-1} \Psi^T Y \tag{7.5}$$

where

$$\Psi = \begin{pmatrix} \psi(x_1, d_1, t_1) & \psi(x_1, d_2, t_2) & \cdots & \psi(x_1, d_m, t_m) \\ \psi(x_2, d_1, t_1) & \cdots & \cdots & \cdots \\ \cdots & \cdots & \cdots & \cdots \\ \psi(x_d, d_1, t_1) & \psi(x_d, d_2, t_2) & \cdots & \psi(x_d, d_m, t_m) \end{pmatrix} \tag{7.6}$$

This procedure for calculating the weight vector is superior to using the backpropagation algorithm as it does not contain any convergence or overfitting threats.

The parameters of the WNN that need to be tuned in every modelling problem are the inputs that should be used, the size of the hidden layer and the activation function that should be used in the hidden layer. The appropriate tuning of all these parameters requires a hard, time-consuming step of trial-and-error procedure. This trial-and-error procedure may lead to overfitting of the algorithms and to the data snooping effects. Both of these phenomenon may lead to overestimating our results.

4.2.3 Adaptive genetic algorithm hybrid techniques

In the present chapter an adaptive genetic algorithm is introduced to locate the optimal feature subset and the optimal structure and parameters of NN topologies.

To fulfil these tasks the application of an advanced evolutionary optimization algorithm to optimize the structure and the aforementioned parameters of MLP NNs and WNNs was proposed. The proposed evolutionary algorithm, which is developed for this purpose, is designed to be adaptive. Specifically, in order to achieve better convergence behaviour, adapting their parameter values during the evolutionary process was attempted.

Genetic algorithms (Holland, 1995) are meta-heuristic algorithms inspired by the principle of natural selection. They are useful and efficient if the search space is big and complicated or there is no available mathematical analysis of the problem. A population of candidate solutions, called chromosomes, is optimized through a number of evolutionary cycles and genetic operations, such as crossovers or mutations. Chromosomes consist of genes, which are the optimizing parameters. At each iteration (generation), a fitness function is used to evaluate each chromosome, measuring the quality of the corresponding solution, and the fittest chromosomes are selected to survive. This evolutionary process is continued until some termination criteria are met. It has been shown that genetic algorithms can deal with large search spaces and do not get trapped in local optimal solutions like other search algorithms (Holland, 1995).

Genetic algorithms, as discussed in Section 2, have been successfully used in the task of optimizing ANNs. However, their performance is highly related to the optimal selection of their parameters, which tune their searching properties. Thus, some parameter settings favour the better exploration of the search space and others favour the exploitation of more promising areas. For these reasons the applications of genetic algorithms in practical problems requires the optimization of a variety of parameters, including population size, mutation probability, number of generations, etc. Moreover, the location of the weights of an ANN parallel to the location of their structure and parameters creates a very large space which is difficult to handle by any existing algorithm.

To overcome these problems a fully adaptive genetic algorithm was proposed to optimize the structure and parameters of ANNs without searching for their weights. These weights are going to be calculated using ANN-specific methodologies: LM backpropagation for MLPs and analytical deterministic methods for WNNs.

The chromosomes are encoded as binary strings. When continuous values are needed, the string genes are transformed to their corresponding decimal value. As for the selection operator, roulette wheel selection was deployed. In order to raise the evolutionary pressure and speed up convergence, the fitness functions were scaled using the exponential function.

A new fitness function to quantify the performance of the population's members was proposed. This fitness function is described in equation (7.7).

$$\text{Fitness} = \text{annualized return} - \text{MSE} - 0.001 * \#\text{selected\_inputs} \qquad (7.7)$$

where annualized return is the annualized profit or loss when trading with the extracted ANN, the MSE is the mean square error of the predictions and the #selected_inputs is the number of inputs which are selected for this specific ANN. This fitness function is appropriate for our task as it incorporates trading and statistical measures and in parallel favours simpler solutions to avoid overfitting.

The two main genetic operators of a genetic algorithm are crossover and mutation. For the crossover operator, two-point crossover was used to create two offspring from every two selected parents. The parents are selected at random; two crossover points are selected at random; and two offspring are produced by exchanging genetic material between the two crossover points of the two parents. The crossover probability was set equal to 0.9 in order to leave some part of the population to survive unchanged to the next generation.

Most studies on the selection of the optimal mutation rate parameter agree that a time-variable mutation rate scheme is usually preferable to a fixed mutation rate (Thierens, 2002). Accordingly, the dynamic control of the mutation parameter is proposed using equation (7.8):

$$P_m(n) = 0.2 - n \cdot \frac{0.2 - \dfrac{1}{P_S}}{MAX_G} \qquad (7.8)$$

where n is the current generation, P_S is the size of the population and MAX_G is the maximum generation specified by the termination criteria. Using equation (7.8), the algorithm starts with a high mutation rate for the first generations and then gradually decreases over the number of generations. In this manner global search characteristics are adopted in the beginning and are gradually switched to local search characteristics for the final iterations. The mutation rate is reduced with a smaller step when a small population size is used in order to avoid stagnation. For bigger population sizes the mutation rate is reduced with a larger step size since a quicker convergence to the global optimum is expected.

The population size was set to 20 candidate solutions. The termination criterion that was applied is a combination of the maximum number of iterations and a convergence criterion. The maximum number of iterations was set to 100 and the convergence criterion is satisfied when the mean population fitness is less than 5 per cent away from the best population fitness for more than five consecutive iterations.

5 Empirical trading results

In this section the results of the studied models in the problem of trading the DJIA and the FTSE100 indices are presented. The trading performance of all the examined models considering the out-of-sample subset is presented in Tables 7.2–7.3.

The trading strategy which was used in the present work is simple and identical for all of the examined models: go or stay long when the forecast return is

Table 7.2 Out-of-sample trading performance results for the DJIE index

	ARMA	MACD	aGA-MLP	aGA-WNN
Information ratio (excluding costs)	0.12	0.37	0.98	1.07
Annualized volatility (excluding costs) (%)	18.04	18.04	18.01	18.00
Annualized return (excluding costs) (%)	2.16	6.61	17.74	19.30
Maximum drawdown (excluding costs) (%)	−28.01	−14.37	−17.19	−13.75
Positions taken (annualized)	34	27	33	64
Transaction costs (%)	0.30	0.24	0.10	0.57
Annualized return (including costs) (%)	1.86	6.37	17.64	18.73

Table 7.3 Out-of-sample trading performance results for the FTSE100 index

	ARMA	MACD	aGA-MLP	aGA-WNN
Information ratio (excluding costs)	0.11	0.30	0.26	0.74
Annualized volatility (excluding costs) (%)	18.14	18.04	18.79	18.77
Annualized return (excluding costs) (%)	2.06	5.45	4.97	13.94
Maximum drawdown (excluding costs) (%)	−29.05	−14.00	−43.74	−26.79
Positions taken (annualized)	36	20	158	67
Transaction costs (%)	1.8	1.0	7.9	3.36
Annualized return (including costs) (%)	0.26	4.45	−2.9	10.58

above zero and go or stay short when the forecast return is below zero. Because of the stochastic nature of the proposed methodologies a simple run is not enough to measure their performance and extract meaningful conclusions. This is the reason why 50 runs were executed and the mean results are presented in Tables 7.2–7.3.

It is easily observed from Tables 7.2 and 7.3 that the hybrid evolutionary–neural network methods clearly outperform the classical ARMA and MACD models. Furthermore, among the hybrid proposed techniques aGA-WNN is the one that prevails. The robustness of WNNs, when combined with the supreme global search characteristics of the proposed adaptive genetic algorithm approach, is able to produce highly profitable trading strategies.

5.1 Transaction costs

The transaction costs for a tradable amount were considered about 5 pips per trade (one way) between market makers for both DJIE and FTSE100 indexes. The pips are the smallest price changes that a given financial index can make.

From Tables 7.2 and 7.3 one can easily see that even when considering transaction costs, the aGA-WNN predictor still significantly outperforms all other examined trading strategies in terms of annualized return.

As the transaction costs deployed in the present study are estimated considering the worst-case scenario, it is worth mentioning that the true profitability potential of the proposed trading strategies is much higher.

5.2 Leverage to exploit high information ratios

In order to further improve the trading performance of our models a 'level of confidence' to our forecasts was deployed, i.e. a leverage based on the test sub-period. The leverage factors applied are calculated in such a way that each model has a common volatility of 18 per cent on the test dataset. Since the proposed models have a volatility of approximately 18 per cent, this level was chosen as our basis.

The cost of leverage (interest payments for the additional capital) is calculated at 4 per cent per annum (that is 0.016 per cent per trading day). The interest costs are calculated by considering a 4 per cent interest rate per annum, divided by 252 trading days. In reality, leverage costs also apply during non-trading days so that we should calculate the interest costs using 360 days per year. But for the sake of simplicity, the approximation of 252 trading days was used to spread the leverage costs of non-trading days equally over the trading days. This approximation prevents us from keeping track of how many non-trading days a position is held.

As it turns out when observing Tables 7.4 and 7.5, when leveraging was used aGA-MLP slightly (but not with statistically important difference) outperformed aGA-WNN in the task of trading with the DJIE index. However, aGA-WNN is clearly more profitable when trading the FTSE100 index. In general the aGA-WNN was clearly superior to aGA-MLP and this is attributed to the advantages of WNNs over the MLP NNs ones.

Table 7.4 Out-of-sample trading performance results for the DJIE index considering leverage

	aGA-MLP	aGA-WNN
Sharpe ratio (excluding costs)	0.98	1.07
Annualized volatility (excluding costs) (%)	18.07	17.65
Annualized return (excluding costs) (%)	18.78	19.05
Maximum drawdown (excluding costs) (%)	18.76	−14.00
Positions taken (annualized)	12	64
Transaction and leverage costs (%)	0.7	3.35
Annualized return (including costs) (%)	18.08	15.7

Table 7.5 Out-of-sample trading performance results for the FTSE100 index considering leverage

	aGA MLP	aGA WNN
Sharpe ratio (excluding costs)	0.26	0.74
Annualized volatility (excluding costs) (%)	18.79	17.67
Annualized return (excluding costs) (%)	4.97	14.78
Maximum drawdown (excluding costs) (%)	−43.74	−23.78
Positions taken (annualized)	158	76
Transaction and leverage costs (%)	7.9	3.89
Annualized return (including costs) (%)	−2.9	10.89

6 Concluding remarks

In the present chapter a computational framework for the combination of evolution-ary algorithms and NNs for the forecasting and trading of financial indices was introduced. Adaptive genetic algorithms were designed, developed and deployed to optimize the NNs' structure and parameters. The proposed evolutionary algorithms use parameters whose values are being adapted during the evolutionary process either to fasten the evolutionary process or to avoid getting trapped in local optimal solutions. The proposed evolutionary algorithm was deployed to optimize the struc-ture and parameters of MLP and wavelet ANNs. The derived hybrid methodologies were applied in the problem of modelling and short-term trading of the DJIA and the FTSE100 financial indexes using a problem-specific fitness function.

Experimental results have proved that the proposed hybrid techniques clearly outperformed statistical techniques in terms of Sharpe ratio and annualized return. Furthermore, as expected, WNNs produced more profitable trading strat-egies than MLP NNs. The optimal hybrid technique, as proved experimentally, is the aGA-WNN method. This technique outperformed the other examined models in the applied trading simulations. The proposed hybrid methodologies were further applied to a more complex trading task including leveraging. Exper-imental results in this trading task indicated that aGA-WNN still outperforms the aGA-MLP method.

Our future plans involve the development of a web platform that will enable users to deploy the proposed models in forecasting and trading tasks through a user-friendly interface.

References

Andreou, A., E. Georgopoulos and S. Likothanassis, 'Exchange-Rates forecasting: a hybrid algorithm based on genetically optimized adaptive neural networks', *Computa-tional Economics* 20(3), 2002, 191–210.

Ardalani-Farsa, M. and S. Zolfaghari, 'Chaotic timeseries prediction with residual ana-lysis method using hybrid Elman–NARX neural networks', *Neurocomputing* 73(13–15), 2010, 2540–2553.

Bozic, J., S. Vukotic and D. Babic, 'Prediction of the RSD exchange rate by using wave-lets and neural networks', in *Proceedings of the 19th Telecommunication Forum*, 2011, 703–706.

Chauhan, N., V. Ravi and D. Chandra, 'Differential evolution trained wavelet neural net-works: application to bankruptcy prediction in banks', *Expert Systems with Applica-tions* 36(4), 2009, 7659–7665.

Dunis, C., J. Laws and A. Karathanasopoulos, 'Modeling and trading the Greek stock market with mixed neural network models', *Applied Financial Economics*, 21(23), 2010, 1793–1808.

Dunis, C., J. Laws and G. Sermpinis, 'Higher order and recurrent neural architectures for trading the EUR/USD exchange rate', *Quantitative Finance* 11(4), 2011, 615–629.

Holland, J., *Adaptation in Natural and Artificial Systems: An Introductory Analysis with Applications to Biology, Control and Artificial Intelligence*, Cambridge, MA: MIT Press, 1995.

Hsieha, T., H. Hsiaob and W. Yeha, 'Forecasting stock markets using wavelet transforms and recurrent neural networks: an integrated system based on artificial bee colony algorithm' *Applied Soft Computing* 11(2), 2011, 2510–2525.

Karathanasopoulos, A., K. Theofilatos, P. Leloudas and S. Likothanassis, 'Modeling the Ase 20 Greek index using artificial neural networks combined with genetic algorithms', In *Proceeding of the 20th International Conference on Artificial Neural Networks*, 15–18 September 2010, Thessaloniki, Greece (ICANN 2010).

Khashei, M., S. Hejazi and M. Bijari, 'A new hybrid artificial neural networks and fuzzy regression model for time series forecasting', *Fuzzy Sets and Systems* 159(7), 2008, 769–786.

Kumar, K., V. Ravi, M. Carr and N. Kiran, 'Software development cost estimation using wavelet neural networks' *Journal of Systems and Software* 81(11), 2008, 1853–1867.

Pino, R., J. Parreno, A. Gomez and P. Priore, 'Forecasting next-day price of electricity in the Spanish energy market using artificial neural networks', *Engineering Applications of Artificial Intelligence* 21(1), 2008, 53–62.

Rumelhart, D., E. Hinton, E. Geoffrey and R. Williams, 'Learning representations by back-propagating errors', *Nature* 323(6088) 1986, 533–536.

Sermpinis, G., K. Theofilatos, A. Karathanasopoulos, E. Georgopoulos and C. Dunis, 'Forecasting foreign exchange rates with adaptive neural networks using radial-basis functions and particle swarm optimization', *European Journal of Operational Research* 225(3), 2013, 528–540.

Shen, W., X. Guo, C. Wub and D. Wuc, 'Forecasting stock indices using radial basis function neural networks optimized by artificial fish swarm algorithm', *Knowledge-Based Systems* 24(3), 2011, 378–385.

Tao, H. 'A wavelet neural network model for forecasting exchange rate integrated with genetic algorithms', *International Journal of Computer Science and Network Security* 6(8), 2006, 60–63.

Thierens, D. 'Adaptive mutation rate control schemes in genetic algorithms', in *Proceedings of the 2002 IEEE World Congress on Computational Intelligence: Congress on Evolutionary Computation*, 2002, 980–985.

Tsai, C. and J. Wu, 'Using neural network ensembles for bankruptcy, prediction and credit scoring', *Expert Systems with Applications* 34(4), 2008, 2639–2649.

Tseng, C., S. Cheng, Y. Wang and J. Peng, 'Artificial neural network model of the hybrid EGARCH volatility of the Taiwan stock index option prices', *Physica A: A Statistical Mechanics and its Applications*, 387(13), 2008, 3192–3200

Tummala, P., P. Srinivasu, P. Avadhani and Y. Murthy, 'Comparison of variable learning rate and Levenberg–Marquardt back-propagation training algorithms for detecting attacks in intrusion detection systems', *International Journal of Computer Science & Engineering* 3(11), 2011, 3572–3581.

Vahidinasab, V., S. Jadid and A. Kazemi, 'Day-ahead price forecasting in restructured power systems using artificial neural networks', *Electric Power Systems Research*, 78(8), 2008, 1332–1342.

Yu, L., K. Lai and S. Wang, 'Multistage RBF neural network ensemble learning, for exchange rates forecasting', *Neurocomputing*, 71(16–18), 2008, 3295–3302.

Zainuddin, Z. and O. Pauline, 'Improved wavelet neural networks for early cancer diagnosis using clustering algorithms', *International Journal of Information and Mathematics Sciences* 6(1), 2010, 30–36.

Zhang, Q. and A. Benveniste, 'Wavelet networks', *IEEE Transactions on Neural Networks* 3, 1982, 889–898.

8 Using argumentation and hybrid evolutionary multi-model partitioning algorithms for efficient portfolio construction

Nikolaos Spanoudakis, Konstantina Pendaraki and Grigorios Beligiannis

1 Introduction

Portfolio management (Markowitz, 1959) is concerned with constructing a portfolio of securities, e.g. stock, bonds, mutual funds (Sharpe, 1966), etc., that maximizes the investor's utility. Traditional portfolio theories (Markowitz, 1959; Ross, 1976; Sharpe, 1964) have been based on unidimensional approaches that do not fit to the multidimensional nature of risk (Colson and Zeleny, 1979), and they do not capture the complexity presented in the relevant dataset.

In a recent work (Spanoudakis and Pendaraki, 2007), where mutual fund (MF) portfolios using an argumentation-based decision-making framework have been constructed, this troublesome situation was resolved. This has been achieved due to the high level of adaptability in the decisions of the portfolio manager or investor, when his environment is changing and the characteristics of the funds are multidimensional, by the use of argumentation. Argumentation can be abstractly defined as the principled interaction of different, potentially conflicting arguments, aiming to arrive at a consistent conclusion (Rahwan *et al.*, 2005). Specifically, rules that determine whether an MF should be included in the portfolio, based on the investment policy, the market context and different investor types policies, are developed using evaluation criteria of fund performance and risk. Also, strategies for resolving conflicts over these rules are defined.

Argumentation was selected among a number of different approaches as it: (1) allows for decision making using conflicting knowledge, (2) allows defining non-static priorities between arguments and (3) the modularity of its representation allows for the easy incorporation of views of different experts. Traditional approaches such as statistical methods need to make strict statistical hypotheses, multi-criteria analysis methods need significantly more effort from experts and neural networks require increased computational effort and are characterized by inability to provide explanations for the results.

It was demonstrated that when taking into account the market context, the results would be better if we could forecast the status of the market of the following investment period. In order to achieve this goal we employed a hybrid system that combines evolutionary algorithms (EAs) (Deb, 2001; Coello *et al.*, 2007), multi-model partitioning (MMP) theory (Pappas *et al.*, 2006, 2008) and the extended Kalman filter (EKF) (Einicke and White, 1999; Prevost *et al.*, 2007). A general description of this algorithm and its application in linear and non-linear data is discussed by Beligiannis *et al.* (2004), while the specific version used in this chapter is presented by Adamopoulos *et al.* (2002), where its successful application to non-linear data is also presented. This algorithm captured our attention because it had been successfully used in the past for accurately predicting the evolution of stock values in the Greek market (Beligiannis *et al.*, 2004). Moreover, there is a lot of work on hybrid EAs and their application to many difficult problems has shown very promising results (Abraham *et al.*, 2007). The problem of predicting the behaviour of the financial market is an open problem and many solutions have been proposed (Markowitz, 1959; Michalewicz, 1996; Patuwo *et al.*, 1993; Spanoudakis and Pendaraki, 2007). However, there isn't any known algorithm able to identify effectively all kinds of behaviours. Also, many traditional methods have been applied to the same problem and the results obtained were not very satisfactory. There are two main difficulties in this problem: first, the search space is huge; second, it comprises many local optima. We chose to apply a hybrid evolutionary system to this problem because EAs comprise a global forecasting technique in the sense that a single formula is sought that allows forecasts of future entries in any series generated by the process, starting at any point in time. In this way they perform well in cases where the search space is huge and/or comprises of many local optima.

In this contribution the PORTRAIT Tool, a hybrid computational intelligence portfolio construction application resulting from the combination of argumentation with hybrid evolutionary multi-model partitioning algorithms, is presented along with the obtained results. Some preliminary results have appeared in Spanoudakis *et al.* (2009). The employed hybrid evolutionary multi-model partitioning algorithms combine the effectiveness of adaptive multi-model partitioning filters of Lainiotis and EAs' robustness and have been successfully applied to many linear and non-linear system identification problems (Beligiannis, 2005; Beligiannis *et al.*, 2004). Specifically, the a-posteriori probability that a specific model, of a bank of the conditional models, is the true model can be used as fitness function for the EAs. In this way, the algorithms identify the true model even in the case where it is not included in the filters' bank. It is clear that the filter's performance is considerably improved through the evolution of the population of the filter's bank, since the algorithms can search the whole parameter space (Beligiannis, 2005; Beligiannis *et al.*, 2004).

The rest of the chapter is organized as follows. Section 2 presents an overview of the investment domain concepts along with a presentation of the dataset used for validating the PORTRAIT Tool. Section 3 outlines the main features of the proposed argumentation-based decision-making framework and the developed argumentation theory. The financial time series forecasting hybrid evolutionary algorithm is presented in Section 4. Section 5 presents the developed tool and discusses the obtained empirical results. Section 6 discusses its added value compared to different approaches in the past and Section 7 summarizes the main findings of this research.

2 Application domain and dataset description

This section first presents the sources of the data that we used for our study. Subsequently, it describes the criteria (or variables) used for creating portfolios.

2.1 The employed dataset

The MF industry has experienced a huge growth at the international level, becoming the primary vehicle through which individuals and most institutions invest in capital markets. Today, there are 20 MF management companies that manage 278 MFs of all types, with assets rising to €6.166 billion (data as of 20 June 2013). Thus, the plethora of possible choices available to investors regarding the investments on MFs makes it very difficult for a simple investor to perform a thorough evaluation of all the investment choices in order to choose funds that lead to superior stock selection in composing efficient portfolios, also according to his decision character.

The sample used in this study is provided by the Association of Greek Institutional Investors and consists of daily data of *domestic equity mutual funds* over the period from January 2000 to December 2008. Daily returns for all domestic equity MFs are examined for this nine-year period. At the end of the examined period, the sample consisted of 80 domestic equity MFs.

For the application of the proposed methodological framework, further information is derived from the official web pages of the Athens Stock Exchange (www.ase.gr) and the Bank of Greece (www.bankofgreece.gr), regarding the return of the market portfolio and the return of the three-month Treasury bill, respectively. This information is very important as the variations of the returns in the ASE-GI, (Athens Stock Exchange – General Index) are expressed through the variation of the prices of the stocks, taking into account the fluctuations and the risk of the financial environment. Furthermore, the three-month Treasury bill is a risk-free asset, and constitutes the benchmark against which the return of an MF or another risky investment is compared.

The database we used is based on the following basic principles: the historical data have been recorded by the MF management companies, and the daily data update is also the responsibility of each company. The net price of a fund is used to calculate the return on investments, as well as the offer and redemption prices.

2.2 Evaluation criteria

According to the portfolio theory of Markowitz (1952), investors are taking into account the two dimensions of risk and return, in order to make an investment decision among alternative funds. According to this theory, the evaluation of MFs should take into account the potentialities that offer the diversification of risk among different funds and the treatment of an MF as portfolio. These two dimensions of risk and return are able to well define the position of a mutual fund in a spectrum of different investments.

The proposed framework is based on five fundamental variables which represent basic characteristics of the examined funds regarding different performance and risk variables. Overall, the return variables measure the expected outcome of the investment in the MFs, while the risk variables measure the uncertainty about the outcome of the investment. Precisely, these variables are the following:

1   the return of the funds,
2   the standard deviation of the returns,
3   the beta coefficient,
4   the Sharpe index,
5   the Treynor index.

These variables are frequently used in the portfolio management research area. Representative studies for the use of these variables are: (1) for the return variable (Brown and Goetzmann, 1995; Simons, 1998); (2) for the beta coefficient (LeClair, 1974; Eun *et al.*, 1991; Elton *et al.*, 1993); (3) for the standard deviation of the returns (Gallo and Swanson, 1996; Simons, 1998); (4) for the Sharpe index (Ippolito, 1989); and (5) for the Treynor index (Redman *et al.*, 2000). A brief description of these criteria follows.

Return of the funds: the final decision of an investor to proceed or not to a certain investment policy is initially taken by the magnitude of return. What an investor really cares for is the actual value of return of an investment defined by the difference between the nominal return and the rate of inflation. The return on an MF investment in a given time period is calculated by taking into account the change in a fund's net asset value. The fund's return in period t is defined in equation (8.1), where R_{pt} is the return of a mutual fund p in period t, NAV_t is the closing net asset value of the fund on the last trading day of the period t, NAV_{t-1} is the closing net asset value of the fund on the last trading day of the period $t-1$ and $DIST_t$ is the income and capital distributions (dividend of the fund) taken during period t.

$$R_{pt} = \frac{NAV_t + DIST_t - NAV_{t-1}}{NAV_{t-1}} \tag{8.1}$$

The *standard deviation* is the most commonly used measure of variability. For an MF the standard deviation σ is used to measure the variability of its daily returns, thus representing the total risk of the fund. The standard deviation of an MF is defined in equation (8.2), where σ is the standard deviation of the MF p in period t, $<Rbar>_{pt}$ is the average return in period t and T is the number of observation (days) in the period for which the standard deviation is being calculated:

$$\sigma = \sqrt{\frac{1}{T} \sum (R_{pt} - \bar{R}_{pt})^2} \tag{8.2}$$

The β coefficient (*β*) is a measure of a fund's risk in relation to the capital risk. It is the slope coefficient in a regression of the return of the portfolio being evaluated against the return of a proxy for the market portfolio. It represents the systematic risk and it is a crucial factor in pricing risky assets and in determining the risk of a totally diversified portfolio. In other words, for an MF, the *β* coefficient represents the variance on the value of the fund in relation to the capital risk, and it precisely measures the relative riskiness (variability) of the fund. Thus, the value that the *β* coefficient is taking is not representative of funds' variability in absolute terms, but it shows its variability in relation to the market index. The higher the value of the *β* coefficient of an investment is, the riskier the investment is. The *β* coefficient shows the sensitivity of mutual funds' value on the increasing and decreasing ratings of financial markets. The *β* coefficient is defined in equation (8.3), where $cov(R_{pt}, R_{Mt})$ is the covariance of the daily return of an MF with the daily return of the market portfolio (Athens Stock Exchange), and $var(R_{Mt})$ is the variance of the daily return of the market portfolio:

$$\beta = cov(R_{pt}, R_{Mt}) / var(R_{Mt}) \tag{8.3}$$

The traditional total performance measure, the *Sharpe index* (Sharpe, 1966), or alternatively the reward-to-variability ratio, is a useful measure of performance for portfolios that are not well diversified. The Sharpe index is used to measure the expected return of a fund per unit of risk, defined by the standard deviation. This measure is defined as the ratio $(R_{pt} - R_{ft}) / \sigma$ where R_{ft} is the return of the risk-free portfolio in period *t*, which is calculated from the three-month Treasury bill. The evaluation of MFs with this index shows that an MF with higher performance per unit of risk is the best-managed fund, while an MF with lower performance per unit of risk is the worst-managed fund.

The *Treynor index* (Treynor, 1965) is obtained by simply substituting volatility for variability in the Sharpe index. Thus, the Treynor index is similar to the Sharpe index except that performance is measured as the risk premium per unit of systematic (*β* coefficient) and not of total risk. This measure is defined as the ratio $(R_{pt} - R_{ft}) / \beta$. The evaluation of MFs with this index shows similarly to the Sharpe index that an MF with higher performance per unit of risk is the best-managed fund, while an MF with lower performance per unit of risk is the worst managed fund.

Table 8.1 reports some useful descriptive statistics of the variables used in the analysis over the period 2000–2008. The examined period contains both bull and bear market sub-periods due to major fluctuations, a considerable decline in all stock prices and high liquidity conditions that characterize the Greek market in the last decade. Thus, negative returns are presented in 2000–2002, where the values of the two traditional indexes, Sharpe and Treynor, are also negative. The period 2003–2007 presented positive returns, with positive Sharpe and Treynor indexes. In 2008 we have negative returns. Additionally, the volatility of returns, presented by the standard deviation, is high over the whole period. Finally, on average, the values of the *β* coefficient fluctuated during the examined period,

Table 8.1 Descriptive statistics for the five variables for each year

Year		Return	σ	β	Sharpe ratio	Treynor ratio
2000	Mean	−40.78	38.24	0.90	−2.63	−0.37
	Standard deviation	11.28	74.82	0.17	0.57	0.20
	Minimum	−62.03	10.79	0.42	−3.41	−0.88
	Maximum	−12.71	606.10	1.77	0.73	0.99
2001	Mean	−23.23	36.12	0.91	−1.42	−0.17
	Standard deviation	6.67	45.25	0.23	0.56	0.11
	Minimum	−38.90	10.29	0.32	−2.41	−0.51
	Maximum	5.80	260.83	1.98	0.53	0.28
2002	Mean	−27.80	13.83	0.77	−3.25	−0.24
	Standard deviation	6.83	2.04	0.10	0.56	0.04
	Minimum	−44.03	5.90	0.56	−4.69	−0.36
	Maximum	−3.53	18.47	0.99	−1.38	−0.14
2003	Mean	19.36	16.31	0.79	0.56	0.05
	Standard deviation	12.49	7.41	0.11	0.83	0.08
	Minimum	−30.61	7.15	0.55	−3.86	−0.30
	Maximum	46.57	72.98	1.31	2.09	0.23
2004	Mean	9.53	12.66	0.80	0.05	0.002
	Standard deviation	8.96	1.09	0.08	0.64	0.04
	Minimum	−8.38	9.83	0.58	−1.32	−0.09
	Maximum	25.27	15.51	1.03	1.01	0.06
2005	Mean	26.33	10.99	0.79	1.36	0.08
	Standard deviation	7.75	1.66	0.12	0.49	0.03
	Minimum	−0.71	4.54	0.33	−0.43	−0.08
	Maximum	38.16	14.56	1.08	2.52	0.17
2006	Mean	25.48	17.37	0.64	0.90	0.90
	Standard deviation	1.11	0.27	0.04	0.01	0.01
	Minimum	−1.14	6.34	−0.17	0.63	0.63
	Maximum	50.09	21.22	1.62	1.02	1.02
2007	Mean	12.61	14.45	−0.35	0.83	−11.53
	Standard deviation	0.73	0.24	0.06	0.02	3.40
	Minimum	−2.35	6.88	−1.98	0.10	−187.76
	Maximum	24.76	20.31	0.88	1.06	10.29
2008	Mean	−57.88	5.05			
	Standard deviation	5.05				
	Minimum	−66.05				
	Maximum	−43.30				

where the highest values of β are reported in the 2000 and 2001 (negative returns), presenting the riskiest investment fund opportunities.

3 Argumentation-based decision making

In this section we first present the argumentation framework that we used and then we focus on the knowledge engineering part of the work.

3.1 The argumentation framework

There are situations where systems need to support decision making under complex preference policies that take into account different factors. Argumentation technology caters for such situations (Bench-Capon and Dunne, 2007). Argumentation can be abstractly defined as the formal interaction of different conflicting arguments for and against some conclusion due to different reasons and provides the appropriate semantics for resolving such conflicts. The conclusion can be an action to take at a specific time, the validity of a proposition, etc. Thus, a decision-making entity (e.g. a program) may use argumentation to perform its individual reasoning when it needs to make decisions under complex preferences policies in a highly dynamic environment (Kakas and Moraitis, 2003).

There are argumentation frameworks that use object-level arguments for representing the decision policies and then they use priority arguments expressing preferences on the object-level arguments in order to resolve possible conflicts. Additional priority arguments can be employed for resolving potential conflicts between priority arguments of the previous level. Therefore, these argumentation frameworks allow for the representation of dynamic preferences under the form of dynamic priorities over arguments.

Such an open-source framework is Gorgias (Kakas and Moraitis, 2003), built in Prolog. We used it for deciding which MFs will be used for composing an investment portfolio (the interested reader can download it from www.cs.ucy. ac.cy/~nkd/gorgias). This framework has been successfully applied in the past in different applications, for determining the pricing policy of a product in the retail business sector (Spanoudakis and Moraitis, 2009) and for selecting the best transportation means for a mobility-impaired person (Moraitis and Spanoudakis, 2007). Gorgias allows defining dynamic priorities between arguments, which means that the priorities of rules can depend on context. To present an example of how we modelled the application domain we need to give some formal definitions, as they were given by Kakas and Moraitis (2003):

Definition 1. A theory is a pair (T, P) whose sentences are formulae in the background monotonic logic $(L, \vdash)$ of the form $L \leftarrow L_1, \ldots, L_n$, where $L, L_1, \ldots, L_n$ are positive or negative ground literals. For rules in P the head L refers to an (irreflexive) higher priority relation, i.e. L has the general form $L = h\_p(rule1, rule2)$. The derivability relation, $\vdash$, of the background logic is given by the simple inference rule of *modus ponens*.

An argument for a literal L in a theory (T, P) is any subset, T, of this theory that derives L, $T \vdash L$, under the background logic. A part of the theory $T_0 \subset T$, is the background theory that contains the facts. Based on these facts the rules will come to new conclusions.

An argument attacks another when they derive a contradictory conclusion. These two arguments are considered as conflicting arguments a. A conflicting argument (from T) is admissible if it counter-attacks all the arguments that attack it. It counter-attacks an argument if it can use priority arguments (from P) and make itself at least as strong as a conflicting argument.

Definition 2. An agent's argumentative policy theory is a theory $T=((T, T_0), P_R, P_C)$ where T contains the argument rules in the form of definite Horn logic rules, P_R contains priority rules which are also definite Horn rules with head $h\_p(r_1, r_2)$ s.t. $r_1, r_2 \in T$ and all rules in P_C are also priority rules with head $h\_p(R_1, R_2)$ s.t. $R_1, R_2 \in P_R \cup P_C$. T_0 contains auxiliary rules of the agent's background knowledge.

All in all, for defining the decision-making theory we specify rules in three different levels. The first level (T) defines the (background theory) rules that refer directly to the subject domain and reflect the knowledge needed for reaching the different goals of the knowledge base, called the *Object-level Decision Rules*. In the second level we use rules to define priorities over the first-level rules for each identified situation resolving possible conflicts. These situations can reflect the needs of a *role* that the decision maker can assume or a *context* in which he finds himself, usually including a *default context*. Finally, the third-level rules define priorities over the rules of the previous level but also over the rules of this level in order to define *specific contexts*, where different contexts can be combined. A comprehensive example on how the rules are developed and deployed in these three levels is given in Section 3.2.2.

3.2 The decision maker's argumentation theory

The first choice that we had to make was what would be the goal of the decision-making process. This goal had to be something that would be the head of the object-level rules. Our problem was to compose portfolios of MFs and we had expert knowledge regarding when an investor should buy or not an MF based on its performance on the different criteria (variables). Thus we defined that the goal of the rule base would be to find out which MFs to select. The facts of our base would be the performance of the MFs on the five different criteria (variables) presented in Section 2, combined with information coming from the environment (context) and the investor profile (role). Therefore, our object-level rules have as their head the predicate *selectFund/1* and its negation.

3.2.1 Experts' knowledge

For capturing the experts' knowledge we consulted the literature from the economics field but also the empirical results of applying the found knowledge in the Greek market. Thus, we identified two types of investors, *aggressive* and *moderate*. An aggressive investor wants to chase the highest returns regardless of the risk related to them; the higher the risk the higher the possible returns on investment (RoI). Thus, an aggressive investor is placing his capital upon funds with high return levels and high systematic risk (high values on the β coefficient criterion). On the other hand, the moderate investor prefers funds with high return levels and low or medium systematic risk. For modelling the roles we defined the *investor/1* predicate. An aggressive investor is expressed with the predicate *investor(aggressive)*, while a moderate investor with the predicate *investor(moderate)*.

The next part was to classify the MFs in three groups for each performance criterion. For example, we needed to have funds with high, medium and low returns, funds with high, medium and low β coefficients, etc. To define this classification we used the following definitions. Let F be a set of MFs. Let the set C^y be the *partially ordered set by* $\leq$ of the values of the performance of the funds on criterion C for a given year y. Thus, there is a function $f : F \rightarrow C^y$ that defines a one-to-one relation from the set of funds F to the set of values C^y. Now that the set C^y is ordered from the least performing MF to the best MF, we can create groups of MFs by selecting subsets. In our case, we wanted to create a set with the 30 per cent best MFs (the set of high-valued funds), a set of the worst 30 per cent of the MFs (the set of low-valued funds) and a set with those remaining if we remove the previous two from C^y (the set of medium-valued funds).

Formally, if $s \in N$ is the size of C^y, then the *set of high-valued funds* $H^y \subset C^y$ can be defined as the last m elements of C^y, where $m = [(3/10)s]$ (m defines how many are the 30 per cent of MFs). Thus, H^y contains the higher 30 per cent (rounded down) of the values in C^y. The *set of low-valued funds* $L^y \subset C^y$ is similarly defined as the first m elements of C^y. Finally, the *set of medium valued funds* $M^y \subset C^y$ is defined as $M^y = (C^y \cap L^{yC}) \cap H^{yC}$, i.e. those funds that belong to C^y but not to H^y or L^y.

Thus, for the return on investment variable we defined the predicates *highR/1*, *mediumR/1* and *lowR/1*, for the β coefficient variable the predicates *highB/1*, *mediumB/1* and *lowB/1*, for the Sharpe index variable the predicates *highSharpe/1*, *mediumSharpe/1* and *lowSharpe/1*, for the Treynor index variable the predicates *highTreynor/1*, *mediumTreynor/1* and *lowTreynor/1*, and for the standard deviation of the returns variable the predicates *highSTDEV/1*, *mediumSTDEV/1* and *lowSTDEV/1*.

Regarding the context of the investment, we defined a default context where the selected funds are those with high returns. To represent the market context we defined the bull market and the bear market. In a bull market, those funds that give larger returns in an increasing market are selected. Such funds have high systematic (the β coefficient) or total risk (standard deviation). In a bear market, we select those funds that have lower risk and their returns are changing more smoothly than market changes (funds with low systematic and total risk). We use the *market/1* predicate with the instances *market(bull)* and *market(bear)* for representing the bull and bear market, respectively.

Investors can be interested not only in a fund's return but also in the risks they are willing to take to achieve these returns. The knowledge of the degree of risk incorporated in the portfolio of a mutual fund gives the investors the opportunity to know how much higher is the return of a fund in relation to the expected one, based on its risk. Therefore, some investors select portfolios with high performance per unit of risk. Such portfolios are characterized by high performance levels, high reward-to-variability ratios (Sharpe ratio) and high reward-to-volatility ratios (Treynor ratio). MFs with these characteristics are considered to be the best managed funds.

3.2.2 Combining contexts and roles

In this third level of modelling rules we needed to define strategies for combining the roles and contexts that we defined previously. We provide a brief summary of the strategies that we developed for the different combinations:

- The combination of the *bull market* context and the *aggressive investor* role expands the aggressive role choices to those of the bull market.
- *The aggressive investor* role *in the bear market* context accepts the union of their preference (all choices of the individual role and context) expanded by those MFs that have medium systematic risk MFs while having low total risk.
- *A moderate investor* role in a *bear market* context no longer selects a medium risk (systematic or total) fund (only low is acceptable). Thus, compared to the bear market context that selects low total and systematic risk, low total or systematic risk funds are accepted.
- *The moderate investor* role in the *bull market* context limits the selections of the bull market context to those of medium or low risk.
- In *bull market* context and *high performance per unit of risk* context, the final portfolio is the union of the individual context and role selections.
- In *bear market* context and *high performance per unit of risk* context, the final portfolio is their union, except that the bear market context no longer selects MFs with low reward-to-variability ratio (Sharpe ratio) or with low reward-to-volatility ratio (Treynor ratio).
- *Aggressive investor* role and *high performance per unit of risk* context. The final portfolio is their union, except that the aggressive investor no longer selects MFs with low reward-to-variability ratio or with low reward-to-volatility ratio.
- *Moderate investor* role and *high performance per unit of risk* context. The final portfolio is their union, except that the moderate investor no longer selects MFs with low reward-to-variability ratio or with low reward-to-volatility ratio.
- Every role and context has higher priority when combined with the general context.

Besides the abovementioned predicates and rules, the knowledge base also contains the facts: the performance and risk variables values for each MF and the thresholds for each group of values for each year. The rules in equations (8.4)–(8.6) are an example of the object-level rules (level 1 rules of the framework – *T*). In presenting the rules we adopt a Prolog-like style, where variables start with a capital letter, while literals start with a lowercase letter.

$$r_1(Fund): selectFund(Fund) \leftarrow highR(Fund) \tag{8.4}$$

$$r_2(Fund): \neg selectFund(Fund) \leftarrow highB(Fund) \tag{8.5}$$

$$r_3(Fund): \neg selectFund(Fund) \leftarrow mediumB(Fund) \tag{8.6}$$

Thus, the r_1 rule (see equation (8.4)) states that a high-performance fund should be selected, while the r_2 rule (see equation (8.5)) states that a high systematic risk MF should not be selected. The r_3 rule (see equation (8.6)) states that an MF with a systematic risk in the medium group should not be selected.

Then, in the second level we assign priorities over the object-level rules. These rules are defined by experts and express their preferences in the form of priorities (P_R) between the object-level rules that should take place within defined contexts and roles. For example, the level 1 rules with signatures r_1 and r_2 are conflicting. In the default context the first one has priority, while the moderate investor role reverses this priority. Similarly, the level 1 rules with signatures r_1 and r_3 are conflicting. In the default context the first one has priority, while the bear market role reverses this priority (see equations (8.7)–(8.10)).

$$R_1: h\_p(r_1(Fund),r_2(Fund)) \leftarrow true \qquad (8.7)$$

$$R_2: h\_p(r_1(Fund),r_3(Fund)) \leftarrow true \qquad (8.8)$$

$$R_3: h\_p(r_2(Fund),r_1(Fund)) \leftarrow investor(moderate) \qquad (8.9)$$

$$R_4: h\_p(r_3(Fund),r_1(Fund)) \leftarrow market(bear) \qquad (8.10)$$

Rules R_1 (see equation (8.7)) and R_2 (equation (8.8)) define the priorities set for the default context, i.e. an investor selects a fund that has high RoI even if it has medium or high risk. Rule R_3 (see equation (8.9)) defines the priorities for the moderate role (within which, the fund selection process is cautious and does not select a high RoI fund if it has high systematic risk). Rule R_4 (see equation (8.10)) is one of the four rules for the bear market context (that does not select a high RoI fund if it has medium systematic risk).

In P_C (level 3 rules) the strategy for integrating the different roles and context rules is defined in the form of priority rules. Both the moderate role and market context take precedence over the default context (rules C_1 and C_2, respectively, see equations (8.11) and (8.12)). When combining the *moderate investor* role (accepts only medium or low systematic risk MFs) and *bear market* context (accepts only low systematic and total risk MFs), for example, the moderate investor role could accept a medium systematic risk MF only if its total risk is low (rule C_3 and C_4, see equation (8.13) and (8.14)).

$$C_1: h\_p(R_3, R_1) \leftarrow true \qquad (8.11)$$

$$C_2: h\_p(R_4, R_2) \leftarrow true \qquad (8.12)$$

$$C_3: h\_p(R_2, R_4) \leftarrow lowSTDEV(Fund), market(bear), investor(moderate) \qquad (8.13)$$

$$C_4: h\_p(C_3, C_2) \leftarrow true \qquad (8.14)$$

Thus, a moderate investor in a bear market context would select an MF with medium systematic risk if the total risk is low. In the latter case, the argument r_1 is the only admissible one, as it takes along the priority arguments R_2, C_3 and C_4 and becomes stronger than the conflicting r_3 argument that can only take along the R_4 and C_2 priority arguments. That is because C_4 states that C_3 is stronger than C_2. Thus, the MF is inserted in the portfolio.

An issue with the above rules is that the facts *market(bear)* or (exclusive) *market(bull)* could not be safely determined for the next investment period. In the application version presented by Spanoudakis and Pendaraki (2007) it was just assumed to remain the same as at the time of the investment. Thus, assuming that the context policy is always valid for the specific context, it would be very convenient if we could forecast the status of the financial market for the next investment period.

4 Forecasting the status of the financial market

The problem of fitting an autoregressive moving average model with exogenous input (ARMAX) or its non-linear version (NARMAX) to a given time series has attracted much attention because it arises in a large variety of applications, such as time series prediction in economic and biomedical data, adaptive control, speech analysis and synthesis, neural networks, radar and sonar, fuzzy systems, wavelets and many more (Haykin, 1991). As a result, a large variety of new methods for modelling static and dynamic linear and non-linear systems has been designed and implemented. Therefore, it is important to understand what are the opportunities, limitations and pitfalls of the several approaches, in order to obtain reliable designs towards real-time applications. Furthermore, the effect of varying process parameters on system performance is of crucial importance, specifically when the desired system performance alters and deteriorates due to the disturbances of the system's parameters every time the design is based on nominal parameter values. Therefore, it is more than desirable to be able to incorporate parameters' variation into system design.

The subject of nonlinear time series modelling has been studied extensively from different points of view, including statistics, identification theory, approximation theory, signal processing, information theory, physics and optimization theory. Consequently, a large number of numerous approximate non-linear estimation algorithms have been proposed for certain data models. One of the most widely known approaches is the so-called EKF (Song and Speyer, 1985). The development of the EKF is based on a linearization procedure performed around the last estimation of the state vector. The idea to handle a non-linear model in this way is quite natural and the filtering procedure is fairly simple and efficient. The performance of the EKF is reduced in the case of low signal-to-noise ratio. A different adaptive approach, based on the partitioning theorem, is the multi-model adaptive filter (MMAF) (Lainiotis, 1976). The MMAF operates on a bank of EKFs, each fitting to a different model. The filter converges to the conditional model that gives the maximum a-posteriori probability. Thus, a non-linear filtering problem can be faced efficiently. Despite its applicability, it is known that the EKF suffers from the proper determination of the initial conditions that affects dramatically the convergence of the algorithm. In the literature (Chui and Chen, 2008) some methods are proposed to determine the initial conditions, but there is no unified framework for the general solution to this problem.

The hybrid evolutionary forecasting algorithm used in this contribution is a generic applied evolutionary hybrid technique, which combines the effectiveness of adaptive multi-model partitioning filters and EAs' robustness (Adamopoulos *et al.*, 2002). Specifically, the a-posteriori probability that a specific model, of a bank of the conditional models, is the true model, can be used as a fitness function for the EA. In this way, the algorithm identifies the true model even in the case where it is not included in the filters' bank. It is clear that the filter's performance is considerably improved through the evolution of the population of the filters' bank, since the algorithm can search the whole parameter space. The proposed hybrid evolutionary algorithm can be applied to linear and non-linear data; is not restricted to the Gaussian case; does not require any knowledge of the model switching law; is practically implementable, computationally efficient and applicable to online/adaptive operation; and, finally, exhibits very satisfactory performance as indicated by simulation experiments (Beligiannis *et al.*, 2004). The structure of the hybrid evolutionary system used is depicted in Figure 8.1.

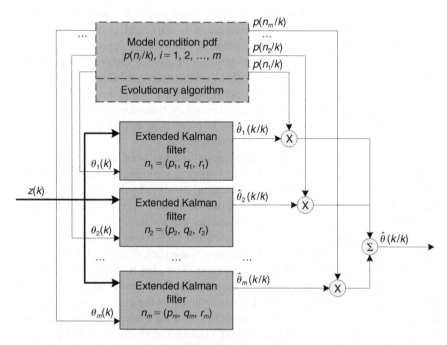

Figure 8.1 The structure of the hybrid evolutionary multi-model partitioning algorithm used for financial time series forecasting.

As presented by Beligiannis *et al.* (2004), there are two major quantities that must be estimated; the model order $n(p,q,r)$ and the unknown parameter vector $Q(t)$. The estimation method used is the MMAF as it is obtained from Lainiotis partition theorem. Our goal is to achieve the optimal estimation for both estimated quantities and particularly for the model order n. The only information we have for these parameters is that they belong to a set or a space (finite or infinite). It is obvious that if the unknown parameters belong to a finite-discrete set with small cardinality, the MMAF is one of the most appropriate and most effective methods to estimate them. It is also widely known that EAs perform well when the space which will be searched has a large number of elements. So, EAs can be used when the unknown parameters belong to a space with large cardinality or belong to an infinite space or follow a probability distribution. Then, we should optimize with EAs the model-conditional probability density function (pdf) for discrete sample space. The pdf is the fitness function for the EA, for the several values of the unknown parameters $n=(p,q,r)$ and $Q(t)$, underlying the above constraints.

The representation used for the genomes of the population of the EA is the following. We use a mapping that transforms a fixed dimensional internal representation to variable dimensional problem instances. Each genome consists of a vector x of real values $xi \in \Re$, $i=1,\ldots, k$ and a bit string b of binary digits $bi \in \{0, 1\}$, $i=1,\ldots, k$. Real values are summed up as long as the corresponding bits are equal. Obviously, k is an upper bound for the dimension of the resulting parameter vector. We use the first $k/3$ real values for the autoreggressive part, the second $k/3$ real values for the moving average part and the last $k/3$ real values for the exogenous input part. An example of this mapping is presented in Figure 8.2. For a more detailed description of this mapping refer to Beligiannis *et al.* (2004). In this specific implementation the number of genes composing each genome of the EA equals 12. Subsequently and according to our model, the first four real values are used for the autoregressive part, the second four real values are used for the moving average part, and the last four real values are used for the exogenous input part.

At first an initial population of m genomes is created at random (each genome consists of a vector of real values and a bit string). In this specific implementation the number of possible solutions that are evolved, that is the population size

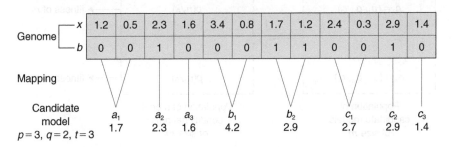

Figure 8.2 Mapping from a fixed dimensional internal representation to a variable length NARMAX parameter vector. The resulting order is $n(p, q, r) = (3, 2, 3)$.

of the EA, equals 20. Since there are no obvious theoretical criteria to determine the population size of the EA, we decided, in order to determine the EA's population size, to follow the approach proposed by former contributions in the literature (Beligiannis, 2005; Beligiannis *et al.*, 2004). As such, we performed exhaustive experiments testing many different values of the EA's population size ranging from 1 to 100. Experimental results showed that the most proper value for the population size of the EA is 20.

As stated before, each vector of real values represents a possible value of the NARMAX model order and its parameters. For each such population we apply an MMAF with EKFs and have as a result the model-conditional pdf of each candidate model. This pdf is the fitness of each candidate model, namely the fitness of each genome of the population (Figure 8.3).

The reproduction operator we decided to use is the classic biased roulette wheel selection according to the fitness function value of each possible model order (Michalewicz, 1996). As far as crossover is concerned, we use the one-point crossover operator for the binary strings and the uniform crossover operator for the real values (Michalewicz, 1996). For both crossover operators a probability equal to 0.9 was used. Finally, we use the flip mutation operator for the binary strings and the Gaussian mutation operator for the real values (Michalewicz, 1996).

As known, in Gaussian mutation, when a gene is selected for mutation, a random value is generated based on a Gaussian distribution, and this value is added onto the existing value of that gene. The width of the Gaussian is a percentage of the range of possible values for that gene and the resulting combined value is truncated if necessary to ensure it remains in the valid range. The use of the Gaussian function ensures that the mutated value is likely to be close to the original value, but also allows occasional larger changes, preventing the mutation operator from being overly disruptive while still maintaining the ability to break free from local optima. Since there are no obvious theoretical criteria to determine the width of the Gaussian mutation operator's width, we decided, in our approach, that the Gaussian function's width be set to 1/20 of the range of

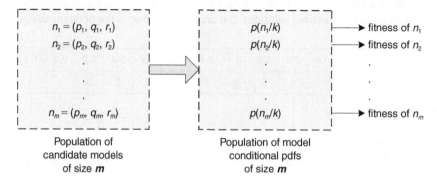

Figure 8.3 The fitness of each candidate model is the model conditional pdf (*m* is the number of the EKFs in the MMAF).

each allele following similar approaches in the literature (Temby *et al.*, 2005; Yoon and Kim, 2012).

For both mutation operators a probability equal to 0.1 was used. Every new generation of possible solutions iterates the same process as the old ones and all this process may be repeated as many generations as we desire or till the fitness function has value 1, which is the maximum value it is able to have as a probability. For a more detailed description of this hybrid evolutionary system, refer to Beligiannis *et al.* (2004).

The approach followed in this contribution is different compared to the one presented by Beligiannis *et al.* (2004). The difference lies in the calculation of the output value xi of each filter i. In Beligiannis *et al.* (2004), at each step of the algorithm, the past values of xi, used in order to estimate the next value of xi, are the ones that have already been estimated by the algorithm up to this step. All these values (outputs of each filter) are then used in order to estimate the next value of the output vector x. The method presented in this contribution uses a different approach in order to estimate x. The number of estimated values of xi, used in order to estimate the next value of xi, is smaller than the total length of the time series that has been estimated till this point. The length of past values used in each generation in order to estimate the next value of x equals to $n/2$, where n is the total length of the time series to be estimated. Every new value of x, estimated by the algorithm, is added to this time series of length $n/2$ and the oldest one is removed in order for this time series to sustain a length of $n/2$. The value of $n/2$ was not selected arbitrarily. We have conducted exhaustive experiments using many different values. The value of $n/2$ that has been finally selected was the most effective one, that is the one that resulted in the best prediction results. In this specific implementation the value of parameter n equals 30, that is 30 semesters are used as past values for forecasting, starting from the first semester of 1985. Of course, as stated before, every new value of x (status of the financial market for a specific semester), estimated by the algorithm, is added to this time series of length 30 and the oldest one is removed in order for this time series to sustain a length of 30.

Thus, the hybrid evolutionary multi-model partitioning algorithm presented in Figure 8.1 is used in order to forecast the behaviour of the financial market in relation to its current status. The market is characterized as a bull market if it is forecast to rise in the next semester, or as a bear market if it is forecast to fall. We used the percentage of the return of the Athens Stock Exchange index for each semester (in relation to the previous semester) starting from 1985 to the years of our sample data (2001–2008). Our algorithm indicates a bull market if this percentage is forecast to be positive or a bear market if it is forecast to be negative. The algorithm performed very well considering that it could forecast the next semester market behaviour with a success rate of 93.33 per cent (14 out of 15 correct predictions), as presented in Table 8.2.

One can argue, after studying the results presented in Table 8.2, that the forecast values of change are far different from the actual values of the change of the financial market index. However, the algorithm is not applied in order to predict

Table 8.2 Results obtained after applying the forecasting algorithm to forecast the sign (positive or negative) of the return of the Athens Stock Exchange index for each semester of the investment period

Semester	RASE change (%)	Forecast value
First semester 2001	−19.112	−2.409
Second semester 2001	−5.267	−2.989
First semester 2002	−14.822	−0.826
Second semester 2002	−21.206	−2.334
First semester 2003	**6.468**	**−3.412**
Second semester 2003	21.190	1.025
First semester 2004	1.535	3.391
Second semester 2004	19.219	6.656
First semester 2005	8.357	3.067
Second semester 2005	19.204	1.343
First semester 2006	0.831	3.118
Second semester 2006	18.984	1.091
First semester 2007	8.440	0.0125
Second semester 2007	6.561	0.3002
First semester 2008	−33.946	−0.002

Note
The row in bold indicates the failed forecast

specific values of the financial market index. It is used, as stated above, in order to predict the next semester financial market behaviour, which is the behaviour of the financial market in relation to its current status (whether the financial market index of the current semester is higher or lower compared to the financial market index of the previous semester). The results presented in Table 8.2 demonstrate that the proposed hybrid evolutionary forecasting algorithm achieves very satisfactory results in doing this.

5 The PORTRAIT tool

The PORTfolio constRuction based on ArgumentatIon Technology (PORTRAIT) tool development and architecture is presented in this section. Then we present the results obtained using this tool.

5.1 System architecture

The portfolio generation application is a Java program creating a human–machine interface and managing its modules, namely the decision-making module, which is a Prolog rule base using the Gorgias framework (we used the SWI-Prolog free software Prolog environment, www.swi-prolog.org), and the forecasting module, which is a Matlab (www.mathworks.com/products/matlab) implementation of the forecasting hybrid system (see Figure 8.4). Moreover, we have developed a tool for a popular spreadsheet program that allows automatic extraction of the MFs' facts from spreadsheet data (see the system architecture in Figure 8.4).

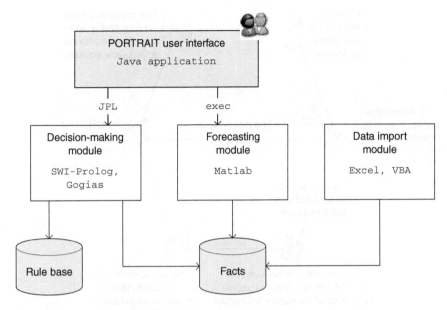

Figure 8.4 The PORTRAIT system architecture.

The application connects to the SWI-Prolog module using the provided Java interface (JPL) that allows for inserting facts to an existing rule base and running it for reaching goals. The goals can be captured and returned to the Java program. The application connects to Matlab by executing it in a system shell. The Matlab program writes the results of the algorithm to a file. The application first executes the forecasting module, then updates the rule base with the needed facts, with the investor profile (selected roles) and, finally, queries the decision-making module, setting as a goal the funds to select for participation in the final portfolio. Thus, after the execution of the forecasting module, the predicate *market/1* is determined as bull or bear and inserted as a fact in the rule base before the decision-making process is launched.

Figure 8.5 shows the business process related to using the PORTRAIT tool and Figure 8.6 shows a screenshot of the integrated system. In the screenshot the reader can see two scenarios for an investment portfolio for the end of 2005. Since the 2006 data are already in the database, the reader can also see the expected return of this portfolio. In a real situation, though, these data are not available, so the client gets only an indication on the return based on the current year's returns. The reader can also notice that in the proposed portfolios each fund participates with an equal share. There are three more options in which the fund participation is related to its performance in the current or previous years. If the reader wants to find out more about the portfolio composition strategies, our related work can be consulted (Pendaraki and Spanoudakis, 2012).

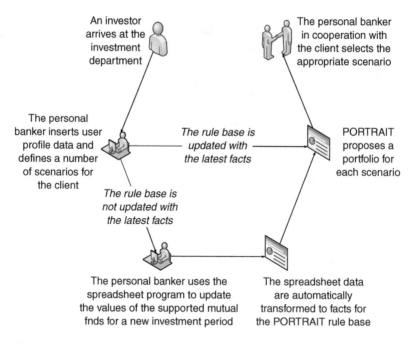

An investor
arrives at the
investment
department

The personal banker
in cooperation with
the client selects the
appropriate scenario

The personal
banker inserts user
profile data and
defines a number
of scenarios for
the client

*The rule base is
updated with
the latest facts*

PORTRAIT
proposes a
portfolio for
each scenario

*The rule base is
not updated with
the latest facts*

The personal banker uses the
spreadsheet program to update
the values of the supported mutual
fnds for a new investment period

The spreadsheet data
are automatically
transformed to facts for
the PORTRAIT rule base

Figure 8.5 The investment process using the PORTRAIT tool.

5.2 System validation

For validating the PORTRAIT tool we defined scenarios for all years for which
we had available data (2000–2008) and for all combinations of contexts. That
resulted in seven simple scenarios (general, forecast market, aggressive investor,
moderate investor, high-performance contexts, bear market and bull market) and
11 specific-context scenarios (the two investor types combined with the market
status, plus the two investor types combined with the high-performance option,
plus the market status combined with the high performance option) all run for
eight years each (we could not run a scenario for 2008 as we did not have the
2009 data for evaluating the scenarios). Each one of the examined scenarios
refers to different investment choices and leads to the selection of different
numbers and combinations of MFs.

In Table 8.3 the reader can inspect the average RoI for all 18 scenarios compared with the average RoI of the General Index of the Athens Stock Exchange
(RASE) and the average return of all the considered MFs. The table data are
sorted according to the 2008 average returns column. In order to compare our
results with our previous works (Spanoudakis and Pendaraki, 2007; Spanoudakis
et al., 2009) we also present the average returns from 2001 to 2006 (five years).

Looking at Table 8.3 it is clear that there have been significant improvements.
We extended our MFs database and we have worked with the knowledge base

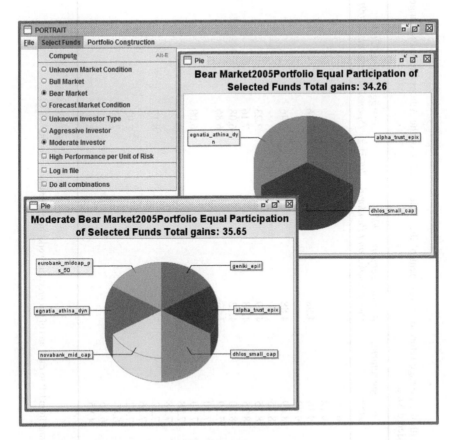

Figure 8.6 A screenshot of the PORTRAIT tool.

and provided better strategies for combining the different contexts. Moreover, we included more scenarios, including the possibility of an investor continuously investing in a bull market or a bear market context, which proved quite success-ful as, in this version, the best scenarios are those of the moderate investor com-bined with the bear market context, and the high performance per unit of risk preference combined with the bull market context.

Thus, we proved that by using effective strategies in the third preference rules layer the decision maker can optimize the combined contexts. In Figure 8.7 we present a detailed graph of the RoI of the bear market context, the moderate investor role and the specific context that combines them for all eight years of our database. Notice that by using effective rules at the third level we can add knowledge and have better results. For example, in 2003, 2005 and 2006 the specific context has better results than both simple contexts. The same holds for other specific contexts, i.e. the market forecast context combined with the moderate role, and the moderate role combined with the bear market context.

Table 8.3 Average RoI for all 18 scenarios compared with the average return on investment of the General Index of the Athens Stock Exchange (RASE) and the average return of all the considered MFs.

Portfolio	Average returns, 2008	Average returns, 2006	Average returns, 2006 (Spanoudakis and Pendaraki, 2007)	Average returns, 2006 (Spanoudakis et al., 2009)
Moderate – bear market	2.30	9.62		
High perfomance – bull market	2.07	9.18		7.16
High perfomance	2.02	9.18		
Bear market	1.91	9.09		
High perfomance – aggressive	1.72	8.69	4.98	7.46
High perfomance – bear market	1.64	8.75	4.88	
High perfomance – market forecast	1.64	8.75		7.23
High perfomance – moderate	1.27	8.25	4.59	7.16
Market forecast – moderate	1.24	8.20	4.98	6.08
General	0.84	7.59	4.72	6.86
Aggressive – bear market	0.77	7.50	3.53	
Moderate	0.71	7.50	4.02	6.09
Bull market	0.65	7.28		
Aggressive – bull market	0.65	7.28		
Market forecast	0.57	7.32	3.72	8.17
Moderate – bull market	0.53	7.26		
Market forecast – aggressive	0.40	7.02	3.56	7.92
Aggressive	0.36	6.89	2.65	7.38
RASE	−1.08	6.85		
All Mutual Funds Average	−1.79	4.95		

Notes
The table data are sorted according to the 2008 average returns.
We also present the 2006 average returns of this work (third column from left to righ) and of our previous works in the next two columns

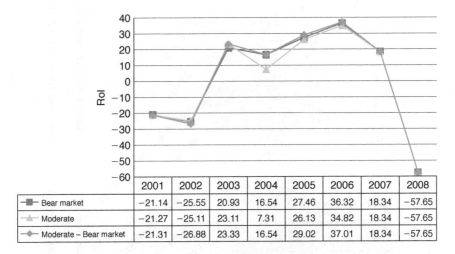

	2001	2002	2003	2004	2005	2006	2007	2008
Bear market	−21.14	−25.55	20.93	16.54	27.46	36.32	18.34	−57.65
Moderate	−21.27	−25.11	23.11	7.31	26.13	34.82	18.34	−57.65
Moderate − Bear market	−21.31	−26.88	23.33	16.54	29.02	37.01	18.34	−57.65

Figure 8.7 The bear market context, the moderate investor role and the specific context that combines them returns for all eight years.

Besides the increase in average return (1 per cent average for all contexts), another important result of this contribution is that the best scenarios do not change as the investment period expands. In Figure 8.8 the reader can see all the different investment scenarios and their compound return (all values are percentages) for two years (2002), four years (2004), six years (2006) and all eight years (2008) of our dataset. The ranking of the best scenarios is generally the same in all investment periods, which means we can somehow extract safe conclusions about the Greek MF market. The average MF return is always far lower than our lowest scenario. The same holds for the RASE, except for 2004, where it beats a few of our scenarios. Looking at Table 8.4, which is sorted according to the 2008 compound return rate, in the 2004 column the reader will notice that in 2004 the RASE greatly outnumbered the average performance of all mutual funds and is only five points below the best MF, while in other years it is 20–30 points below the best MF (see Table 8.4).

Summarizing, we evaluated our system along three major axes. First, we compared its performance with our previous works (Spanoudakis and Pendaraki, 2007; Spanoudakis *et al.*, 2009). Then, we compared it with the performance of the Athens General Index and the average performance of all MFs in our database. The benchmark data have been retrieved from the Athens Stock Exchange and such data have been used in the past for evaluating the performance of similar systems. For example, other existing systems (Brockett *et al.*, 1992; Loviscek and Jordan, 2000; Morton *et al.*, 2006) have been evaluated in comparison to the S&P500, an index of the prices of 500 large cap common stocks actively traded in the two largest American stock markets, the New York Stock Exchange and NASDAQ.

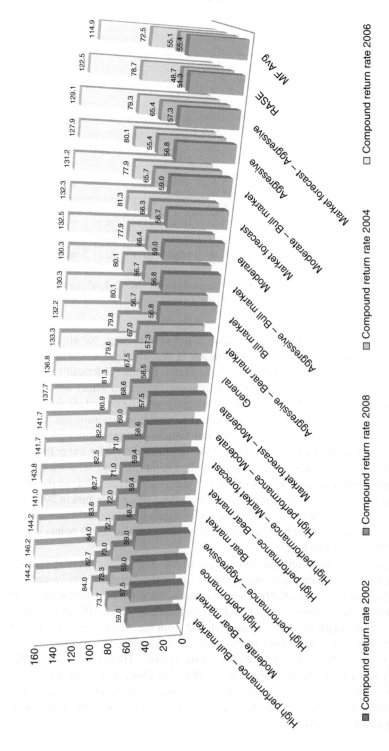

Figure 8.8 The compound return of all scenarios sorted according to the compound return of 2008, compared to the compound return of the RASE and the average return of all MFs.

- ■ Compound return rate 2002
- ■ Compound return rate 2008
- ■ Compound return rate 2004
- □ Compound return rate 2006

Table 8.4 Returns of the different scenarios for each year compared to the RASE and the average MFs returns

	2001	2002	2003	2004	2005	2006	2007	2008	Average returns, 2008	Compound return rate 2008
High perfomance – bull market	-21.09	-25.19	28.31	10.88	27.74	34.43	18.30	-56.77	2.07	73.7
Moderate – bear market	-21.31	-26.88	23.33	16.54	29.02	37.01	18.34	-57.65	2.30	73.3
High perfomance	-21.09	-25.19	28.31	10.88	27.74	34.43	18.30	-57.20	2.02	73.0
High perfomance – aggressive	-21.09	-25.19	28.31	10.44	27.46	32.23	18.34	-56.77	1.72	72.1
Bear market	-21.14	-25.55	20.93	16.54	27.46	36.32	18.34	-57.65	1.91	72.0
High perfomance – bear market	-20.67	-25.08	25.21	10.88	27.74	34.43	18.30	-57.65	1.64	71.0
High perfomance – market forecast	-20.67	-25.08	25.21	10.88	27.74	34.43	18.30	-57.65	1.64	71.0
High perfomance – moderate	-21.09	-25.68	24.47	10.88	27.74	33.17	18.30	-57.65	1.27	69.0
Market forecast – moderate	-21.31	-26.88	23.33	14.51	29.38	30.16	18.34	-57.65	1.24	68.6
General	-21.27	-25.68	23.11	10.44	27.46	31.50	18.34	-57.20	0.84	67.5
Aggressive – bear market	-21.31	-27.20	20.93	15.21	28.89	28.51	18.34	-57.20	0.77	67.0
Bull market	-21.27	-27.86	23.11	14.51	28.89	26.28	18.34	-56.77	0.65	66.7
Aggressive – bull market	-21.27	-27.86	23.11	14.51	28.89	26.28	18.34	-56.77	0.65	66.7
Moderate	-21.27	-25.11	23.11	7.32	26.13	34.82	18.34	-57.65	0.71	66.4
Market forecast	-21.14	-25.55	20.93	14.51	28.89	26.28	18.34	-57.65	0.57	66.3
Moderate – bull market	-21.27	-25.11	23.11	7.32	29.38	30.16	18.34	-57.65	0.53	65.7
Aggressive	-21.27	-27.86	23.11	14.51	28.85	23.99	18.34	-56.77	0.36	65.4
Market forecast – aggressive	-21.31	-27.20	20.93	14.51	28.89	26.28	18.34	-57.20	0.40	65.4
RASE	-22.88	-33.45	27.38	20.42	29.71	19.95	15.95	-65.69	-1.08	48.7
All mutual funds average	-23.23	-27.80	19.36	9.53	26.33	25.48	13.87	-57.88	-1.79	55.1

6 Related work and discussion

We chose argumentation because it allows for decision making using conflicting knowledge, thus different experts can express their knowledge without needing to be consistent with the opinions of the others. It allows for defining non-static priorities between arguments, which means that the priorities of rules can depend on context. Finally, the modularity of its representation allows for the easy incorporation of views of different experts (Altman *et al.*, 1981).

Traditional approaches do not provide these benefits; on the contrary, they pose specific limitations. Statistical methods need to make a strict statistical hypothesis not allowing for flexibility (Altman *et al.*, 1981). Multi-criteria analysis methods need significantly more effort from experts, e.g. Electre-tri (Yu, 1992), as they need to define criteria, weights, preference, indifference, veto thresholds and profiles, leading, in some cases, to troublesome situations due to time constraints or the reluctance of the decision makers to actively contribute in a direct interrogation process managed by an expert analyst (see Doumpos and Zopounidis, 2002) for a complete comparison between decision support methods. Neural networks have also been used in the past (in Patuwo *et al.*, 1993, for example), but they require increased computational effort and are characterized by their inability to provide meaningful explanations for the produced results (Subramanian *et al.*, 1993). In the last decade, many interesting financial forecasting machine learning techniques have been proposed in the literature (Krollner *et al.*, 2010; Karathanasopoulos *et al.*, 2010). Most of them are very promising and manage to overcome drawbacks and limitations posed by traditional approaches, as demonstrated by their experimental results (Antoniou *et al.*, 2010; Theofilatos *et al.*, 2012).

The reasons for using the Gorgias argumentation framework (Kakas and Moraitis, 2003) among others (see, e.g. Prakken and Vreeswijk, 2002), are (1) the Gorgias open-source library, which is available at the website of the University of Cyprus, and (2) the possibility for dynamic preference selection in different levels that allowed for the modular conception of the rules.

The hybrid evolutionary multi-model partitioning algorithms (Beligiannis *et al.*, 2004; Beligianis, 2005) are selected as they comprise a global forecasting technique, in the sense that a single formula is sought that allows forecasts of future entries in any series generated by the process, starting at any point in time. Local approximation schemes, on the other hand, deal only with data that lie in a close neighbourhood in the embedding space, and require separate computations for forecasts in different regions. Obviously, a conventional search for the actual equation of the data-generating process is hopeless, since the dynamics underlying most data, especially financial series, are far too complicated. The usability of classical regression analysis techniques is also very limited. During the past decade various non-linear techniques have been developed to accomplish the task of forecasting. The nearest neighbour technique (Hübinger *et al.*, 1994) which requires massive amounts of data, embeds the time series in a space of sufficiently high dimension and then seeks vectors in the historical series that are similar to the one that is to be predicted. Neural nets also use historical series that are similar to the one that is to be predicted, along with the backpropagation of errors, to finetune a set of parameters, and thereby build a forecasting function that links past values of the time series with future values (Casdagli and Eubank, 1992; Weigend and Gershenfeld, 1995). Predictions based on radial basis functions (Moody and Darken, 1989) use global interpolation techniques and have proven useful in practice when only sparse data are available. Finally, wavelet analysis – like the Fourier transform – decomposes a time series into its basic components, thus allowing insight into its fine structure, and then uses a weighted sum of these wavelets for forecasting purposes (Ramsey and Zhang, 1997).

Except for that, the hybrid evolutionary multi-model partitioning algorithms selected combine the effectiveness of adaptive multi-model partitioning filters of Lainiotis and EAs' robustness and have been successfully applied to many linear and non-linear system identification and time series prediction problems (Beligiannis *et al.*, 2004; Beligiannis, 2005). The proposed algorithms can be applied to linear and non-linear data, are not restricted to the Gaussian case, do not require any knowledge of the model switching law, are practically implementable, computationally efficient and applicable to online/adaptive operation and exhibit excellent performance, as indicated by experimental results (Beligiannis *et al.*, 2004; Beligiannis, 2005).

7 Conclusion

In this contribution we presented the PORTRAIT tool, which allows a decision maker (fund manager) to construct effective multi-portfolios of MFs under different, possibly conflicting contexts.

The empirical results of our study showed that the proposed methodology, which integrates an argumentation system with a hybrid evolutionary multi-model partitioning algorithm, is well suited for this type of application.

The PORTRAIT tool has been validated using a dataset of Greek MFs for 2000–2008. It gives the opportunity to a decision maker (fund manager) to construct multi-portfolios of MFs that perform better than the average MF and achieve higher returns than the Athens Stock Exchange – General Index for medium- to long-term investments. PORTRAIT is intended for use by banks, investment institutions and consultants and the public sector.

We are currently exploring the possibility of developing a rule base for solving the problem of determining when to construct a new portfolio for an investor. In that case we will need to make the application web-based so that it can retrieve online financial data from the internet for computing the decision variables and to allow investors to insert their profiles by completing online forms.

Part of our future work would be, on one hand, to include the transaction costs in our study, in order to have a clearer view of the profitability of the proposed models, and on the other hand, to compare the proposed portfolio constructing methodology with other machine learning methods.

References

Abraham, A., C. Grosan and H. Ishibuchi, eds., *Hybrid Evolutionary Algorithms*, Berlin, Heidelberg: Springer, 2007.

Adamopoulos, A., P. Anninos, S. Likothanassis, G. Beligiannis, L. Skarlas, E. Demiris and D. Papadopoulos, 'Evolutionary self-adaptive multimodel prediction algorithms of the fetal magnetocardiogram'. In *14th International Conference on Digital Signal Processing Proceedings* (DSP 2002). Santorini, 2002, 1149–1152.

Altman, E., R. Eisenbeis and J. Sinkey, *Applications of Classification Techniques in Business, Banking, and Finance*, Greenwich, CT: JAI Press, 1981.

Antoniou, M., E. Georgopoulos, K. Theofilatos and S. Likothanassis, 'Forecasting euro–United States dollar exchange rate with gene expression programming'. In H. Papadopoulos, A.S. Andreou and M. Bramer, (eds), *Artificial Intelligence Applications and Innovations*, Berlin, Heidelberg: Springer, 2010.

Beligiannis, G., 'Evolutionary Lainiotis' algorithms for system identification: a survey'. In *12th International Workshop on Systems, Signals & Image Processing* (IWSSIP 2005), Chalkida, 2005, 63–67.

Beligiannis, G., L. Skarlas and S. Likothanassis, 'A generic applied evolutionary hybrid technique for adaptive system modeling and information mining', *IEEE Signal Processing Magazine* 21(3), 2004, 28–38.

Bench-Capon, T. and P. Dunne, 'Argumentation in artificial intelligence', *Artificial Intelligence* 171(10–15), 2007, 619–641.

Brockett, P., A. Chames, W. Cooper, K.-H. Kwon and T. Ruefli, 'Chance constrained programming approach to empirical analyses of mutual fund investment strategies', *Decision Sciences* 23(2), 1992, 385–408.

Brown, S. and W. Goetzmann, 'Performance persistence', *The Journal of Finance* 50(2), 1995, 679–698.

Casdagli, M. and S. Eubank (eds), 'Nonlinear modeling and forecasting', *Proceedings of the Workshop on Nonlinear Modeling and Forecasting*, September, 1990, Santa Fe, NM: Addison-Wesley, 1992.

Chui, C. and G. Chen, *Kalman Filtering: With Real-Time Applications*, New York: Springer, 2008.

Coello, C., G. Lamont and D. Veldhuizen, *Evolutionary Algorithms for Solving Multi-Objective Problems*, New York: Springer, 2007.

Colson, G. and M. Zeleny, 'Uncertain prospects ranking and portfolio analysis under the condition of partial information', *Mathematical Systems in Economics* 44, 1979, 1–9.

Deb, K., *Multi-Objective Optimization Using Evolutionary Algorithms*, New York: Wiley, 2001.

Doumpos, M. and C. Zopounidis, *Multicriteria Decision Aid Classification Methods*, New York: Springer, 2002.

Einicke, G. and L. White, 'Robust extended Kalman filtering', *IEEE Transactions on Signal Processing* 47(9), 1999, 2596–2599.

Elton, E., M. Gruber, S. Das and M. Hlavka, 'Efficiency with costly information: a reinterpretation of evidence from managed portfolios', *Review of Financial Studies* 6(1), 1993, 1–22.

Eun, C., R. Kolodny and B. Resnick, 'U.S.-based international mutual funds: a performance evaluation', *Journal of Portfolio Management* 17, 1991, 88–94.

Gallo, J. and P. Swanson, 'Comparative measures of performance for U.S.-based international equity mutual funds', *Journal of Banking & Finance* 20(10), 1996, 1635–1650.

Haykin, S., *Adaptive Filter Theory*, Englewood Cliffs, NJ: Prentice-Hall, 1991.

Hübinger, B., R. Doerner, W. Martienssen, M. Herdering, R. Pitka and U. Dressler, 'Controlling chaos experimentally in systems exhibiting large effective Lyapunov exponents', *Physical Review* E50(2), 1994, 932–948.

Ippolito, R., 'Efficiency with costly information: a study of mutual fund performance, 1965–1984', *Quarterly Journal of Economics* 104(1), 1989, 1–23.

Kakas, A. and P. Moraitis, 'Argumentation based decision making for autonomous agents'. In *Proceedings of the 2nd International Joint Conference on Autonomous Agents and Multi-Agent Systems* (AAMAS'03). New York: ACM Press, 2003, 883–890.

Karathanasopoulos, A., K. Theofilatos, P. Leloudas and S. Likothanassis, 'Modeling the Ase 20 Greek index using artificial neural nerworks combined with genetic algorithms'. In K. Diamantaras, W. Duch and L.S. Iliadis (eds), *Artificial Neural Networks: ICANN 2010*. Berlin, Heidelberg: Springer, 2010, 428–435.

Krollner, B., B. Vanstone and G. Finnie, 'Financial time series forecasting with machine learning techniques: a survey'. In *European Symposium on Artificial Neural Networks: Computational and Machine Learning* 2010, 25–30.

Lainiotis, D., 'Partitioning: a unifying framework for adaptive systems', *Estimation: Proceedings of the IEEE* 64(8), 1976, 1126–1143.

LeClair, R., 'Discriminant analysis and the classification of mutual funds', *Journal of Economics and Business* 26(3), 1974, 220–224.

Loviscek, A. and W. Jordan, 'Stock selection based on Morningstar's ten-year, five-star general equity mutual funds', *Financial Services Review* 9(2), 2000, 145–157.

Markowitz, H., 'Portfolio Selection', *The Journal of Finance* 7(1), 1952, 77–91.

Markowitz, H., *Portfolio Selection: Efficient Diversification of Investments*, New York: Wiley, 1959.

Michalewicz, Z., *Genetic Algorithms + Data Structures = Evolution Programs*, New York: Springer, 1996.

Moody, C. and C. Darken, 'Fast learning in networks of locally-tuned processing units', *Neural Computation* 1(2), 1989, 281–294.

Moraitis, P. and N. Spanoudakis, 'Argumentation-based agent interaction in an ambient-intelligence context', *IEEE Intelligent Systems* 22(6), 2007, 84–93.

Morton, D., E. Popova and I. Popova, 'Efficient fund of hedge funds construction under downside risk measures', *Journal of Banking & Finance* 30(2), 2006, 503–518.

Pappas, S., A. Leros and S. Katsikas, 'Joint order and parameter estimation of multivariate autoregressive models using multi-model partitioning theory', *Digital Signal Processing* 16(6), 2006, 782–795.

Pappas, S., N. Harkioakis, P. Karampelas, L. Ekonomou and S. Katsikas, 'A new algorithm for on-line multivariate ARMA identification using multimodel partitioning theory'. In *2008 Panhellenic Conference on Informatics (PCI 2008)*. IEEE, 2008, 222–226.

Patuwo, E., M. Hu and M. Hung, 'Two-group classification using neural networks', *Decision Sciences* 24(4), 1993, 825–845.

Pendaraki, K. and N. Spanoudakis, 'An interactive tool for mutual funds portfolio composition using argumentation', *Journal of Business Economics & Finance* 1(3), 2012, 33–51.

Prakken, H. and G. Vreeswijk, 'Logics for defeasible argumentation'. In D. Gabbay and F. Guenthner (eds), *Handbook of Philosophical Logic*, volume 4. New York: Kluwer Academic Publishers, 2002, 218–319.

Prevost, C., A. Desbiens and E. Gagnon, 'Extended Kalman filter for state estimation and trajectory prediction of a moving object detected by an unmanned aerial vehicle'. In *American Control Conference, 2007.* ACC '07, 2007, 1805–1810.

Rahwan, I., P. Moraïtis and C. Reed, eds, *Argumentation in Multi-Agent Systems*, Berlin, Heidelberg: Springer, 2005.

Ramsey, J. and Z. Zhang, 'The analysis of foreign exchange data using waveform dictionaries', *Journal of Empirical Finance* 4(4), 1997, 341–372.

Redman, A., N. Gullett and H. Manakyan, 'The performance of global and international mutual funds', *Journal of Financial and Strategic Decisions* 13(1), 2000, 75–85.

Ross, S., 'The arbitrage theory of capital asset pricing', *Journal of Economic Theory* 13(3), 1976, 341–360.

Sharpe, W., 'Capital asset prices: a theory of market equilibrium under conditions of risk', *Journal of Finance* 19(3), 1964, 425–442.

Sharpe, W., 'Mutual fund performance', *The Journal of Business* 39(1), 1966, 119–138.

Simons, K., 'Risk-adjusted performance of mutual funds', *New England Economic Review*, (September/October) 1998, 33–48.

Song, T. and J. Speyer, 'A stochastic analysis of a modified gain extended Kalman filter with applications to estimation with bearings only measurements', *IEEE Transactions on Automatic Control* 30(10), 1985, 940–949.

Spanoudakis, N. and P. Moraitis, 'Engineering an agent-based system for product pricing automation', *Engineering Intelligent Systems for Electrical Engineering and Communications* 17(2–3), 2009, 139–151.

Spanoudakis, N. and K. Pendaraki, 'A tool for portfolio generation using an argumentation based decision making framework'. In *19th IEEE International Conference on Tools with Artificial Intelligence (ICTAI 2007)*. IEEE, 2007, 270–273.

Spanoudakis, N., K. Pendaraki and G. Beligiannis, 'Portfolio construction using argumentation and hybrid evolutionary forecasting algorithms', *International Journal of Hybrid Intelligent Systems* 6(4), 2009, 231–243.

Subramanian, V., M. Hung and M. Hu, 'An experimental evaluation of neural networks for classification', *Computers & Operations Research* 20(7), 1993, 769–782.

Temby, L., P. Vamplew and A. Berry, 'Accelerating real-valued genetic algorithms using mutation-with-momentum'. In S. Zhang and R. Jarvis (eds), *AI 2005: Advances in Artificial Intelligence. Proceedings of the 18th Australian Joint Conference on Artificial Intelligence*, Sydney, Australia, 5–9 December 2005. Berlin, Heidelberg: Springer, 2005, 1108–1111.

Theofilatos, K., S. Likothanassis and A. Karathanasopoulos, 'Modeling and trading the EUR/USD exchange rate using machine learning techniques', *Engineering, Technology & Applied Science Research* 2(5), 2012, 269–272.

Treynor, J. 'How to rate management of investment funds', *Harvard Business Review* 43, 1965, 63–75.

Weigend, A. and N. Gershenfeld, eds., *Time Series Prediction*, Reading, MA: Addison-Wesley 1995.

Yoon, Y. and Y. Kim, 'The roles of crossover and mutation in real-coded genetic algorithms'. In S. Gao (ed.), *Bio-Inspired Computational Algorithms and Their Applications*, InTech, 2012.

Yu, W., 'ELECTRE TRI: Aspects methodologiques et manuel d'utilisation', *Document du Lamsade, No. 74*, Universite de Paris-Dauphine, Paris, 1992.

Part V

Trading and investments with advanced computational intelligence modelling techniques

9 Forecasting DAX 30 using support vector machines and VDAX

Rafael Rosillo, Javier Giner and
David de la Fuente

1 Introduction

Quantitative decision making in financial markets is a topic of constant innovation, in which artificial intelligence (AI) is playing a key role as a decision-making support for the investors. Several AI techniques have been applied to this topic, such as neural networks (NNs), genetic algorithms (GA)s, fuzzy logic and more recently support vector machines (SVMs). In this chapter, the latter are used for the development of a trading system.

SVMs are a supervised learning technique used for data analysis and pattern recognition, mainly in classification problems with an increasing number of real-world applications, including finance. The parameters of the SVM, such as kernel and C parameters, are changed in order to achieve better results.

Technical analysis is widely used by investors (Taylor and Allen, 1992) to make decisions. Two of the main indicators of this analysis have been considered to be inputs of this SVM: relative strength index (RSI) and moving average convergence/divergence (MACD).

An intelligent stock trading system based on SVMs using technical analysis and the volatility index of DAX 30 (VDAX) is shown in this chapter. The results demonstrate that this algorithm obtains better profits than buy and hold strategies in bear markets.

The rest of the chapter is structured as follows. In Section 2 we present the literature review relevant to the SVM, VDAX and technical analysis. Section 3 explains the trading algorithm created. Section 4 shows the empirical results of the trading system. Section 5 provides some concluding remarks.

2 Literature review

In this section, the literature review relevant to SVMs, VDAX and technical analysis is presented.

2.1 Support vector machines

A basic theory of the SVM classifier model is presented here. SVMs are specific learning algorithms characterized by the capacity for control of the decision function and the use of kernel functions (Vapnik, 1999; Cristianini and Taylor, 2000). The correct selection of the kernel function is very important.

SVMs were originally developed by Vapnik (1998). For a detailed introduction to the subject, Burges (1998) and Evgeniou *et al.* (2000) are recommended.

The methods based on kernel functions suggest that instead of attaching to each element an algebraic correspondence of the input domain represented by

$$\Phi : X \rightarrow F \tag{9.1}$$

a kernel function

$$K : X \times X \rightarrow R \tag{9.2}$$

is used to calculate the similarity of each pair of objects in the input set. An example is given in Figure 9.1.

The biggest difference between SVMs and other traditional methods of learning is that SVMs do not focus on an optimization protocol that makes few errors, like other techniques. SVMs try to make forecasts in which the user can be very confident of obtaining the correct results, although it can have a lot of errors for a specific period.

Traditionally, most learning algorithms have focused on minimizing errors generated by the model. They are based on what is called the principle of empirical risk minimization (ERM). The focus of SVM is different. It does not seek to reduce the empirical risk of making just a few mistakes, but intends to build reliable models. This principle is called structural risk minimization. The SVM searches for a structural model that has little risk of making mistakes with future data.

The main idea of SVMs is to construct a hyperplane as the decision surface so that the margin of separation between positive and negative examples is maximized; it is called the optimum separation hyperplane (OSH), as shown in Figure 9.1.

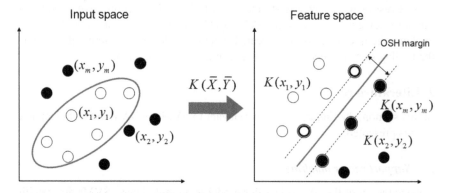

Figure 9.1 An example of how a kernel function works.

Given a training set of instance-label pairs $(\mathbf{x}_i, y_i)$, $i=1,\ldots, m$ where $\mathbf{x}_i \in \Re^n$ and $y_i \in \{1, -1\}$, indicating y_i as the class to which the point $\mathbf{x}_i$ belongs, the SVMs require the solution of the following problem:

$$\min_{\mathbf{w},\xi,b}\left\{\frac{1}{2}\|\mathbf{w}\|^2 + C\sum_{i=1}^{n}\xi_i\right\} \tag{9.3}$$

subject to:

$$y_i(\mathbf{w}\cdot\mathbf{x}_i - b) \geq 1 - \xi_i \tag{9.4}$$

$$\xi_i \geq 0$$

where ξ_i are the slack variables introduced by the method, which measure the degree of misclassification of the data $\mathbf{x}_i$, $\mathbf{w}$ is the normal vector to the hyperplane; b is the offset of the hyperplane from the origin along the normal vector $\mathbf{w}$; and $C>0$ is the penalty parameter of the error term. Different values of parameter C are tested in order to achieve the best results to forecast the movement. The value of C was set by cross-validation. The training period has been split into ten parts. Then the SVM is trained with nine parts and the remaining is used for testing. This procedure is repeated nine more times using different parts of the training period for testing on each. Finally, the value of C is chosen from the best case out of ten.

SVMs can be used in two different ways: classification or regression. Some applications of SVMs to financial forecasting problems have been reported recently. Two applications on SVM financial time series forecasting were developed in 2003: in Cao and Tay (2003), SVM are applied to the problem of forecasting several futures contracts from the Chicago Mercantile Market, showing the superiority of SVMs over backpropagation and regularized radial basis function NNs; in Kim (2003), SVMs are used to predict the direction of change in the daily Korean composite stock index and they are benchmarked against backpropagation NNs and case based reasoning. The experimental results show that SVMs outperform the other methods and that they should be considered as a promising methodology for financial time series forecasting. In Huang *et al.* (2005), an SVM classifier is used to predict the directional movement of the Nikkei 225 index with extremely promising results. Lastly, Lee (2009) explains a prediction model based on SVM, with a hybrid feature selection to predict the trend of stock markets. It is shown that SVM outperforms backpropagation NNS in the problem of stock trend prediction.

In previous studies, such as Dunis *et al.* (2012), we have applied this AI technique to show that it is possible to forecast some periods of the IBEX-35 index under some chosen risk-aversion parameters using an SVM classifier.

2.2 VDAX

The VDAX indicates in percentage points the volatility to be expected in the next 45 days for the DAX. The basis for the calculation of this index is provided by the DAX option contracts and it is analogous to the VIX, the volatility index on the S&P 500.

Volatility indices have several characteristics that make them interesting to use in order to forecast stock markets. They are used when uncertainty and risk increase. Volatility indices revert to the mean after high volatility situations and also after low volatility situations, like the dynamic of interest rates. Finally, volatility is often negatively correlated with stock or index level, and it usually stays high after large downward moves in the market. These tendencies will be studied below in order to improve the trading strategy. They can be seen in Figure 9.2.

2.3 Technical analysis

The main literature review on technical analysis is from Menkhoff and Taylor (2007). Four arguments are analysed: technical analysis may exploit the influence of central bank interventions; the foreign exchange markets may be characterized by not-fully-rational behaviour; technical analysis may be an efficient form of information processing; and it may provide information on non-fundamental influences on foreign exchange movements. This study will be focused on the last two arguments.

Almost all foreign exchange professional traders use technical analysis as a tool in decision making, at least to some degree, and the relative weight given to technical analysis as opposed to fundamental analysis rises as the trading or forecast horizon declines, as shown by Menkhoff and Taylor (2007). Technical analysis is used more than fundamental analysis; according to Taylor and Allen

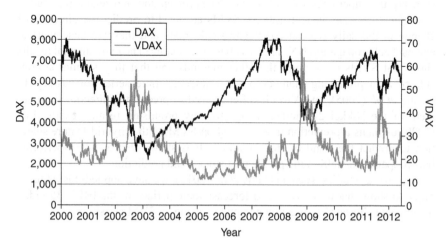

Figure 9.2 DAX (left axis) and VDAX (right axis).

(1992), 90 per cent of polled investors use it. Allen and Taylor (1990) and Taylor and Allen (1992) document systematically for the first time that technical analysis is, indeed, an important tool in decision making in the foreign exchange market.

There are many more recent studies which recommend the use of technical analysis for trading rules. Brock *et al.* (1992) proved that using moving averages and supports and resistances such as trading tools for technical analysis of companies of the Dow Jones Index (DJI) from 1897 to 1986 generated better profitability than the buy and hold strategy in the same index. Mills (1997) showed a similar result to Brock *et al.* (1992), but for the FT30 index. Kwon and Kish (2002) document that technical trading rules achieve better profitability than the buy and hold strategy in the NYSE, while Chong and Ng (2008) recommend the use of technical trading rules using the RSI and MACD indicators for the FT30 index, and they show that the use of both oscillators generates a greater profitability than the buy and hold strategy. Rosillo *et al.* (2013) recommend the use of technical trading rules using the RSI indicator for blue chips and momentum indicator for small caps; they show that the use of both oscillators generates a greater profitability.

There are a lot of studies which support the validity of technical analysis and stochastic indicators in order to forecast stock markets, and this is the main motivation to use RSI and MACD as inputs of the SVM.

3 Trading rule design

In this section the trading rule design is explained. The algorithm was developed in Matlab.[1] An outline of the design of the trading rule is shown in Figure 9.3.

3.1 The data

The dataset used in this study was obtained from Datastream. The daily data cover the period between 3 January 2000 and 30 December 2011.

The SVM is trained on different periods of time with this database in order to achieve different results for comparison. Although our database uses data from a daily basis, the trading strategy relies on a weekly prediction of the DAX 30 price move. A weekly forecast was selected as the expected price move, up or down, over a week is more significant.

3.2 The inputs

The inputs of the SVM are the VDAX, the RSI and the MACD indicators. RSI and MACD indicators have been chosen because they are the most frequently used in quantitative technical analysis. VDAX has been chosen because it includes relevant volatility information of the DAX 30.

The daily return has also been included in the inputs, because in this research we are trying to forecast the DAX 30 index and this variable improves the final results. It is better to use returns in the inputs instead of daily prices because

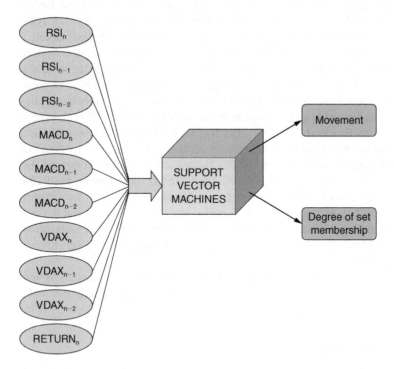

RSI$_n$

RSI$_{n-1}$

RSI$_{n-2}$

MACD$_n$

MACD$_{n-1}$

MACD$_{n-2}$

VDAX$_n$

VDAX$_{n-1}$

VDAX$_{n-2}$

RETURN$_n$

SUPPORT
VECTOR
MACHINES

Movement

Degree of set
membership

Figure 9.3 Design of the trading rule.

daily prices can cause errors in the SVM with scale problems. The inputs have
been normalized from −1 to +1.

3.2.1 MACD

The *MACD* is designed mainly to identify trend changes. It is constructed based
on moving averages and is calculated by subtracting a longer exponential moving
average (*EMA*) from a shorter *EMA*. The *MACD* is shown in equation (9.5):

$$MACD = EMA_k(i) - EMA_d(i) \tag{9.5}$$

where:

$$EMA_n(i) = \alpha * S_i + (1 - \alpha) * EMA_n(i - 1)$$

$$\alpha = \frac{2}{1 + n}$$

and where *n* is the number of days in the exponential average and S_i is the asset
price on *i*th day.

In this chapter, $k=12$ and $d=26$-day *EMA*s are selected, which are commonly used time spans in order to calculate *MACD* (Murphy, 1999).

The range of *MACD* has been normalized between −1 and +1 in order to use it in the SVM.

3.2.2 *RSI*

The RSI was designed by J. Welles Wilder Jr. (1978). A brief explanation of this indicator is shown in equation (9.6). If more details are needed, it can be seen in J. Welles Wilder Jr. (1978).

The RSI is an oscillator that shows the strength or speed of the asset price by means of the comparison of the individual upward or downward movements of the consecutive closing prices.

For each day, an upward change (*U*) or downward change (*D*) is calculated. 'Up days' are characterized by the daily close S_t being higher than the close of previous day S_{t-1}.

$$U_t = S_t - S_{t-1}$$

$$D_t = 0$$

'Down days' are characterized by the daily close being lower than the close of the previous day.

$$U_t = 0$$

$$D_t = S_{t-1} - S_t$$

The average U_t and D_t are calculated using an *n*-period exponential moving average (EMA_n).

Relative Strength Index at time t (RSI_t) is the following ratio between 0 and 100:

$$RSI_t = 100 \frac{EMA_n^U}{EMA_n^U + EMA_n^D} \tag{9.6}$$

The 14-day RSI, a popular length of time utilized by traders, is also applied in this study. The RSI ranges from 0 to 100; however, the range has been normalized between −1 and +1 in order to place it in the SVM.

3.2.3 *VDAX*

The VDAX calculation method has changed since its introduction in 1994. The original VDAX was constructed using the implied volatilities of eight different DAX index options, using the Black–Scholes option pricing model, trying to represent the implied volatility of a hypothetical at-the-money option with exactly 45 days to expiration. In 2005 Deutsche Börse introduced the VDAX-NEW, which is calculated on the basis of a more recent model developed in a similar way that the new VIX index. It has replaced implied volatilities of at-the-money DAX options with the square root of implied variance across at-the-money and out-of-money options on a given time to expiration. An option is called at-the-money when the price of the underlying security is equal to the strike price, and out-of-money if the strike price is greater than the market price of the underlying security. This index has a fixed remaining time to expiration of 30 days. We have used the VDAX old index in this research, reserving the VDAX-NEW for further works.

One of the main VDAX characteristics really relevant for investors is that it shows a strong negative correlation with DAX.

In Figure 9.4 daily data between 1992 and 2011 are analysed. The correlation between the daily returns of the S&P 500 and the VDAX changes is –0.63383; it is a result that is worth highlighting because it is a strong negative value. However, there is only instantaneous correlation and there is no remarkable lead–lag effects. This evidence merely documents correlation and is not intended to express causality. Consequently, VDAX is included in the trading strategy.

In order to be processed in the SVM, the range of VDAX, typically in the range of a yearly standard deviation, has been normalized between –1 and +1. When daily VDAX data are not available, we have used the previous daily data available.

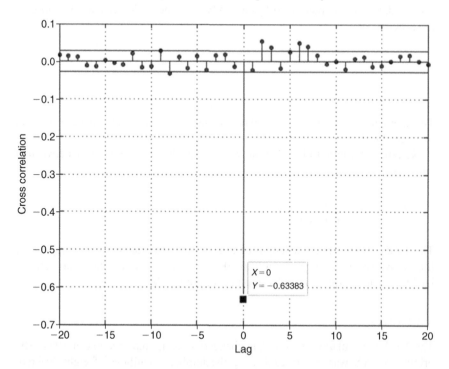

Figure 9.4 Cross correlation DAX returns and VDAX changes.

3.3 The SVM trading rule

The design of the trading rule is the hardest section. In order to achieve better results, some of the parameters of the SVM have been modified, such as kernel function and C parameter.

An SVM has been chosen in order to make the quantitative decision. As it was explained in Section 2, SVMs are helping investors in decision making and many experiments demonstrate that SVMs generate better results than other AI techniques. An SVM classifier has been used.

The training period has been designed with 249 days; the next day is tested by the SVM to see if the result is a good decision or not. Other periods, such as 200 days, 300 days and 500 days, have been tested too, but the best results are achieved with 250. So, the training period is 249 days and the testing period is one day. The total of data for each experiment is 250 days, very similar to one business year.

Although our dataset is daily, the trading strategy relies on a weekly prediction of the DAX 30 price move. A weekly forecast was selected as the expected price move, up or down, over a week is more significant.

The only problem that has been detected is the situation in which the SVM is being trained and it does not have data to compare in order to make the decision to buy or sell. This situation happens for the last five days of the training period. In this way, the study is more real. In order to fix this, four experiments have been done, such as: compare these five days with the last day known; delete these five days, compare these five days with a simple moving average of that five days; and compare these five days with a weighted average of that five days. The best results achieved are shown in the results section.

The following example is presented in order to clarify the previous explanation. Let us start with the situation shown in Table 9.1.

Training data are from day 1 to day 249. In Table 9.1, data from day 241 to 250 are shown. Sell/buy decision is done by comparing the current day value with the value of five days ahead. In the case of days 245 to 249, the five days ahead value is unknown. Thus, to have a value to compare with, a simple moving average with values of days 245 to 249 is used.

Table 9.2 would be as follows: simple moving average: $4+6+10+8+1 = 29/5 = 5.8$

In consequence, the SVM would be trained using Table 9.2. The day 250 decision would be taken by the SVM.

Table 9.1 Training data with unknown values

	Training									Testing
Day	241	242	243	244	245	246	247	248	249	250
Daily close price	7	5	3	3	4	6	10	8	1	7
Decision	Sell	Buy	Buy	Sell	?	?	?	?	?	?

Table 9.2 Training data with known values

	Training									Testing
Day	241	242	243	244	245	246	247	248	249	250
Daily close price	7	5	3	3	4	6	10	8	1	7
Decision	Sell	Buy	Buy	Sell	Buy	Sell	Sell	Sell	Buy	SVM decision

The SVM procedure can be described as follows. First, the SVM analyses the inputs classified in purchase situations or sell situations. Second, the SVM tries to separate the different prices of the DAX 30 into two classes using the inputs mentioned earlier: buying and selling situations.

Third, the SVM uses the kernel function heavy tailed radial basis function (HTRBF, equation (9.7)) developed by Chapelle *et al.* (1999) and the SVM-KM Matlab toolbox developed by Canu *et al.* (2005) in order to make the forecast. The C parameter of the SVM is chosen by cross-validation. Fourth, the hit ratio is calculated for the different testing periods.

$$e^{-\rho \sum_j |x_j^a - y_j^a|^b} \quad \text{with } a \le 1 \text{ and } b \le 2 \tag{9.7}$$

Finally, given a value of the RSI, MACD and VDAX, the SVM predicts the upward or downward movement for the following week and the intensity of that movement.

3.4 The outputs

The outputs of the SVM are the up or down movements expected for the index weekly change, and its degree of set membership (bullish or bearish class). For instance, the SVM output is 0.85. This means that the DAX 30 value will be higher for the next week than now, and the value of 0.85 is the degree of set membership for the bullish class because it is positive. Negative values are associated with the bearish class. The degree of set membership is stronger if the value is further from 0.

4 Results

In Table 9.3 the results of the different implemented tests are shown.

Two trading strategies are compared, holding five contracts at the same time at most. They are explained below:

SVM strategy: all the inputs which appear in Figure 9.2 are used.
BH (buy and hold) strategy: it is the buy and hold strategy that holds five contracts all the time in order to follow the SVM trading strategy. It is used as a benchmark.

Table 9.3 Yearly results of the two strategies

Year	DAX points		R		σ		SR		MDD (points)	
	SVM	B&H	SVM	B&H	SVM	B&H	SVM	B&H	SVM	B&H
2000	-258	-2,703	-0.003	-0.078	0.0978	0.1057	-0.03	-0.74	4,420	8,540
2001	-390	-6,352	-0.007	-0.211	0.0973	0.134	-0.077	-1.573	5,100	14,204
2002	173	-10,525	0.0128	-0.495	0.1126	0.1528	0.1136	-3.24	6,195	13,686
2003	-1,748	4,877	-0.109	0.2794	0.1418	0.1268	-0.766	2.2034	4,368	3,856
2004	2,830	1,656	0.1296	0.0792	0.058	0.069	2.2333	1.1485	1,350	2,316
2005	2,922	5,925	0.1255	0.2386	0.0505	0.0501	2.4874	4.7603	843	1,048
2006	4,506	5,717	0.1507	0.1875	0.0611	0.0662	2.466	2.8305	1,519	3,763
2007	3,920	6,920	0.113	0.19	0.0704	0.0691	1.6055	2.7519	2,052	3,312
2008	6,854	-16,335	0.1644	-0.521	0.0997	0.1465	1.6479	-3.557	2,757	18,150
2009	-2,464	6,395	-0.095	0.2331	0.1243	0.1206	-0.767	1.932	4,527	6,165
2010	2,348	5,035	0.0757	0.1536	0.071	0.0759	1.0668	2.0235	2,551	2,714
2011	5,346	-5,623	0.1442	-0.162	0.103	0.1338	1.4005	-1.213	3,686	11,246
2000–2005	3,529	-7,121	0.0193	-0.032	0.074	0.1243	0.2612	-0.257	8,300	28,370
2006–2011	20,510	2,109	0.0943	0.018	0.0773	0.108	1.2199	0.1663	4,607	21,603
2000–2011	24,040	-5,012	0.0471	-0.006	0.0684	0.1193	0.6875	-0.053	8,300	28,370

For each day, the DAX 30 index is purchased or sold depending on the trading system recommendation. After five days, the reverse operation over the DAX 30 is applied in order to be out of the market. This sequence is repeated every day.

A little variation of the buy and hold strategy is used as a benchmark. It consists of purchasing the DAX 30 index daily and selling the DAX 30 index after five days. The profit or loss after n periods would be:

$$\sum_{i=6}^{n} \Delta_i = (S_n + S_{n-1} + S_{n-2} + S_{n-3} + S_{n-4}) - (S_5 + S_4 + S_3 + S_2 + S_1) \qquad (9.8)$$

where $\Delta_i = S_i - S_{i-1}$ is the daily profit or loss of DAX 30.

Different ratios have been calculated in order to compare the two strategies. They are shown in the Appendix.

In Table 9.3 the yearly results of the two strategies with the different ratios appear. Furthermore, at the end of table 9.3, three different period groups are shown.

In the first column of Table 9.3 the DAX 30 points that can be achieved with each strategy are shown, in the second column the annualized return, in the third column the annualized standard deviation of daily returns, in the fourth column the Sharpe ratio and in the fifth column the maximum drawdown are shown.

The bold numbers present the best result of each strategy for a determinate indicator.

As can be seen in Table 9.3, the SVM strategy is better in years with a bearish trend than the buy and hold strategy. Furthermore, the volatility is lower in the SVM strategy than the buy and hold strategy.

In Figure 9.5 the global period of analysis, 2000–2011, is shown.

Figure 9.5 Cumulative DAX 30 points for each strategy from 2000 to 2011.

As can be seen in Figure 9.5, the crisis periods had a negative influence in the buy and hold strategy, but not the SVM strategy, though in bull movements the SVM strategy cannot improve the buy and hold strategy results.

5 Conclusions

An intelligent stock trading system based on SVMs using VDAX and technical analysis indicators such as RSI and MACD in order to forecast DAX 30 is shown in this chapter.

Overall, this study shows that the SVM strategy produces better results than the buy and hold strategy when a bearish movement is produced. This may be caused by the influence of VDAX in the bearish movement. It is usual that in a bearish movement, the volatility increases more than a bullish movement, so VDAX helps the SVM more in a bearish than bullish situation. It is worth noting that during the 2008 stock market crisis the algorithm increased the profits significantly. The SVM allows for a reduction in the maximum drawdown indicator and a better Sharpe ratio is also achieved using SVM.

The trading system that has been developed will be useful when a bearish movement appears.

Appendix

Daily return:

$$r_i = \frac{S_i}{S_{i-1}} - 1 \tag{9.9}$$

Annualized return:

$$R^A = 250 * \frac{1}{n} \sum_{i=1}^{n} r_i \tag{9.10}$$

Standard deviation:

$$\sigma^A = \sqrt{250} \sqrt{\frac{1}{n-1} \sum_{i=1}^{n} (r_i - \bar{r})^2} \tag{9.11}$$

Sharpe ratio:

$$SR = \frac{R^A}{\sigma^A} \tag{9.12}$$

Maximum drawdown calculated in DAX points:

$$MDD = \min_{t=1,\ldots,n} \left(F_t - \max_{\tau=1,\ldots,t} (F_\tau) \right) \tag{9.13}$$

where F_t is the accumulated fund with each different strategy.

Acknowledgement

Financial support given by the Government of the Principality of Asturias is gratefully acknowledged. The authors would like to thank the reviewers for their comments, which have greatly contributed to improving our chapter.

Note

1   The software used is MATLAB 7.8.0 (R2009a).

References

Allen, H. and M. Taylor, 'Charts, noise and fundamentals in the London foreign exchange market', *Economic Journal* 100, 1990, 49–59.

Brock, W., J. Lakonishok and B. LeBaron, 'Simple technical trading rules and the stochastic properties of stock returns', *Journal of Finance* 47, 1992, 1731–1764.

Burges, C., 'A tutorial on support vector machines for pattern recognition', *Data Mining and Knowledge Discovery*, 2, 1998, 121–167.

Canu, S., Y. Grandvalet, V. Guigue and A. Rakotomamonjy, *SVM and Kernel Methods Matlab Toolbox, Perception Systèmes et Information*, INSA de Rouen, Rouen, France, 2005.

Cao, L. and F. Tay 'Support vector machine with adaptive parameters in financial time series forecasting', *IEEE Transactions on Neural Networks* 14, 2003, 1506–1518.

Chapelle, O., P. Haner and V. Vapnik, 'Support vector machines for histogram-based image classification', *IEEE Transactions on Neural Networks* 10(5), 1999, 1055–1064.

Chong, T. and W. Ng, 'Technical analysis and the London stock exchange: testing the MACD and RSI rules using the FT30', *Applied Economics Letters* 15, 2008, 1111–1114.

Cristianini, N. and J. Taylor, *An Introduction to Support Vector Machines and Other Kernel-based Learning Methods*, New York: Cambridge University Press, 2000.

Dunis, C., R. Rosillo, D. De la Fuente and R. Pino, 'Forecasting IBEX-35 moves using support vector machines', *Neural Computing and Applications*, 2012. DOI: 10.1007/s00521-012-0821-9.

Evgeniou, T., M. Pontil and T. Poggio, 'Regularization networks and support vector machines', *Advances in Computational Mathematics* 13, 2000, 1–50.

Huang, W., Y. Nakamori and S. Wang, 'Forecasting stock market movement direction with support vector machine', *Computers & Operations Research* 32, 2005, 2513–2522.

Kim, K., 'Financial time series forecasting using support vector machines', *Neurocomputing* 55, 2003, 307–319.

Kwon, K. and R. Kish, 'Technical trading strategies and return predictability: NYSE', *Applied Financial Economics* 12, 2002, 639–653.

Lee, M., 'Using support vector machine with a hybrid feature selection method to the stock trend prediction', *Expert Systems with Applications* 36(8), 2009, 10896–10904.

Menkhoff, L. and M. Taylor 'The obstinate passion of foreign exchange professionals: technical analysis', *Journal of Economic Literature* 45, 2007, 936–972.

Mills, T., 'Technical analysis and the London stock exchange: testing trading rules using the FT30', *International Journal of Finance and Economics* 2, 1997, 319–331.

Murphy, J., *Technical Analysis of the Financial Markets*, New York: Institute of Finance, 1999.

Rosillo, R., D. De la Fuente and J. Brugos, 'Technical analysis and the Spanish stock exchange: testing the RSI, MACD, momentum and stochastic rules using Spanish market companies', *Applied Economics* 45, 2013, 1541–1550.

Taylor, M. and H. Allen, 'The use of technical analysis in the foreign exchange market', *Journal of International Money and Finance* 11, 1992, 304–314.

Vapnik, V., *Statistical Learning Theory*, New York: Wiley, 1998.

Vapnik, V., 'An overview of statistical learning theory', *IEEE Transactions of Neural Networks* 10, 1999, 988–999.

Welles Wilder Jr., J., *New Concepts in Technical Trading Systems*, Greensboro, NC: Hunter Publishing Company, 1978.

10 Ensemble learning of high-dimensional stock market data

Manolis Maragoudakis and Dimitrios Serpanos

1 Introduction

Stock market analysis using ICT methods is a dynamic and volatile domain. Over the past years there has been an increasing focus on the development of modelling tools, especially when the expected outcomes appear to yield significant profits to the investors' portfolios. In alignment with the modern globalized economy, the available resources are becoming gradually more plentiful, and thus difficult to analyse by standard statistical tools. Therefore, technical analysis experts judge that the stock market is an excellent representative field of application with strong dynamics in research through data mining, mainly due to the quantity and the increased rate at which that data are being created. Thus far, there have been a number of research papers that emphasize solely past data from stock bond prices and other technical indicators. Throughout recent studies, prediction is also based on textual information, based on the logical assumption that the course of a stock price can also be affected by news articles. Nowadays, news is easily accessible, access to important data such as inside company information is relatively cheap and estimations emerge from a large resource such as economists, statisticians, journalists, etc., through the internet. Stock market research encapsulates two main philosophical attitudes, i.e. fundamental and technical approaches (Technical-Analysis, 2005). The former states that stock market movement of prices derives from a security's relative data. In a fundamentalist trading philosophy, the price of a security can be determined through the nuts and bolts of financial numbers. These numbers are derived from the overall economy, the particular industry's sector or, most typically, from the company itself. Figures such as inflation, joblessness, return on equity (ROE), debt levels and individual price to earnings (PE) ratios can all play a part in determining the price of a stock.

In technical analysis, it is believed that market timing is the key concept. Technicians utilize charts and modelling techniques from past data to identify trends in price and volume. These strategists believe that market timing is critical and opportunities can be found through the careful averaging of historical price and volume movements and comparing them against current prices. Technicians also believe that there are certain high/low psychological price barriers such as support and resistance levels where opportunities may exist. They further reason that price movements are not totally random. According to several researchers, the goal is not to question the predictability of financial time series but to discover a good model that is capable of describing the dynamics of stock markets.

Towards the latter direction, stock market analysis using information techno-logy techniques is a dynamic and unpredictable domain. Over the past years there has been an increasing focus on the development of modelling systems, especially when the expected outcomes appear to yield significant profits to the investors' portfolios.

Throughout recent studies, prediction is also based on textual records, based on the logical assumption that the course of a stock price can be influenced by news articles, ranging from companies' releases and local politics to news of superpower economies (Ng and Fu, 2003).

However, unrestricted access to news information was not possible until the early 1990s. Despite the large amount of data, advances in natural language processing and knowledge discovery from data (also known as data mining) allow for effective computerized representation of unstructured document col-lections, analysis for pattern extraction and discovery of relationships between document terms and time-stamped datastreams of stock market quotes.

When data tend to grow both in number of records and attributes, numerous mining algorithms face significant difficulties, resulting in poor forecast ability. The aim of this study is to propose a potential answer to the problem, by consid-ering the well-known ensemble algorithm of random forests (Breiman, 2001) and altering their construction phase by utilizing a Markov blanket approach, which rejects irrelevant features. The novelty of this study is based on the fact that technical analysis contains the event and not the cause of the change, while textual data may interpret that cause. The chapter takes into account a large number of technical indices, accompanied with features that are extracted by a text-mining methodology, from financial news articles. Previous research has demonstrated that due to the high-dimensionality and sparseness of such data, the majority of widespread data mining algorithms suffer from either conver-gence or accuracy problems. The problem of several non-informative features occurs in normal random forests, as well as in other tree-based algorithms, such as CART or C4.5, due to the fact that, if simple random sampling is used for selecting the subset of m eligible features at each node, almost all these subsets are likely to contain a predominance of non-informative features

The importance of this study lies in the fact that technical analysis contains the event and not the cause of the change, while textual data may interpret that cause. The chapter takes into account a large number of technical indices, accompanied by features that are extracted by a textual analysis phase from fin-ancial news articles. Previous research has demonstrated that due to the high-dimensionality and sparseness of such data, the majority of popular data mining algorithms suffer from either convergence or accuracy problems. Even though particular feature reduction techniques exist, such as principal component analysis (PCA) (Hotelling, 1933) or latent semantic indexing (LSI) (Deerwester *et al.*, 1990), stock market datasets that incorporate both textual and technical data face the following problem: from the total set of input features, usually a small subset of them is truly informative as regards to the prediction of the class label. For example, for a given security, when someone takes more than 20 indices and 300 terms from financial articles into account, in order to predict the security's price, usually a small subset of the aforementioned features have significant influence on the prediction outcome. The problem of several non-informative features occurs in the standard random forests technique, as well as in other tree-based algorithms such as CART (Breiman *et al.*, 1984) or C4.5 (Quinlan, 1993), due to the fact that, if simple random sampling is used for selecting the subset of *m* eligible features at each node, almost all these subsets are likely to contain a predominance of non-informative features.

Our proposed methodology is called '*Markov blanket random forests – MBRF*'. MBRF deals with high-dimensional datasets and is proven to be robust in particular cases where a large number of non-informative features exist. The notion of the Markov blanket is not innovative. However, to the best of our knowledge, it is the first time the Markov blanket has been used as a focal filtering element within the training phase of random forests. Results obtained from the experimental phase, including a virtual trading experiment, are very promising. Certainly, as it is tedious for a human investor to read all daily news concerning a company and other financial information, a prediction system that could analyse such textual resources and find relationships with price movement at future time windows is beneficial.

2 Related work

The use of data mining techniques in stock market modelling and prediction has gained significant attention from academic and business stakeholders. Due to the large number of available studies in traditional technical analysis, we shall highlight research that studies the influence of news articles on stock markets. Chung *et al.* (2002) were among the first to confirm the reaction of the market to news articles. They used salient political and economic news as proxies for public information. They have found that both types of news have impacts on measures of trading activity, including return volatility, price volatility, number of shares traded and trading frequency. Klibanof *et al.* (1998) dealt with closed-end country funds prices and country-specific salient news. They stated that there is a positive relationship between trading volume and news. News that occupies at least two columns of the *New York Times* front page was considered as salient. Similar to the aforementioned approach, Chan and Wei (1996) found that news that is placed on the front page of the *South China Post* increased return volatility in the Hong Kong stock market. Mitchell and Mulherin (2002) used the daily number of headlines of Dow Jones as a measure of public information. They mentioned the positive impact of news on absolute price changes. Cho (1999) used the number of news released by Reuter's News Service measured per unit of time as a proxy for public information. In contrast to Mitchell and Mulherin, Cho examined the impact of news on the intraday market activity. Their results suggest that there is a significant positive relationship between news arrivals and trading volume. Mittermayer (2004) proposed a prediction system called *NEWS-CATS*, which provides an estimate of the price after the publication of press releases. Schumaker and Chen (2006) examined three different textual representation formalisms and studied their abilities to predict discrete stock prices 20 minutes after an article release.

A notable approach that incorporates genetic algorithms was suggested by Thomas and Sycara (2000). In their approach, they attempted to classify stock prices using the number of postings and size of related articles on a daily basis (textual data were originated from discussion boards on a financial forum). It was found that positive share price movement was correlated to stocks with more than 10,000 posts. However, discussion board postings are quite susceptible to bias and noise.

Another popular classifier, Naïve Bayes, was used by Wüthrich *et al.* (1998) in order to represent each article as a weighted vector of keywords. Phrase co-occurrence and price directionality was learned from example articles, which led to the training data. One problem with this algorithm is that articles may focus their attention on some other event and superficially reference a particular stock security. These types of problems can cloud the results of training by unintentionally attaching weight to a casually mentioned security.

One of the most interesting approaches incorporated support vector machines (SVM). In the work of Fung *et al.* (2003), regression analysis of technical data was used to identify price trends, while SVM analysis of textual news articles was used to perform a binary classification in two predefined categories: stock price rise and drop. In cases where conflicting SVM classification follows, such that both rise and drop classifiers are determined to be positive, the system returns a 'no recommendation' decision. From their research using 350,000 financial news articles and a simulated buy and hold strategy based upon their SVM classifications, they showed that their technique was mildly profitable. Mittermayer (2004) also used SVM is his research to find an optimal profit trading engine. While relying on a three-tier classification system, his research focused on empirically establishing trading limits. It was found that profits can be maximized by buying or shorting stocks and taking profit on them at 1 per cent up movement or 3 per cent down movement. This method slightly beat random trading by yielding a 0.11 per cent average return.

The Arizona Financial Text System (AZFinText), proposed by Schumaker and Chen (2010), extracts proper nouns and selects the proper nouns that occur three or more times to be used as features. AZFinText is a regression system that attempts to forecast feature prices and does not perform true sentiment analysis, in the sense that this system labels each news article with a price value instead of sentiment label. The AZFinText system does this by labelling each news article with the stock price 20 minutes after it is published. The AZFinText system was tested on S&P 500 and compared against the top quantitative funds. It had an 8.5

per cent return in the given period, while the S&P 500 had a lesser return of 5.62 per cent. It ranked as number four against all the other quant funds. However, those quant funds that ranked above it traded in different markets than the AZFinText system.

Another system, developed by Falinouss (2007), consists of identifying price trends by time series segmentation, then each news document is sentiment labelled by aligning it up with the price trend. The document preprocessing part consists of the three standard methods; tokenizing, stop-word removal and stemming. Document representation is accomplished by using the standard method of using a vector space model with *tf-idf* as the term weighting method. The system is reported to achieve an accuracy of 83 per cent for correctly labelling a news article as rise or drop. The recall of rise predictions is stated to be 67 per cent, and for drop predictions it is 93 per cent. The precision for rise predictions is claimed to be 87 per cent and for drop 81 per cent. However, the author did not include an evaluation on how good this system is when used for trading stocks.

In the work of Preis *et al.* (2013) it is suggested that within a given time period, Google Trends data did not only reflect the current state of the stock markets but may have also been able to forecast certain future trends. Their findings are consistent with the intriguing proposal that notable drops in the financial market are preceded by periods of investor concern. In such periods investors may search for additional information about the market, before eventually deciding to buy or sell. By following this logic, during the period 2004 to 2011, Google Trends search query volumes for certain terms could have been used in the construction of profitable trading strategies. They compared their approach against the 'buy and hold' strategy and a purely random investment strategy on the Dow Jones Industrial Average (DJIA). The proposed Google Trends strategy utilizing the search volume of the term debt has yielded a profit of 326 per cent.

To sum up, while many of the previous studies have focused mainly on classifications based on historical stock prices, none of them have clearly managed to harness data mining algorithms in order to accurately and effectively determine a discrete stock price prediction, based on both stock prices and financial news articles. For existing approaches that relied on a 'bag of words' textual representation format, the plethora of input variables has obviously presented algorithms with problems, and this could be a reason for the small improvements that are reported in literature regarding to stock market forecasting.

Undoubtedly, semantically rich text representation of articles is more beneficial, since less noise and outlier parameters are inserted to the classifier. However, for the majority of languages such as modern Greek, semantic annotation tools and resources such as WordNet (Fellbaum, 1998) are not available. Thus, we have focused our effort on improving the ability of existing data mining algorithms to handle the 'bag of words' problem, augmented by numerous additional parameters, obtained from technical indices. The proposed approach discusses both theoretical and experimental issues of the new, hybrid algorithm we propose, which is suitable for large datasets, particularly when the number of non-informative input features is large.

3 Background

The present section introduces the elementary machine learning practices that formed the background for our proposed hybrid algorithm, MBRF. We introduce the notion of ensemble classification and, more specifically, random forests, followed by some preliminary description on Bayesian networks, as well as on the notion of the Markov blanket of a node within a Bayesian network, which is exploited in the proposed approach.

3.1 Ensemble classification

Recently, ensemble classification has gained much popularity within the machine learning and data mining community. The idea behind the aggregation of multiple single classifiers is based on the statement that non-correlated classifiers have the ability to outperform the total prediction error when aggregated. The following scenario exemplifies how an ensemble method can improve a classifier's performance. Suppose a set of K binary classifiers is constructed, each of which predicts the class with an average error rate of ε. As previously mentioned, an ensemble classifier performs the classification based on the majority vote of each base classifier. In the case that all base classifiers are identical, the error rate of the ensemble will remain ε, while, if the base classifiers are independent (i.e. they portray non-correlated error), then the ensemble will make false prediction if and only if more than half of the base classifiers predict incorrectly. From a mathematical view, the estimate error rate of the ensemble classifier can be calculated using equation (10.1):

$$\varepsilon_{ensemble} = \sum_{[K/i]}^{K} \binom{K}{i} \varepsilon^i (1-\varepsilon)^{K-i} \tag{10.1}$$

As an example, consider the case where the error ε is 0.35 and there are $K=25$ base classifiers. According to the above equation, i would be 13 and the total error of the ensemble classifier would be only 0.06, which is significantly lower than the error rate of the base classifiers.

The random forest algorithm is a popular classification technique whose classifier is an ensemble of classification trees. It is considered particularly well suited to situations characterized by a large number of features, a circumstance that is becoming more prevalent as the ability to collect and store vast amounts of data becomes easier and increasingly common (Breimen, 2001). In such instances, the classical classification approaches tend to become overwhelmed by the number of features and fail, while random forests continue to do well. For instance, with DNA microarray data, work by Dudoit (2002), shows that random forests outperform most of the other classification techniques. However, when, in addition to having a large number of features, the proportion of truly informative features is small, its performance tends to decline as well (Freund and Shapire, 1996). In this chapter, a solution for this problem is proposed, which is founded on the notion of a feature selection and reasoning algorithm, based on the *Markov blanket* of the class attribute.

3.2 Random forests

Despite the fact that random forests have been quite successful in classification and regression tasks, to the best of our knowledge, there has been no research in using the aforementioned algorithm for Greeklish to Greek transformation. Nowadays, numerous attempts in constructing ensemble of classifiers towards increasing the performance of the task at hand have been introduced. A plethora of them have portrayed promising results as regards classification approaches. Examples of such techniques are adaboost, bagging and random forests (Breimen, 2001). Random forests are a combination of tree classifiers such that each tree depends on the values of a random vector sampled independently and with the same distribution for all trees in the forest. The generalization error of a forest of tree classifiers depends on the strength of the individual trees within the forest and their intercorrelation. Using a random selection of features in order to split each node yields output error rates that compare equally to adaboost, yet they are more robust with respect to noise. While traditional tree algorithms spend a lot of time choosing how to split at a node, random forests perform this task with little computational effort. Compared with adaboost, random forests portray the following characteristics:

- the accuracy is as good as adaboost and sometimes better;
- they are relatively robust to outliers and noise;
- they are faster than bagging or boosting;
- they provide useful internal estimates of error, strength, correlation and variable importance;
- they are simple and easily parallelized.

A random forest classifier $\Theta(x)$ consists of a number of trees, with each tree grown using some form of randomization, where x is an input instance. The leaf nodes of each tree are labelled by estimates of the posterior distribution over the data class labels. Each internal node contains a test that best splits the space of data to be classified. A new, unseen instance is classified by sending it down every tree and aggregating the reached leaf distributions. The process is described in Figure 10.1. Each tree is grown as follows:

- If the number of cases in the training set is N, sample N cases at random but with *replacement*, from the original data. This sample will be the training set for growing the tree.
- If there are M input variables, a number $m \ll M$ is specified such that at each node, m variables are selected at random out of the M and the best split on these m is used to split the node. The value of m is held constant during the forest growing.

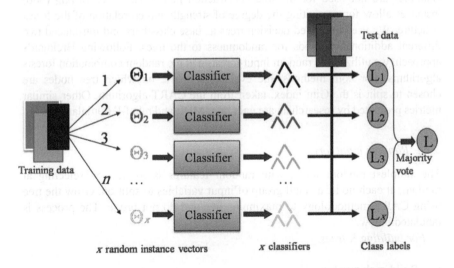

Figure 10.1 Hierarchical decomposition of a random forests classifier on a dataset.

- Each tree is grown to the largest extent possible. Therefore, no pruning is applied.

As regards the overall error rate of the random forests, this is affected by two different factors:

1   Tree *inter-correlation*: highly correlated trees result in high error rate.
2   *Robustness* (strength) of each individual tree within the forest: higher strength results in lower error rates.

Upon completion of the tree construction step, the set of data are run down the tree, and proximity values are computed for each pair of cases. If two cases occupy the same terminal tree node, their proximity is augmented by one. At the end of the run, proximities are normalized, divided by the number of trees.

In order to make the classification process more formal, suppose that the joint classifier $\Theta(x)$ contains x individual classifiers $\Theta_1(x)$, $\Theta_2(x)$,..., $\Theta_x(x)$. Let us also assume that each data instance is a pair (x,y), where x denotes the input attributes, taken from a set Ai, $i=1,...,M$ and y symbolizes the set of class labels L_j, $j=1,...,$ c (c is the number of class values). For reasons of simplicity, the correct class will be denoted as y, without any indices. Each discrete attribute A_i takes values from a set V_i, $i=1$ to m_i (m_i is the number of values attribute A_i has). Finally, the probability that an attribute A_i has value v_k is denoted by $p(v_i,k)$, the probability of a class value y_j is denoted by $p(y_j)$ and the probability of an instance with attribute A_i having value v_k and class label y_j is symbolized by $p(y_j|v_i,k)$. Each training example is picked up from a set of N instances at random with replacement. By this procedure, called bootstrap replication, a pool of 36.6 per cent of the training examples are not used for the tree construction phase. These *out-of-bag* (oob) instances allow for computing the degree of strength and correlation of the forest structure. We used unpruned decision trees as base classifiers and introduced two different additional methods for randomness to the trees. Following Breiman's approach, we utilized the random input forests and the random combination forests algorithms. For both methods, the evaluation metric on which tree nodes are chosen to split is the Gini index, taken from the CART algorithm. Other similar metrics presented by researchers are gain ratio MDL and relief-F (Quinlan, 1993).

3.2.1 Random input forests

The simplest random forest with random features is formed by selecting at random, at each node, a small group of input variables to split on. Grow the tree using CART methodology to maximum size and do not prune. The process is tabulated below.

For building K trees:

- Build each tree by:

    - Selecting, at random, at each node a small set of features (F) to split on (given M features). Common values of F are:

        - $F=1$
        - $F=\log_2(M)+1$.

    - For each node, split on the best of this subset (using *oob* instances).
    - Grow tree to full length.

3.2.2 Random combination forests

This approach consists of defining more features by taking random linear combinations of a number of the input variables. That is, a feature is generated by specifying L, the number of variables to be combined. At a given node, L variables are randomly selected and added together with coefficients that are uniform random numbers on $[-1,1]$. F linear combinations are generated, and then a search is made over these for the best split. The complete procedure is as follows.

For building K trees:

- Build each tree by:

    - Create F random linear sums of L variables:

$$A_f = \sum_{i=1}^{L} b_{fj} x_i, \text{ where } b_{fj} = \text{uniform random number on the space of } [-1, +1]$$

    - At each node, split on the best of these linear boundaries.
    - Grow tree to full length.

3.3 Markov blanket property

In order to better capture the significant properties of a Markov blanket, a brief introductory section on Bayesian networks (BNs) is integrated. BNs graphically represent the joint probability distribution over a set of random variables. A BN is composed of a qualitative portion (its structure) and a quantitative portion (its conditional probabilities). The structure BS is a directed acyclic graph where the nodes correspond to domain variables $x_1,\ldots, x_n$ and the arcs between nodes represent direct dependencies between the variables (Heckerman *et al.*, 1995). Likewise, the absence of an arc between two nodes x_i and x_j denotes that x_j is independent of x_i given its parent nodes. Following the notation of Cooper and Herskovits (1992), the set of parent nodes of a node x_i in BS is denoted as π_i. The structure is annotated with a set of conditional probabilities, containing a term $P(x_i=X_i|\pi_i=\Pi_i)$ for each possible value X_i of x_i and each possible instantiation Π_i of π_i. In a BN, the structure BS encodes the Markov condition if each node x_i is probabilistically independent of all non-descendants given its parent nodes. From this condition, the so-called 'chain rule' for BNs follows immediately: a BN can be factorized as a product, for all variables in the network, of their probabilities conditionally on their parents only, i.e.:

$$p(x_1 = X_1,\ldots,x_n = X_n) = \prod_{i=1}^{n} p(x_i = X_i \mid \pi_i = \Pi_i) \qquad (10.2)$$

The example network of Figure 10.2 encodes the joint probability distribution $p(X_1, X_2, X_3, X_4, X_5)$ which, based on the previous equation, is estimated as:

$$p(X_1,X_2,X_3,X_4,X_5) = p(X_2 \mid X_1)p(X_3 \mid X_1)p(X_4 \mid X_2,X_3)p(X_5 \mid X_3)(10.3)$$

A Markov blanket of a node x_i, denoted as $MB(x_i)$, is a minimal set of attributes, containing the immediate parent of the node, its child nodes and the immediate parent nodes of its child nodes. Mathematically, the above statement is translated into:

$$\forall x_k \in \{x_1,\ldots,x_n\} \setminus MB(x_i) \cup \{x_i\}, x_i \vdots x_k \mid MB(x_i)$$

where $\vdots$ denotes the conditional independence of x_i with x_k, given $MB(x_i)$.

Suppose B_i and B_j are two BNs that have the same probability distribution, then $MB_{Bi}(x_k)=MB_{Bj}(x_k)$ for any variable x_k. Certainly, MBs are not exclusive and may vary in size, but any given BN has a unique $MB(x_i)$ for any x_i, which is the set of parents, children and parents of children of x_i. In Figure 10.3, a BN is depicted along with the Markov blanket of a target node x. As regards to the dataset interpretation, feature x is independent of all other features given its $MB(x)=\{U_i,U_j,Y_k,Y_l,Z_{km},Z_{ln}\}$. BN theory has proven (Heckerman *et al.*, 1995) that if a BN B_N is faithful to its corresponding joint probability distribution, then for every variable x, $MB(x)$ is unique. This important attribute is exploited in the next section, in order to alleviate the problem of picking non-informative features at the random forests construction phase.

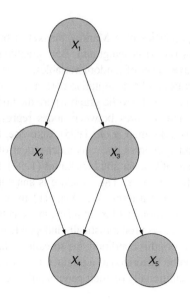

Figure 10.2 A simple Bayesian network depicting the interelation of five random variables.

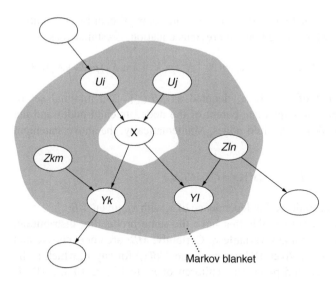

Figure 10.3 An example of a Bayesian network with the Markov blanket of node *x*.

4 Markov blanket random forests

Based on the existing implementations of random forests and taking our initial concerns on feature relevance into consideration, we propose a novel algorithm for classification using RF. The algorithm is entitled '*Markov blanket random forests – MBRF*', since the danger of selecting irrelevant and misleading features is remedied by using the Markov blanket of the class node to provide the best splitting criteria for each tree. By selecting random samples and obtaining the extracted Markov blanket of the target node, the probability of the tree containing more informative features is increased. In the case of high-dimensional datasets, the diversity of the ensemble is not compromised and is more robust that other pre-filtering or weighting schemes. The algorithm consists of two distinct phases: the former regards the construction of the Markov blanket and the latter is about constructing the trees. Its basic procedure can be sketched in the following steps:

MBRF (Data *D*, Features *F*, Target *C*)

1 Draw n_{tree} bootstrap samples from the original data *D*.
2 Build an unconstrained BN without learning the conditional probability table.
3 Obtain the Markov blanket of the class node *C*.
4 For each of the bootstrap samples, grow an unpruned classification or regression tree, with the following modification: at each node, rather than choosing the best split among all predictors, use m_{try} of the Markov blanket and choose the best split from among those variables.
5 Predict new data by aggregating the predictions of the n_{tree} trees (i.e. majority votes for classification, average for regression).

An important variation of the proposed algorithm in comparison with previous random forests implementation is located on the second and third steps, respectively. In the following section, we provide the mathematical explanation of the aforementioned phases.

4.1 Determining the Bayesian network structure and the Markov blanket of the class node

Based on the framework of Cooper and Herskovits (1992), the most probable BN structure is obtained by performing a hill-climb search over the space of candidate BN structures. The following equation, along with Bayes' theorem, provides a metric of relation *r* among two candidate network structures BS_i and $BS_{j,}$ respectively:

$$r = \frac{P(BS_i \mid D)}{P(BS_j \mid D)} = \frac{\dfrac{P(BS_i, D)}{P(D)}}{\dfrac{P(BS_j, D)}{P(D)}} \tag{10.4}$$

Therefore, the problem of calculating $P(BS|D)$ reduces to that of calculating $P(BS,D)$. In order to estimate the above probability, the following assumptions have to be taken into consideration:

1   Variables are discrete and all are observed and complete (i.e. there are no hidden variables or missing data).
2   Instances from the database (i.e. examples) occur independently, given a directed network model.
3   The density function $f(BS_i|BS_j)$ is uniform, i.e. the prior probabilities to place on a network structure BS is unconcerned.

According to the notation used so far, suppose F be a set of m discrete variables, where a variable x_i in F has r_i possible value assignments: $(v_{i1}, \dots, v_{ir_i})$. Let D be a database of n cases, where each case contains a value assignment for each variable in F. Let BS denote a network structure containing just the variables in F. Each variable x_i in BS has a set of parents, represented as a list of variables π_i. Let w_{ij} denote the jth unique instantiation of π_i relative to D. Suppose there are q_i such unique instantiations of π_i. Let N_{ijk} be defined as the number of cases in D in which variable x_i has the value v_{ik} and π_i is instantiated as w_{ij}. N_{ijk} is calculated as:

$$N_{ijk} = \prod_{i=1}^{n} p(x_i = X_i \mid \pi_i) = \prod_i N_{ij} \sum_{k=1}^{n} N_{ij} \tag{10.5}$$

Then, given the assumptions outlined above,

$$p(BS,D) = \prod_{i=1}^{m} \prod_{j=1}^{qi} \frac{(r_i - 1)!}{(N_{ij} + r_i - 1)!} \prod_{k=1}^{n} N_{ijk}! \tag{10.6}$$

Equation (10.6) can be combined with equation (10.4) to give a computable method of comparing the probabilities of two network structures, when given a database of cases for the variables in the structures. Since, by the third assumption listed above, the prior probabilities of all valid network structures are equal, $P(BS)$ is a constant. Therefore, to maximize $P(BS,D)$ just requires finding the set of parents for each node that maximizes the second inner product of equation (10.6). The search strategy operates by initially assuming that a node has no parents, and then adding incrementally that parent whose addition most increases the probability of the resulting network. Parents are added greedily to a node until the addition of no one parent can increase the network structure probability. The function used in this procedure is taken from the second inner product of equation (10.7):

$$gain(x_i, \pi_i) = \prod_{j=1}^{qi} \frac{(r_i - 1)!}{(N_{ij} + r_i - 1)!} \prod_{k=1}^{n} N_{ijk}! \tag{10.7}$$

In a single iteration, an arc is added to node i from the node z that maximizes $gain(x_i, \pi_i \cup \{z\})$. If $gain(x_i, \pi_i) > gain(x_i, \pi_i \cup \{z\})$ then no arc is added.

Since, as the number of nodes is increased (the window size is expanded), the population of possible networks becomes cumbersome, a more robust search strategy had to be followed. Our modified search strategy is as follows: initially, the most probable forest-structured network is constructed (i.e. a network in which every node has at most one parent). A greedy search is performed by adding, deleting or reversing the arcs randomly. In the case that a change results in a more probable network it is accepted, otherwise cancelled. Throughout this process, a repository of networks with high probability is maintained. When the search reaches a local maximum, a network is randomly selected from the repository and the search process is activated again. It should be noted that in order to avoid the convergence to the previous local maximum the network is slightly modified, meaning that we delete some arcs. Since the training dataset is large we also sub-sample the data to speed the network evaluation process up. During the search, the size of the sub-samples is increased. A restriction on the network complexity is also applied during the search, so that a limited number of arcs is allowed in the beginning and, as the process progresses, more and more arcs are approved. These two annealing schemes (sub-sampling and complexity restrictions) have been proven to have the effect of avoiding many bad local maxima.

Upon creation of the structure, the time-consuming process of calculating the conditional probabilities is not needed, since the proposed methodology is basically focused on identifying the Markov blanket of the class node. Therefore, the slow process of learning the conditional probability table on the created BN is omitted and the procedure of identifying the Markov blanket of the class node within the network can be straightforwardly implemented by considering the set of parents, children and parents of children nodes of the class node.

5 Data and preprocessing

As mentioned earlier, articles containing financial news were combined with a plethora of technical indices in order to search for direct influence patterns of the former to the latter. More specifically, we focused on three heterogeneous stock securities from the Greek stock market (Athens Stock Exchange, *.ATG*), a large Greek bank (Piraeus Bank, *.TPEIR*), the principal telecommunication provider of Greece (OTE, *.OTE*) and one of the biggest Greek airline companies (Aegean, *.AEGN*). We have included past data from the major European, Asian and American stock markets, as well as data from energy and metal commodities. Finally, for each of the aforementioned three stock securities, a variety of major technical indices was employed. News articles were automatically extracted from the electronic versions of the leading Greek financial newspapers, i.e. *Naftemporiki* (www.naftemporiki.gr) and *Capital* (www.capital.gr). The time period for all collected data was from *January 2011* to *April 2013*. The technical indices were specified using the *AnalyzerXL* (www.analyzerxl.com) software tool. Table 10.1 tabulates data regarding the three benchmark stocks and their corresponding articles that were collected, while Table 10.2 contains data about historical data of other, main markets and commodities. Tables 10.3 and 10.4 refer to metal and

Table 10.1 The benchmark tickers

Name	Category	Number of articles	Number of days	Symbol
OTE	Telecommunications	1,432	502	.OTE
Bank of Piraeus	Bank	1,323	498	.TPEIR
Aegean Airlines	Airline	256	512	.AEGN

Table 10.2 Market and commodities data

Category	Description	Number of days	Symbol
European markets	^FCHI-CAC 40 Index	513	.FCHI
	^FTSE-FTSE 100 Index	543	.FTSE
	^GDAXI-Xetra Dax Index	529	.GDAXI
	^ATG-Athens Stock Exchange	504	.ATG
Asia/Pacific markets	^HIS-Hang Seng Index	527	.HSI
	^AORD-All Ordinaries Index	519	.AORD
	^N225-Nikkei 225 Average Index	543	.N225
United States markets	^GSPC-S&P 500 Index	515	.GSPC
	^IXIC-Nasdaq Composite Index	531	.IXIC
	^DJI-Dow Jones Industrial Average Index	530	.DJI
Energy	Brent DTD	532	BRT-
	WTI CUSHING	517	WTC-
Metals	Silver	505	XAG-HH
	Gold bullion	505	XAU-B-HH

Table 10.3 Metals data

Name	Number of quotes
Silver	522
Gold bullion	522

Table 10.4 Energy fuel data

Name	Number of quotes
Brent DTD	543
WTI CUSHING	541

energy fuel data considered, respectively, while Table 10.5 depicts a categorized list of the technical indices that were also taken into consideration.

Stock quotes are gathered on a per day basis and articles are aligned according to their release date. In the case that an article was published on a Friday evening (after the closing time of the Athens stock market) or during the weekend, it was considered as being published on the following Monday.

5.1 Sentiment analysis

The large amount of available textual information in general, as well as in news articles, has shifted the focus of researchers to mining information from unstructured and semi-structured information sources (Falinouss, 2007). The text content of the latest news articles and financial reports is taken into account when trying to automatically predict stock behaviour. The web sentiment, i.e. 'positive', 'neutral' or 'negative' content of web articles regarding a stock, has been exploited previously using a 'bag of words' model or a more sophisticated language model (Sehgal and Song, 2007). Automated approaches to sentiment analysis also include the use of WordNet in order to estimate the sentiment of words appearing in the text by measuring their semantic similarity with proto-type positive and negative words (e.g. 'good' or 'bad'). Due to the lack of such

Table 10.5 Technical Indices categorized list

Group name	Function or indicator name
Basic functions	Median price (AKA typical price indicator)
Statistical functions	Standard deviation
Trend indicators	MACD indicator
	Simple moving average
	Exponential moving average
	Line weighted moving average
Volatility indicators	Average true range
	Bollinger band width
Momentum indicators	Williams %R
	TRIX indicator
	Wilder RSI indicator
	Chande momentum oscillator
	Price rate-of-charge indicator
	Cutler's relative strength index
	DX (directional movement indicator)
	Stochastic oscillator
	Price oscillator percentage difference
Market strength indicators	Chaikin A/D oscillator
	Average of volume ROC
	Market facilitation index (MFI)
Support and resistance indicators	Envelope

sophisticated resources for modern Greek, in the present work the sentiment of a word is determined manually, by a financial analysis expert, and the cumulative weight of word sentiments is used to estimate the sentiment of the entire text. The words in the acquired lexicon with an occurrence frequency of at least five times have been semantically annotated by domain experts, according to their positive or negative meaning for stock value prediction. One of five discrete weights, i.e. –2 (clearly negative), –1 (relatively negative), 0 (neutral), +1 (relatively positive), +2 (clearly positive) was assigned to each word. The aforementioned weighting scheme was previously applied by Klibanoff *et al.* (1998) and provided satisfactory results. The reason for selecting five as a threshold for term frequency was mainly attributed to the fact that it balances the number of extracted words with the painstaking process of manual annotation by the domain expert. Table 10.6 displays the most frequent words for each semantic label.

The textual analysis phase consisted of three activities:

1   removal of stop words (i.e. words that are filtered out since they do not provide any special meaning to the text mining concept – usually they contain articles, pronouns, special characters, etc.);
2   lemmatization (i.e. the process of grouping together the various inflected forms of a word so they can be analysed as a single item) of words using a Levenshtein distance-based Greek lemmatizer (Lyras *et al.*, 2007);
3   removal of terms appearing fewer than 30 times within the complete article corpus and taking the 150 most frequent of them.

The class attribute to be predicted contained three discrete labels, namely *UP*, *STEADY* and *DOWN*, if the stock quote closed at a price more than 1 per cent, between 1 per cent and –1 per cent and less than –1 per cent in the following day, respectively. A window of five days was chosen empirically in order to predict the class, resulting in a high-dimensional dataset of more than 620 features.

Table 10.7 summarizes the properties of the system described above. It is organized in four parts: the first two parts provide a rough idea about our

Table 10.6 A sample of frequent terms and their annotated weight

+2	+1	0	–1	–2
Profit	Income	Euro	Cost	Decrease
Increase	Sponsorship	Piraeus	Low	Crisis
Development	Deposit	Bank	Critical	Loss
Profitability	High	Million	Problem	Drop
Ascension	Strong	Stock	Pressure	Deceleration
Improvement	Expansion	Billion	Retreat	Degradation
Positive	Yield	Value	Unscheduled	Damage
Upgrade	Interest	Cyprus	Delay	Danger
Success	Offer	Announcement	Consequence	Negative
Strengthening	Agreement	Buy	Difficult	Deterioration

Table 10.7 Summarized properties of our prototype

Prototype idea	
Aims to forecast…	Price trends
Underlying	Technical indices
Forecast horizon	24 hours
Text mining	
Feature definition	Manually
Number of features	150
Feature granularity	Words
Primary classifier	MBRF
Number of class labels	3
Stock market parameters	
Number of Features	40
Input data	
Information age	0–24 hours
Text analysed	Head, body
Labeling	Manually
Price frequency	Daily close
Test set	
Period	January 2011 to April 2013
Training/test ratio	Tenfold cross validation
Market	Three stocks (Athens Stock Exchange, Greece)
Prototype accuracy vs regression model	21 per cent gain

prototype and a description of the deployed text mining technique; the second part details the parameter settings for the techniques used; the third part summarizes the data used for training; and the final part gives an overview of the major performance figures reported, explained in more detail in the following section.

6 Experimental results

Textual as well as stock quotes data was processed by our proposed methodology (MBRF) and evaluated against several well-known classifiers. More specifically, we considered traditional random forests, naïve Bayes (NB), radial basis functions neural networks (RBF) and a derivative of support vector machines, namely sequential minimal optimization (SMO), which can handle discrete values and acts similarly to regression. Since the latter machine learning algorithms do not reduce features by default, in order to compare the MBRF technique against them, a PCA feature reduction approach was carried out using the Nmath library for .NET platforms (www.centerspace.net/products/nmath). As regards to traditional random forests, we have applied both implementations, random input forests and random combination forests, as they are presented in Section 3. However, since their difference was found to be non-significant, the symbolization of random forests in the results below refers to the most accurate implementation, which was found to belong to random combination forests. Regarding the experimental design, two different approaches were followed.

Experiment 1: the first approach dealt with standard, tenfold cross validation, classification in terms of stock quotes closing price, using datasets with articles and without articles, in order to evaluate the impact of articles on the predictability of a stock quote. We used the *F-measure* metric for evaluation, which is the harmonic mean of *precision* and *recall*, two fundamental metrics of data mining algorithms as regards to classification evaluation. In particular, the *precision* metric of a classifier about a class label is defined as the percentage of correctly classified instances among those that the algorithm classifies as belonging to this class. As *recall* on a class is then defined as the fraction of correctly classified instances among all instances that actually belong to this class. These definitions are illustrated in Table 10.8, showing a 'confusion matrix' which exemplifies the performance of a classification algorithm in terms of its predictions (the columns of the table) against the actual class labels (the rows of the table) for a binary classification problem that contains class labels **A** and **C**.

Table 10.9 tabularizes the *F-measure* score of all machine learning algorithms against traditional linear regression (LR) models. From these outcomes, we could initially observe that combining information from both time series and textual data leads to improvement of the performance for all methodologies. Furthermore, by using only technical analysis data, SMO performs similar to MBRF and significantly outperforms all other approaches, while when incorporating textual information, MBRF is noticeably the best classification approach, a fact that could be attributed to the dimensionality reduction when applying the Markov blanket pre-processing step. According to Table 10.9, the performance

Table 10.8 Confusion matrix and recall and precision metrics for each class (A and C)

		Predicted as…	
		A	*C*
Actual class	**A**	a	b
	C	c	d

$$\text{precision A} = \frac{a}{a+c} \qquad \text{recall A} = \frac{a}{a+b} \qquad \text{precision C} = \frac{d}{b+d} \qquad \text{recall C} = \frac{d}{c+d}$$

$$f-measure = \frac{2*(precision*recall)}{(precision+recall)}$$

Table 10.9 Classification performance in terms of *F-measure*

Dataset	MBRF	RF	SMO	NB	RBF	LR
No articles	65.59	57.83	62.92	55.21	51.61	47.06
Including articles	76.38	59.45	63.69	56.67	56.80	49.94

of MBRF is one of the highest ever reported, with the drawback of a time- and resource-consuming training phase. Training times for each algorithm are mentioned in the following sub-section.

Experiment 2: this experimental design developed a simulated trading strategy in an attempt to further study if the MBRF model could practically be applied to generate higher profits than those earned by employing the traditional regression model of simply following a *buy-and-hold* (passive) investment strategy.

The operational details of the trading simulation are explained as follows: the trading simulation assumes that the investor has €100,000 to create a portfolio by selecting a balanced percentage of each of the three Greek stock quotes mentioned earlier. Each day, the investor could buy, sell or wait, according to the class prediction of the MBRF model. We assume that transactional costs apply when buying or selling, according to Table 10.10. More specifically, the transactional costs of buying are estimated according to the following type:

TransactionCosts(BUY) = Commission + ExpensesASE +
TransferCosts = 0.335 per cent

while the transactional costs of selling are given by:

TransactionCosts(SELL) = Commission + ExpensesASE +
TransferCosts + salesTax = 0.35 per cent

Furthermore, a random choice between 5 per cent and 10 per cent of the current portfolio volume was allowed to be traded each day. The time period was set to the last 50 weekdays (ten weeks) of the aforementioned dataset. As Figure 10.4 depicts, the dashed line, which represents the portfolio budget for the MBRF investing strategy, is clearly outperforming the solid line of the *buy-and-hold* investment strategy by an average factor of 9.5 per cent to 23 per cent for the first five weeks and from 16 per cent to 48 per cent for the remaining five, resulting in a profit of approximately €28,000 rather than €9,000 from the *buy-and-hold* approach.

6.1 Training time

The experimental section concludes with a comparison of training time of all methodologies for each evaluation approach. Time is measured in seconds. The

Table 10.10 Transaction costs

Parameter	Value (%)
Commission	0.250
ASE expenses	0.025
Sales tax	0.015
Transfer costs	0.060

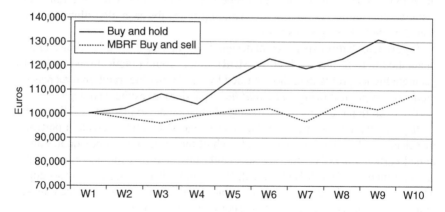

Figure 10.4 Plot of virtual portfolio balance of two different trading strategies.

hardware configuration of the setting includes a modest workstation PC of an Intel I3®, quad-core processor, at 2.4 GHz with 4 GB of available memory. MBRF is obviously the slowest of the selected algorithms as regards to training time. This is attributed to the time-consuming process of finding the most probable BN structure, from which the Markov blanket is extracted at each run. Note, however, that this process is executed in an offline manner, while the improvement of accuracy is of major importance, especially in financial domains, and finally, this process could straightforwardly be parallelized as in each run different instances are selected for BN training. Table 10.11 presents the performance metric of each methodology during training in terms of seconds needed. Note that the process of evaluating the class label of a previously unseen instance was performed instantaneously for each algorithm; therefore, it is not considered in the results.

7 Conclusions

Stock market prediction based on historical data and textual information can result in datasets of high volume, both in attributes and instances. Towards this

Table 10.11 Training time for each algorithm

Methodology	Training time (in seconds)
Markov blanket random forests (MBRF)	6,201
Random input forests	69
Random combination forests	67
Sequential minimization optimization (SMO)	73
Naïve bayesian classifier (NB)	49
Radial basis functions (RBF)	350
Linear regression (LR)	88

phenomenon, a hybrid approach was presented, which alters the random forests implementation strategy by considering the Markov blanket attribute. For this purpose we used a global and heterogeneous dataset of more than 620 features, acquired from various financial articles and equity indices. This first prototype gave encouraging results, taking into account the high levels of noise that such heterogeneity of our dataset in terms of acquisition method and conditions adds, and the difficulties this creates for forecasting. In particular, the proposed ensemble classification technique exhibited a higher classification performance than the traditional RF algorithms, and also other, widely used classifiers. This can be attributed to the incorporation of the Markov blanket, thus suppressing poorly correlated trees. Despite the fact that a plethora of sentiment-related features were manually annotated, we believe that utilizing sophisticated natural language processing tools for modern Greek could automate the laborious tasks of hand-labelling features.

The above preliminary results provide some first evidence of the potential of random forests in general, and the proposed extension of them based on Markov blankets in particular, for trend classification. Taking into account the increasing trend for the electronic/digital acquisition of various data from financial resources, the development of such advanced and high-performing classification techniques contributes to the emergence of the 'intelligent' investing tools. Further research is required for validation of this potential in other financial problems using various types of features, which will probably lead to improvement of the proposed technique.

An important drawback of MBRF is obviously the time-consuming process of extracting the Markov blanket at each tree construction phase. Even though this process can be parallelized and improved, and even though testing an unknown instance is a rapid process, we believe that when the learning phase is improved MBRF could be applied to datasets with massive numbers of features. In addition to supervised classification by MBRF, the idea of using semantic random sampling of features instead of simple random sampling has the potential to be effective in the unsupervised classification problem as well. Hence, we are of the belief that the proposed methodology could be incorporated into other ensemble and machine learning techniques such as regression, RBF neural networks and SVMs. It is our future plan to continue developing this work in that direction. An additional planned future research direction is a different representation of text sentiment. Always respecting the low-resource policy for processing text, more representative text sentiment features and a more balanced proportion of these features in the dataset (they are under-represented in the current approach compared to the historical, technical data) will most likely lead to even more promising prediction results. One idea would be the use of features that denote the incidence of vocabulary words in each article set (or their frequency of appearance, or the even more sophisticated *tf-idf* score, that takes into account not only the word frequency in a given article set, but also its popularity, i.e. how many other article sets it appears in). The number of sentiment features would then equal the vocabulary words, and become comparable to the number of technical features. Another avenue worth exploring is the use of a language model approach that identifies the linguistic features (e.g. words) that depict a significant difference in their statistical properties across the different types of article sentiment (positive, negative, neutral). Again, technical and non-technical features would be comparable in number.

References

Breiman, L., 'Random forests', *Machine Learning Journal* 45, 2001, 532.

Breiman, L., J. Friedman, R. Olshen and C. Stone, *Classification and regression trees*, Monterey, CA: Wadsworth & Brooks/Cole Advanced Books & Software, 1984.

Chan, Y. and K. John-Wei, 'Political risk and stock price volatility: the case of Hong-Kong', *Pacific-Basin Finance Journal* 4(2–3), 1996, 259–275.

Cho, V., 'Knowledge discovery from distributed and textual data', Dissertation Hong Kong University of Science and Technology. Hong Kong, 1999.

Chung, F., T. Fu, R. Luk and V. Ng, 'Evolutionary time series segmentation for stock data mining', In *Proceedings of IEEE International Conference on Data Mining*, 2002, 83–91.

Cooper, G. and E. Herskovits, 'A Bayesian method for the induction of probabilistic networks from data', *Machine Learning* 9, 1992, 309–347.

Deerwester, S., S. Dumais, T. Landauer, G. Furnas and R. Harshman, 'Indexing by latent semantic analysis', *Journal of the Society for Information Science* 41(6), 1990, 391–407.

Dudoit, S., 'Comparison of discrimination methods for the classification of tumors using gene expression data' *Journal of the American Statistics Association* 97, 2002, 77–87.

Falinouss, P., 'Stock trend prediction using news articles: a text mining approach', MSc Thesis. Lulea University of Technology, 2007.

Fellbaum, C. (ed.), *WordNet: An Electronic Lexical Database*, Cambridge, MA: MIT Press, 1998.

Freund, Y. and R. Shapire, 'Experiments with a new boosting algorithm', in Lorenza Saitta (ed.), *Machine Learning: Proceedings of the Thirteenth International Conference (ICML96)*, San Franciso, CA: Morgan Kaufmann, 1996.

Fung, G., J. Yu and W. Lam, 'Stock prediction: integrating text mining approach using real-time news', In: *Proceedings IEEE International Conference on Computational Intelligence for Financial Engineering*, Hong Kong: IEEE Neural Networks Society, 2003, 395–402.

Heckerman, D., D. Geiger and D. Chickering, 'Learning Bayesian networks: the combination of knowledge and statistical data', *Machine Learning* 20, 1995, 197–243.

Hotelling, H., 'Analysis of a complex of statistical variable into principal components', *Journal of Educational Psychology* 24, 1933, 417–444.

Klibanoff, P., O. Laymont and T. Wizman, 'Investor reaction to salient news in closed-end country funds', *Journal of Finance* 53(2), 1998, 673–699.

Lee, J., 'An extensive evaluation of recent classification tools applied to microarray data', *Computational Statistics and Data Analysis* 48, 2005, 869–885.

Lyras, D., K. Sgarbas and N. Fakotakis, 'Using the Levenshtein edit distance for automatic lemmatization: a case study for modern Greek and English,' in *19th IEEE International Conference on Tools with Artificial Intelligence: Vol. 2* (ICTAI 2007) Los Alamitos, CA: IEEE Computer Society, 2007, 428–435.

Mitchell, M. and J. Mulherin, 'The impact of public information on the stock market', *Journal of Finance* 49(3), 2002, 923–950.

Mittermayer, M., 'Forecasting intraday stock price trends with text mining techniques', *Proceedings of the 37th Annual Hawaii International Conference on System Sciences (HICS), IEEE Computer Society* 3(3), 2004, 30064.2.

Ng, A. and A. Fu, 'Mining frequent episodes for relating financial events and stock trends'. *Proceedings of the 7th Pacific-Asia Conference on Advances in Knowledge Discovery and Data Mining, Lectures Notes in Computer Science* 2637, 2003, 27–39.

Preis, T., H. Moat and H. Stanley, 'Quantifying trading behavior in financial markets using google trends', *Scientific Reports* 3(1684), 2013, DOI: 10.1038/srep01684.

Quinlan, J., *C4.5: Programs for Machine Learning*, San Franciso, CA: Morgan Kaufmann Publishers, 1993.

Schumaker, R. and H. Chen, 'Textual analysis of stock market prediction using financial news articles', In *12th American Conference on Information Systems (AMCIS)*, Los Alamitos, CA: IEEE Computer Society, 2006.

Schumaker, R. and H. Chen, 'A discrete stock price prediction engine based on financial news', *Computer* 43(1), 2010, 51–56.

Sehgal, V. and C. Song, 'SOPS: stock prediction using web sentiment', In *Proceedings of the Seventh IEEE International Conference on Data Mining Workshops*, Los Alamitos, CA: IEEE Computer Society, 2007.

Technical-Analysis. The Trader's Glossary of Technical Terms and Topics, www.traders. com, 2005.

Thomas, J. and K. Sycara, 'Integrating genetic algorithms and text learning for financial prediction'. In *Proceedings of the GECCO-2000 Workshop on Data Mining with Evolutionary Algorithms*, Las Vegas, 2000, 72–75.

Wüthrich, B., V. Cho, S. Leung, D. Peramunetilleke, K. Sankaran, J. Zhang and W. Lam, 'Daily prediction of major stock indices from textual WWW data'. In: *Proceedings of the 4th ACM SIGKDD International Conference on Knowledge Discovery and Data Mining*. New York: ACM Press, 1998, 364–368.

Index

Page numbers in *italics* denote tables, those in **bold** denote figures.

For Product Safety Concerns and Information please contact our
EU representative GPSR@taylorandfrancis.com Taylor & Francis
Verlag GmbH, Kaufingerstraße 24, 80331 München, Germany.

For Product Safety Concerns and Information please contact our
EU representative GPSR@taylorandfrancis.com Taylor & Francis
Verlag GmbH, Kaufingerstraße 24, 80331 München, Germany